St. Louis Community College

Forest Park
Florissant Valley
Meramec

Instructional Resources
St. Louis, Missouri

GAYLORD

Sweet, Hot and Blue

Sweet, Hot and Blue
St. Louis' Musical Heritage

by

Lyn Driggs Cunningham
and
Jimmy Jones

INDEX BY TERI HAINES

McFarland & Company, Inc., Publishers
Jefferson, North Carolina, and London

Frontispiece by Teri Shull Haines.

British Library Cataloguing-in-Publication data available

Library of Congress Cataloguing-in-Publication Data

Cunningham, Lyn Driggs, 1926–1988
  Sweet, hot and blue.

  Includes index.
  1. Musicians—Biography. 2. Musicians—Missouri—
Saint Louis Metropolitan Area—Biography. 3. Musicians—
Interviews. 4. Musicians—Missouri—Saint Louis
Metropolitan Area—Interviews. I. Jones, Jimmy,
1930–   . II. Title.
ML394.C86   1989   780'.92'2   [B]   88-27353

ISBN 0-89950-302-0 (lib. bdg.; 50# acid-free natural paper)

Printed in the United States of America.

McFarland & Company, Inc., Publishers
  Box 611, Jefferson, North Carolina 28640

To my Mother and Father
who brought me into this world . . . (L.D.C.)

To Miss Marjorie Oliver
who has always been my inspiration and teacher . . . (J.J.)

In Memory of
Elijah Shaw
Fred "Horsecollar" Lee
Oliver Nelson
Ralph Williams
Sonny Little
Richard Martin
Flora Bush Smith

Acknowledgments

To Carol Brady and all the wonderful people at the Florissant, Mo., County Library for their infinite patience and understanding; Mike Lohmar, Music Reference Department at University of Missouri–St. Louis; Teri Shull Haines for the frontispiece drawing, the index, and wonderful friendship; Marilyn Cornelius for being able to spell, having a good musical ear, plus lots of help in all departments; Maggi Speer for always being there and she knows how to spell too! Duane R. Sneddeker, Missouri Historical Society, Curator of Photographs and Prints; Al Jones for his help with some photographs; and most of all, thanks to Jimmy Jones, my co-author and my friend, whose faith in me and us never failed once through the years...

A special thanks goes to Leo Cheers who down through the years has been the radio connection between music and most of the musicians in the St. Louis and Metro East area. He has always been there to help promote their music.

Leo Cheers writes a column for the *Monitor Newspaper* in East St. Louis. In that column he spotlights the itinerary of these musicians. If you want to know about a person or a group, Leo will know where they are and all you have to do is ask and he will be happy to tell you.

No written thanks here will ever be able to express the feeling that we all feel for you, Leo, but we just want you to know how grateful we are and how much we appreciate you and the goodwill you have always shown us through the years. —L.D.C.

Leo Cheers

Table of Contents

Introduction

Sweet, Hot and Blue is a book written by musicians, about musicians, for all musicians and music lovers all over the world.

It lists 124 musicians from jazz to classical, their lives, careers, bands they performed with in the United States and all over the world, their recording credits, clubs and dates where they performed (then and now), and pictures of their earlier times.

Most of the material, including the interviews and photographs, is new and direct from the entertainers themselves. They were all born in the cities of St. Louis and Metro East (East St. Louis, Illinois).

This book will be a valuable addition to school and public libraries, as well as a timeless asset to the collections of all music lovers. Included in the back of the book is a musician's glossary of terms.

I wrote this book because I love music, all types of music. Throughout these pages you will find all kinds of musicians, although the majority covered lean toward jazz and blues. A good part of these musicians play it all however.

I know I will never regret the time and work it took to gather this material or the pure experience of it. I've been welcomed into musicians' homes and clubs to get "on the wing" interviews. They are a very rare breed of men and women and they love doing what they do best—making us feel good. Each and every one of them is a "great" in his or her own field.

Fame is the ability to please one's listeners in spite of the locale, economy or conditions of employment, the length of engagement, or degree of the artist's popularity. They do their job. On the following pages you will find the musicians born in St. Louis and Metro East who make this possible.

The interviews contained here were gathered over several years, but unfortunately, it was not possible to interview every musician listed herein. Scheduling conflicts presented the biggest obstacle, followed by illness and even death in a few instances.—L.D.C.

Music is a divine version of one soul's expression to another soul.

Lyn Cunningham

The Musicians

Willie Akins Tenor saxophone/Born April 10, 1939, Webster Groves, Mo./Interviewed by Jimmy Jones.

Willie, what were your mother and father's names?

My mother's name was Bettie Addella Akins.

And your dad's name?

Willie Akins Sr.

Where were they born?

My mother was born in Raleigh, Missouri. My father was born in Tennessee somewhere, I'm not sure.

Were they musically inclined?

No.

Where were you born, Willie?

I was born on April 10, 1939 in Webster Groves, Missouri.

Where did you go to school?

I went to Webster Douglas Elementary, Douglas High and Webster High in my last two years of high school.

At what grade did you start thinking about music?

I guess in about the fifth or sixth grade. Walter Layton was my instructor. He was a music teacher in St. Louis, a fine bass saxophone player who used to work with George Hudson.

Did you start on sax?

No, a tonette. Looked like a little toy instrument, I guess about a foot long. It has one octave.

In high school I started playing E Flat Clarinet. Walter said if my father would buy me an Alto Sax I could go to Jefferson and compete in a band contest. After that Walter Layton started recommending me to certain musicians that he knew and I started getting jobs.

Do you remember the first gig you got paid for?

Oh, no, I don't remember that. But while I was in high school the first band I played with was, Eddie Ramblin and his Blue Devils.

Oh, yes, I've heard his name a lot.

I learned a lot from him and he had people like Oliver Nelson working

1

with him. We used to play a certain kind of music, you know? I worked with
Elizabeth Young, piano, Ray Draper, a tuba player and Paul "Hucklebuck"
Williams in New York. He was the one that made "The Honey-Dripper"
popular. We traveled mostly on the East Coast, but went to Canada and all
down South. I stayed in New York from 1957 until about 1968. That's a
pretty good stretch.

That's a musical town, isn't it?

Yeah, that's mainly where everybody goes to see if they got what it
takes to make it. 'Cause you've got the best there, you know?

They give you a good raking over in New York.

Staying there that long I built up enough confidence to reach out and
get into that jazz world, because it was very tough, competitive wise.

Did you record with any of the people you played for?

No, no name folks. Most of the stuff I did along recording lines was
Rand B stuff and it was just like sitting in a session. It wasn't anything I got
credit for by name you see.

What are you doing now, Willie?

For the past four or five years, I've been working with a group called
the St. Louis Jazz Quartette. We have concerts at schools and play all kinds
of music.

*Before we close, do you have any professional advice to pass on to the young
musicians coming up?*

Get as much formal training as you can, it helps.

Harold "Shorty" Baker Trumpet (originally drums)/Born May 26,
1914, St. Louis, Mo., died November 8, 1966, New York, N.Y.

Harold Baker studied with P.G. Lankford in St. Louis. After he
switched to trumpet he played with his brother Winfield's band. He played
with Fate Marable in 1930 in St. Louis and went to Chicago with Erskine
Tate. He returned to St. Louis and played with Eddie Johnson's Crackerjacks between 1932 and 1933. Between 1933 and early 1936 he played again
with a band led by his brother, Winfield Baker. He was with Don Redman
from late 1936 to 1938, playing briefly with Duke Ellington in the latter part
of 1938. He joined Teddy Wilson's Big Band in April of 1939 but left him
early in 1940 to join Andy Kirk where he remained until the spring of 1942.
He co-led a sextet with his wife, Mary Lou Williams. He was with Duke Ellington from September, 1942, until the spring of 1944, at which time he
joined the Army.

Harold guested for Duke Ellington in 1945 and played with him regularly between 1946 and 1952. Before he joined Johnny Hodge's Band in late
1954, he played with the Teddy Wilson Quartet, Ben Webster, and
freelanced in New York City. He still worked occasionally for Duke Ellington in the late '50s, Dick Vance, Claude Hopkins, Bud Freeman,

Willie Akins

George Wein, and also led his own quartet. He played the Metropole in New York in 1964 and his last club dates were at The Embers in New York. Then regular playing was halted by illness in 1965. He was not able to continue playing and died of throat cancer in the New York Veteran's Hospital on November 8, 1966.

Josephine Baker Vocalist, exotic dancer, actress/Born June 3, 1906, St. Louis, Mo., died April 12, 1975, Paris, France.

Josephine Baker was born on June 3, 1906, on the corner of Targee and Gratiot streets in the Mill Valley area on the near South Side of St. Louis, Mo. She lived in a one room shack and stole coal from the railyards at Union Station to keep warm, and raked through garbage cans at the Soulard Market so that the family had enough to eat.

She attended Lincoln School near her home, but got her real education from the streets and the musicians playing in taverns, dance halls and theaters in her neighborhood.

This emaciated, buck-toothed black girl from the slums became an international sex symbol before her twenty-first birthday and owned a thirty-room house in Paris, France.

She did her first performing on the sidewalks outside the Booker T. Washington Theater (St. Louis, Mo.) where she played a banjo made from a cigar box and rubber bands, and a comb covered with tissue paper. The people waiting in line to see professionals gave her pennies. She worked her way into a family vaudeville act and on into the chorus line as a supporting singer and dancer where she performed the intermissions for the main acts.

Her overwhelming desire to succeed led her to copy the stars. She learned the songs and lines and was ready to step in for them if they became ill. This happened, and led to her discovery and a part in Eubie Blake and Noble Sissle's "Shuffle Along," an all black musical hit in New York in 1921.

Four years later Josephine Baker was a sensation in Paris, as an exotic dancer in the Folies Bergere. Paris audiences were wild over Josephine's exotic beauty and eroticism. She performed nearly nude in her numbers and to the European racists and sexists the black woman represented primitive lust and sensuality. Europe offered opportunities denied a black woman in America and Josephine Baker took advantage of it, making films and becoming a confidante to such European intellectuals as Max Reinhardt, Albert Einstein and Le Corbusier. "La Ba-kair," as the French called her, became the essence of the spirit of hot jazz.

She repaid the French people for their affection by calling Paris her home and working for a number of French patriotic causes. When the war broke out in 1939 and Paris fell in 1940, Josephine went to North Africa to work for the Free French. She served as a sub-lieutenant in the Free French Army and received a Rosette of the Resistance for her work in the anti–Nazi cause in France.

Having always been against racism, she vowed to devote all her energies to the postwar years in an all out battle against race hatred. If part of that battle meant returning to St. Louis, return she would, because she still remembered that in 1916 in St. Louis blacks and whites were not allowed to live on the same block and whites rioted in East St. Louis, Ill. because of the presence of black people in their midst.

So at age forty-five she came home. Her return in 1951 brought her professional and political triumphs. She would perform only before integrated audiences and succeeded in breaking the color barrier in many cities. She refused a $12,000 a week offer from the Chase Hotel in St. Louis because they refused to go along with her seating policies. She did return, however, to appear at a rally for the NAACP and Harold Gibbons of the Teamsters Union, both working for school desegregation.

She loaned her name and money to many civil rights causes and adopted fourteen children of different nationalities to show the world that a "rainbow family" could live in peace and set an example for the world.

Josephine Baker died penniless, just as she had been born, at age sixty-nine in Paris, France, on April 12, 1975, but this gutsy rebel of a girl from St. Louis had survived fortune, misfortune, fame, ultimate success, honor and dishonor, all in the years of one lifetime.

Billy Banks Vocalist/Born 1908, Alton, Illinois, died Oct. 19, 1967, Tokyo, Japan.

"Billy Banks, Alton Negro musician, continues to advance in his professional career and is now with the Sixth Club Orchestra in Cleveland, Ohio. Their concerts are broadcast Tuesday, Friday, and Sunday evenings at 10:45 central standard time from station WTAM. Alton relatives who have received station programs find Banks carded as vocalist with the orchestra, but have had some difficulty in tuning him in because WTAM's wavelength is so close to KMOX in St. Louis, Mo." (The *Alton Daily Telegraph*, Feb. 2, 1929.)

Billy did open at Connie's Inn in New York City on June 29, 1932. He returned to Cleveland in 1933 and worked in the family shoe shop.

He joined Noble Sissle in 1934 and he remained with Sissle's Band until he moved to Billy Rose's Diamond Horseshoe for an unbroken residency of over 7,000 performances between December 1938 and June 1948. He also appeared at the Diamond Horseshoe in 1949 and 1950.

He left for Europe in 1952 and spent several years in Holland, England, France and Germany.

He toured Asia extensively before settling in Japan, where he remained until his death in 1967.

William "Bill" Benson Piano/Born November 12, 1936/Interviewed by Jimmy Jones and Lyn Cunningham.

Bill, how are you doing today?

Just fine. Thank you.

Good. First we'd like to get some information on your mother and father, if you'd tell us what their names were.

My father's name was Bill Benson also. He was from Sioux City, Iowa. My mother's maiden name was Mildred Johnson, and then she had another marriage, so her name was Mildred Helliker.

Okay, and do you remember their birthdates?

No, my father I don't have much information about. He was killed about three months before I was born. He was killed in a car accident. My mother's birthdate was December 9, 1910.

That's good, and were they musically inclined?

I understand that my father played some. Played banjo some, but not professionally. My mother didn't at all.

I see. Now we'd like to have your birthdate.

Mine's November 12, 1936.

Where did you go to grade school and high school?

I went to school at the Missouri School for the Blind, which is a state school located here in St. Louis. My home was in Mt. Vernon, Mo., and I came here to go to school from first grade through high school.

I see, I see. Do you remember the name of the school?

It's just called Missouri School for the Blind.

All right. When did you first acquire the musical background that we know about you?

Well, I think that started in high school. In junior high I started playing trumpet, they had a school band that I was in; they had a dance band that I became leader of, did arranging for.

Are there any particular names we should mention from those days, that we would want to mention? That you studied with or under or anything pertaining to the musical . . .

I think our band director there was Lester Best, and our . . . we had two piano and choral teachers, Emannuel Sueter who's still here in St. Louis, and a Noel Chase who is here, and I think all of them influenced me some. I don't know how much of this you want, but I was intending on going into radio writing, continuity writing, and was all set to go to Northwestern University, and KMOX [a St. Louis radio station] had a Saturday morning show they called "Teen O'Clock Time."

I remember that.

And I got into the finals playing a trumpet solo and I didn't win. The winner was a girl named Shirley Rascus who was a singer. She was a protégée of Eddie Cantor, and he had somehow procured a scholarship for her to

Indiana State University so the prize that she won was a two year scholarship to St. Louis School of Music, and as she didn't have a need for it, she gave it to me. Well, that kinda changed my plans. I had a two year scholarship so I thought well, I'll do that at least and then we can see about the other. So after two years I was pretty well ensconced into the music end of things and I went on to get my B.A. in Musical Education, and I have a few hours towards a Masters in that. At that time I was primarily thinking about teaching, not the performing end at all. There was a fellow I had gone to school with whose name was Glen Mueller. He had formed a rock group and he asked me if I would play keyboard. Well I hadn't had that much piano, a little bit of keyboard classes at the Institute and just some foolin' around on my own. I thought, no, I can't do that, but he kept on me and I finally said I would try, so that was really the beginning of my performing thing, I guess, and it just sorta branched and grew from that.

Was that the first paid one, or did you get paid on that?

Yeah, we did. You know the jobs bands used to do, like "Teen Town"? We did a lot of those. Wedding receptions and that sort of thing.

Were there any big names, Bill, that you were affiliated with?

Back in those days of that rock group, there was a few times when Bob Kuban was our drummer.

I see.

He was still in high school at that time. And I don't recall any other big names.

Did you ever do any recording with anybody?

No, I did a couple of albums just locally here on a label that I had set up. None with a major label, or out of town.

I see.

What was the name of that label?

Sepele label.

Technosonic is real close to you here.

Yeah. These were done at Premier on Locust and Jefferson, I think. That's been several years ago. Twelve to fifteen years ago.

Now your musical ambition when you were small; did you ever . . . everybody has an idea in their head about what they want to do, something to reach for in their career. Did you ever think about anything like that?

Not really, because I wasn't thinking in terms of music. It's funny how things can happen along the way in your life to point you in certain directions. Had it not been for Shirley Rascus giving me that scholarship, I don't think music would even have been the direction.

Right.

So I don't think it was until later on, in my twenties perhaps I had some ambition or ideas of things I would like to do.

What was it you did want to be before you . . .

I wanted to go into radio and I thought the best way to be involved with radio would be through writing. Continuity writing.

I see. That would have been interesting.

Not as interesting as what I'm doing.

And right now, you're into what?

Well, I've been at Cheshire for fifteen years.

Oh, really?

Yeah, playing nightly in a lounge called the Fox and Hounds.

All the aforementioned are St. Louis restaurants and since we are going into that, could you name some more St. Louis restaurants and lounges where you played?

Where I've played?

Yeah, where you've played.

There was one on highway 270 and Graham Rd. which was a Holiday Inn at that time and it was . . . now it's something else, I don't know what it was. There was a lounge in the Albert Pick Motel on Lindberg that I worked for a while. A place in Berkely called Velvet Downs. Downtown, a place called The Four-Fifteen Club. It was at 415 Chestnut.

I was at the Six-O Lounge at Sixth and Chestnut.

I worked Al Baker's at cocktail hour, a couple of stints there.

He's still going strong.

Yeah, he's still going strong. There's no others that come to mind right away. There were several little spots that maybe are just as well left nameless. *(They laugh.)*

Bill, is there any advice or any statements that you'd want the readers to know, advice that you would give any young person that's striving to do something musically or maybe help their career in whatever they want to do?

Well, I think two things, maybe. People who sing, I would say, I notice a tendency on the part of a lot of singers; I'm talking about professional singers, to get caught up in the sound, to be very concerned with the sound, and in doing so pass over the lyric content a lot. I think for a singer the only reason for having words is to get the meaning of those words across and I think otherwise you might as well have instrumental music, and I think they should be very conscious of what their words are saying and try to get that across to the listener. I think that's extremely important and I think versatility is extremely important. I think the more kinds of things you can do the better stead it will stand you, with club owners, with patrons, with anybody. I would say, branch out as much as you can, do as many different kinds of things as you can. Styles of music . . .

Do you work with a vocalist, or are you a vocalist?

I am my vocalist.

That's a plus. Being a keyboard artist, you can sing and accompany yourself, and that's a plus. A lot of pianists go out there and they're really good on the keyboard, but they can't sing. Most of the time they either have to hire a singer or pass the job up, you know?

Well I like to think of myself as an entertainer rather than a musician. I think because I try to feel out the crowd and see the type of thing they want. Some nights I might be doing a lot of comedy stuff, or other times meaningful stuff but it's . . . it all goes under the banner of entertaining the crowd, so I like to refer to myself as an entertainer, more than a pianist or a singer.

Right. That's what it's all about, really.

You do not teach music to anyone, do you?

I did teach for about five years in the Lutheran Elementary Schools. I taught intrumental music in ten schools, but it became a problem. The hours began at eight o'clock in the morning, and with my playing every night I finally had to decide which I was really going to do. Was I going to teach, or was I going to the performing end, and I just took that end, and I don't teach any more.

From now on do you intend to do the same thing or do you have a future goal in mind that you're working toward? Do you write music?

I do write music. I haven't been really persistent about getting the music to the sources; publishers; or performers. I think persist is one of the main things I haven't done. I do write and I enjoy doing that.

What kind of music do you write; classical?

No. Popular.

I call it easy listening.

Yeah.

Meaningful music.

I think a lot are getting caught up in sound. They want to get a certain sound, and that may be fine but if it isn't getting the words across, then something's wrong. That's the only reason for them singing.

You're missing the whole thing, when you don't do that. When an artist writes something, they want it heard and they want it understood.

Words are very important.

Are there any more comments you want to make, Bill, before we close?

I don't know what it would be. Thank you very much, and I certainly enjoyed talking with you.

I'm going to treasure this visit, and hopefully you'll give us permission to use this in our research book.

I'll be happy to be a part of it.

We thank you very much.

Yes, we thank you for giving us your time and the interview.

Charles Edward "Chuck" Berry Vocalist, guitar, composer/
Born January 15, 1926, San Jose, Calif.

Chuck Berry was born in San Jose, California, on January 15, 1926, but
was brought to St. Louis when he was only a few months old. He was raised
and educated in St. Louis and had his earliest musical training as a member
of the city's Antioch Baptist Church choir as a lead singer of a religious vocal
quartet.

The first Chuck Berry Combo appeared in 1952 in an East St. Louis
club. A meeting with Muddy Waters in 1955 led to the recording of
"Maybelline," which marked the beginning of his distinctive style. Berry's
music, like the earlier rhythm and blues, was based in the traditional earthy
Negro blues, but he colored them with a wry, good humor, a sense of joyous
affirmation and a forceful rhythmic power.

At age seven when Chuck Berry sat down at the family's upright piano
armed with the recordings of Art Tatum and other jazz giants, it could
hardly have been known that the seeds of great rock and roll were being
planted right in the middle of St. Louis during the Great Depression, nor
could it have been known that this musician would become one of the most
accepted pianists in early rock music. Nor could it have been known that
many years later a professional musician named John Clyde Johnson, and
leader of the Johnnie Johnson Trio, would replace an ailing saxophone
player with that young guitarist/singer/songwriter, Chuck Berry.

Chuck's unbridled talent thrust him to the foreground and that band
changed its name to the Chuck Berry Trio. With Chuck Berry's blaring
guitar riffs and Johnson's deft pianistic texturing the duo was dynamic and
exciting. Such prestigious giants as Muddy Waters, the incomparable
keyboardist Otis Spann and the fabled Layfayette Leake played Berry's
sessions.

In Chicago, Chuck took some tapes to the Chess Record Company;
Leonard Chess liked them and asked him to come in and make a live recording of it. They recorded "Maybelline," with "Wee Wee Hours" on the
flip side, and from then on it was Chuck Berry all the way.

The Chuck Berry Trio started traveling after that record came out.
Chuck Berry wrote "Brown Eyed Handsome Man" while riding in the back
seat of Carl Perkins' new Cadillac. It is said you don't fool with Chuck
Berry when it comes to writing lyrics, the words just roll off his tongue
effortlessly.

Chuck has an intimate understanding of the country and western
idiom. He developed a fascination with Caribbean music in 1956 and in-
jected the rock and roll with a Latin beat, mixing musical forms in "Havana
Moon" and "Hey Pedro," this all taking place some five or six years before
America discovered the calypso stylings of Harry Belafonte that brought
him to star status.

To this day Chuck Berry is still reelin' and rockin' as only he can do.

Diane Bolden Operatic soprano/Born 1959, East St. Louis, Ill.

Diane Bolden is the daughter of Mr. and Mrs. Richard Bolden of East St. Louis, Illinois. She attended grade school there, and as a child wanted to be a nurse, not an opera singer. She always sang in her church, the Mount Zion Missionary Baptist Church. Her brother Richard writes music and at home Diane, Richard, Roderick (another brother) and her sister Pam would gather around an old upright piano and sing four-part harmony.

She attended East St. Louis Senior High School and there she began to think of music as a career. In her senior year she studied voice with Irene Chambers in St. Louis. After high school, Miss Bolden studied music on scholarship at Millikin University in Decatur, Illinois. From there she went to Indiana University in Bloomington, Indiana.

While touring western Europe with the Indiana University Choir, she first auditioned for the Zurich International Opera House in Switzerland. After graduating college she returned to Zurich and spent two years in Switzerland. She moved on to Bonn, Germany, and finally to Hof, Germany. She has said that if she had a favorite composer, it would be Mozart: "His music fits my voice best." She now lives in Europe, spending her summers with the family in East St. Louis, pursuing her career in opera and bringing much musical joy to the operagoers in Hof.

James Boyd, Jr. Saxophone/Born November 19, 1922, Memphis, Tenn./Interviewed by Jimmy Jones.

Do you remember your dad and mother? What were their names?

My dad was James Boyd, Sr. I'm James Boyd, Jr.

And your mother's name?

Florene Boyd.

Florene Boyd? Were they St. Louisans, James?

No, my father came from Mason, Tennessee and my mother came from Memphis, Tennessee.

You don't remember their birthdates, do you?

My father in 1894 in Mason, Tennessee and my mother was born in Memphis, Tennessee in 1900.

Fantastic. You were born here in St. Louis?

I was born in Memphis too, but my parents moved here when I was approximately a year old.

Okay, well, then you are a St. Louisan.

Yeah.

Then you went to grade school...

I went to grade school at the old Waring School to the sixth grade and then I went to Vashon High School.
That's in St. Louis here, right?
Right.
All right Jim, at what point in your school career did you decide to do anything musical?

It was in my second year of high school when I took up saxophone. Prior to that my parents had given me piano lessons which I didn't take to too well. So when I told them I wanted to take saxophone, they weren't too cool about that. *(He laughs.)*
Yeah.

Because they said I was wastin' money so I ended up finally with little odd jobs and what not; I began to get a little money together to buy a saxophone and when they saw I was serious about it, they helped me. And I got a saxophone and I went over to the high school at that time and tried to get into the band.
Do you remember at that time where you lived when you were attending high school?

I lived at number 10 Cardinal right around the corner from the Vashon High.
Number 10 Cardinal? Okay. Was sax the only instrument you played in high school?

Yeah, that was the only one I played in high school.
Now is there any name you would like to mention that maybe inspired you or that you would want to mention that started you out or was tutoring you with sax or anything like that, that you want to mention?

Well, actually, I just liked the sound of the saxophone, and I was listening to people like Lester Young and Coleman Hawkins and I just liked the sound of the instrument and I thought I would like it.
I see, I see. Now what were your first major jobs? Do you remember your first job? As a saxophonist.

I didn't get my first job 'til, actually what happened was, let's put it this way; I did have, when I was in high school I got into the high school band. At the particular time I was there the leader was a guy named Brady Hodge. He was a St. Louisan who played trumpet.
Brady Hodge.

Brady Hodge, uh-huh. Later he moved to Newark, New Jersey and happened to have one of the leading bands around that territory; eleven piece band. That was his career. But while I was in high school I did have help from one of local musicians who is still in St. Louis: Hershel Gilham.
Yeah, I talked to Hershel the other day.

Also there was a guy named Leroy Kirksey; was an excellent

saxophonist who helped me quite a bit but right out of high school I went into the Army. When I was in the Army I went into the 237th Corps battalion, 4th Company, rather, 237th, 4th Company, 493rd, 4th battalion and while I was there I ran into a guy who was an excellent pianist and saxophonist whose name was Jimmy Cole. Jimmy Cole formed a band over there. We used to play for the officers' dances and so on and make a little extra money.
Yeah.
The man, the commanding general over there at that time over in Bilnerbay, New Guinea liked us so well that he made us the nucleus of the army band and we became the 415 Army Service Forces Band. And so that is where I gained most of my experience.
And then coming out of the service, Jim, do you remember whether you got with a group or, if so, what was the name of the group or the club you played in?
Actually when I came out of service I had a problem with my teeth and I was playin' with a bridge and was afraid. My friend, Brady Hodge, wanted me to go to Newark with him 'cause I was a member of his band, and I was afraid to go 'cause I had a problem with my teeth; and any saxophonist needs good teeth. *(He laughs.)*
Right, right.
So I was afraid to go. And I didn't go and I didn't really play anything for about eleven years after. At that time a local guy named Laddie Wilfolk was just takin' up guitar and he told me to come up and help him.
What was his name, Jim?
Laddie Wilfolk.
Laddie Wilfolk?
Yeah. Now deceased. He died in May of 1981.
Uh-huh. Laddie Wilfolk, okay.
Bass player. But he was beginning to start guitar at that time and he asked me to come over and help him and in trying to help him I got myself into pretty good shape and began to play again myself and in 1956 I joined the union.
In 1956. And at that time the union was...
The union was Local 197 for blacks only.
Yeah, right. I remember that.
I joined the union and then I began to play. At that time the first band I played with was a band led by Red Daniels, a local St. Louisan who played guitar and vocalized.
Do you remember the name of the club; the first job?
Oh, I think the first job was the Moonlight Tavern. Red Daniels was the guy who really played jazz and ragtime, and so we played rhythm and blues.

And the name of that place was the Moonlight Tavern. Now we'll go back and try to recapture the days you were in the Army and there's some names we should mention; that you want to mention about that.

Right. As I was mentioning, Jimmy Cole who I played with in the Army, was a baritone man with the J.B. Sand Orchestra and the first alto man with Tiny Bradshaw and also an arranger. And while we were in the Army at one point we were in Manila in the Philippine Islands; we recorded music over there because they liked our band so well. And as the band broke up we were supposed to get back together. We ran across some people who said they wanted to be the backer of the band but it never did come off too well. We done very little together.

And in coming out of service did you travel any, with any name people?

No, didn't travel any. After I got out, because of the problem with my teeth, I wasn't sure I could handle it so I laid off; it was about eleven years before I got back into music, and that was the point where I met Laddie Wilfolk, and in the process of trying to help him, I got more confidence that my teeth wasn't going to bother me.

Right.

See what I had was, I had five teeth out in front, which are the teeth that sit right on the mouthpiece, which made me think I might not be able to handle it.

But you found out . . .

Actually I found out that in spite of that I could overcome it and it didn't really bother me. But by this time I had got married in about 1949 so that I got a job and that kinda stopped the travlin'.

Yeah, I know. (They laugh.) I did too. So from that point on . . .

After that I played with lots of St. Louis musicians. Like I said I played with Red Daniels off and on for a period, at least twelve years, and various other musicians around St. Louis; almost anybody you could name. Almost all of them know me except for the ultra-modern. Now we kept playin' main stream so the ultra moderns probably don't know much about me. But any of those who played the main stream standard ballad type of thing . . .

They had to know Jim Boyd.

Yeah. And I also played with Archie Bursides' Big Band for several years.

Now, Jim, you are kinda semi-retired but you still play right now.

Well, the last band I played with regularly was George "Peekin" Lewis, piano player, combo and he died in 1975 and I wasn't playin' with him very long.

And the last job we did, and I played with you was at this, what was the name of the affair?

Well that was a charitable affair we played for the King Finelan Mental Health Center, a fund-raising project and everybody donated his services.

And that particular thing had Jimmy Jones and Raymond Gay on piano and Melvin Bellups on drums, "Sonny" Little on bass, and the horn was Charlie Hill on trumpet and me, Jimmy Boyd on saxophone.
Right. Okay.
Well let's see. I have played also with, at one time we did have a group where the musical director was Vernon Nashville.
Yeah.
Vern Nashville was the musical director of the group but the group was led by a football player. Crenshaw. Crenshaw, what was his name? Crenshaw would use me on the _____ and in that band we also had Charlie Brown of the New Orleans Saints, and actually we played sort of a mix of music; quite a bit of it rock.
Yeah.
But because of the football players in there we had such jobs. We'd get jobs like at the Playboy Club, but it was a pretty nice group.
Uh huh.
And at one time we thought we were going to go someplace with that group because the football players were in the group.
Right. Right. The name people.
At the time, I think his name was Willis Crenshaw.
Willis Crenshaw, yeah. Of the football Cards.
Willis Crenshaw got off the Cardinals and that seemed like it affected the group altogether 'cause at one time we were thinkin' we were going to be on the Johnny Carson Show and the agency who was gonna sponsor this seemed to have backed off when Willis Crenshaw got out of St. Louis.
Naturally. The name left so everything went down. Right. I guess, Jimmy, if there's anything else you want to mention before we close this interview, name people that you want to name, we'll try to, and if you think of anything else you know between now and publishing time you jot it down for me and I can add it to what we got. This has been an interview . . .
At one time I did have a few jobs with, the only name person was Baby Face Willette.
Baby Face Willette?
The organ player, and that was when he was in St. Louis and needed somebody at the time, and I played several jobs with him, other than that . . .
Where was he from, Jim?
I don't know where Baby Face was from.
But he was appearing in St. Louis at the time?
He was at the time pretty widely recorded and doing pretty well.
I see, I see.
I haven't heard anything about him lately, so I don't know what happened to him.

Okay. We're going to close this interview and this has been an interview with Mr. Jim Boyd Jr., a saxophonist of the St. Louis area, and my name is Jimmy Jones and we thank you all for listening to our interview.

George Leslie Brazier, Sr. Bass, singer, trombone/Born September 26, 1913, St. Louis, Mo./Interviewed by Jimmy Jones.

This is Jimmy Jones and I'm in the home of Mr. George Brazier, Sr. on the first month of the year 1982. George, what's your full name?

George Leslie Brazier, Senior.

George Brazier, okay. How about a birthdate . . .

Well, I was born September 26, 1913.

How about mom and pop? What were their names?

Well, my dad's name was Clyde David Brazier; my mother, Dora Brazier.

Were they born here too, George?

No, no. I think my dad was born in Kentucky and my mother was born in Delhi, Illinois.

I see, but they weren't musically inclined?

No, no.

In your early years of grade school, would you tell me what school you attended.

I attended Dunbar.

Dunbar? I guess we all did. (He laughs.)

And then from there to Lincoln.

To Lincoln High School, okay.

Then all of, well I used to enjoy music but I was never able to play so I got my dad interested in acquiring an instrument for me.

What kind of work did he do?

My dad was a chauffeur for one of the high-classed families in St. Louis. The Ager family.

In high school now, you got kind of thrown into the band or were you interested in some kind of music?

I was interested in playing, although the instrument that I liked best was the saxophone, but during the conditions that there wasn't very much money, of course at that time lessons wasn't but thirty-five cents, but you wasn't able to continue taking lessons. I started, you know, but then I— before that though I was able to acquire an instrument from our ice man, which he played trombone, and he had one so he tried, you know; he knew that about me wanting to play so he tried to get me interested in taking the trombone so my dad, well I say I would rather have a saxophone, but my dad says all instruments are the same. If you want a trombone, you get the trombone. It wasn't but ten dollars but you know— In them days ten dollars was quite a bit. So I bought the trombone and I took it to school

George Brazier on bass, Jimmy Johnson playing guitar, and Joe Johnson on piano.

Left to right: **Willie Akins, Gene "Stumpy" Washington, Jimmy Jones, George Brazier and Mae Wheeler.**

and with me and started takin' lessons from Mr. Harris and I got pretty good on it, and I was able to play and . . .

Harris was the ice man at that time?

No, Harris was the music man teacher down at Lincoln School.

Down at Lincoln and his name . . . ?

M.L. Harris.

M.L. Harris, okay; at Lincoln High School, okay.

Yeah.

And from that point on you were probably in the band.

Yes, I played in; oh; about one or two concerts and then things got a little tough for me and I had to come out of school. I didn't want to, but under the conditions I had to come out. I found a job and I didn't do anything in music until way later on after I left school. I used to go up to a place where all the guys would gather and they had a piano in an old pool room and one of my buddies was a pretty good pianist, you know? Bilsarth? Moore and he, there wasn't anything to do and he'd sit around and play and I'd sing, you know, so pretty soon he said, "Hey, why don't you come on and go out on a job with me?" I said, "No, I'm not that good"; and he said, "Oh yes you could make us a lot of money in tips doin' that"; in those years you could go in a place and though the salary wasn't very much, you could make it up in tips, you know? You could come up with a nice salary for a week's worth of work, you know. So I decided I'd go out. So I done all right, so pretty soon I went from that thing to another thing; you know, able to go in other clubs and sing so I found myself, man I was singing all over town you know. *Yeah, yeah.*

So then, uh, Harold Pickett; he was a musician piano player on the east side here, and he had a band, so we came out one night and he heard me, and he said how would you like to come out to the club where I am? He says I could pay you pretty good money. During that time I think I was makin' about eight dollars a week salary at the place where I was at; of course gettin' a few tips 'cause it was a black club, you know? *Right.*

So Harold Pickett was workin' at this white club and they used to cater to all the guys like people...
Up-tee-ups?

Yeah, like gangsters; sporting class of people. Gamblers.
Do you remember the name of that club?

Yeah. That was Halsteads Club out on the Collinsville Road. About 8400 Collinsville Road.
Okay.

Okay, that's really when I began to get into things because Harold Pickett spent a lot of time with me and he taught me a lot of things and I kept up on the latest in music, you know, and he had some good musicians in the band, such as Al Hickman; one of the very finest saxophonists around the city at the time. And James Beard and King; Clifford King; myself and also he had Ebbie Hardy and so I went on out and started workin' with him and so I made good money out there. The salary was ten dollars a week and our tips used to run about, about 75 dollars a night, so at the end of the week we'd have a nice little sum.
Yeah, a nice little sum.

So I went on from there, well we worked for George Halstead. He was like almost, I'd say almost, like a father to me because he took up a lot of time and anything I needed I could always get it. So he tried to interest me into playin' an instrument. He said, "George, you are a heck of a singer; you got a good voice but it's gettin' so now that everybody can sing. Why don't you learn how to play something?" So I said, "I don't know what instrument I'd like." He said, "I'll tell you what. If you find the instrument you like, I'll get it for you." So during that time there wasn't very many bass players and I always liked the sound of bass cause I'd be on the bandstand kinda' hittin' on an old megaphone you used to sing out of and you know I'd kind of; like I was the bass player.
Pretending...

They didn't have a bass, so finally I found the bass, I think I paid about ten dollars for the bass over in St. Louis at Tony Platt's pawn shop. So I came

on back and told him, he said well okay, he gave me the money and I went on back and got it. So I got me a Carl Fisher instructor and with the help of Al Hickman who was a very good musician, he taught me a lot in less time than a year and I was able to follow the band because I had a good ear, although my ability in reading and like that wasn't up to par, but I could make up the difference with the ear.
Yeah, right.

So I stayed there, I guess around about three years and I began to get so they'd feature me on the floor show playin' bass and singin' you know, so then Howard Gant, a bandleader in St. Louis heard about me and he wanted me to come over for an audition and I went over and made the audition, and he was impressed. He said I'll hire you. So I made up my mind to leave this job and to venture out a little and see what it was all about, because it was a bigger band, you see, and I was used to smaller groups and to get into about a seven or eight piece band; that was the thing about that time, so, uh . . ."
At that time, yeah.

I joined his band and we worked ever' place around St. Louis, all the big spots, the Masonic Hall, West End Waiters, The Dance Box, oh, a number of places, so then later on Eddie Randall was short, well his brother-in-law was gonna lead the band. His brother-in-law was a bass player but he was going into ministry and so my brother was playin' drums with Eddie and so he said, "Why don't you let George come on in? He could help me with this vocal, the vocals and; uh, he's playin' pretty good bass, now he's not good but we can work with him, you know," so anyway Eddie hired me . . .
On your brother's recommendation.

Right.
Now his name, George? Your brother?

Jesse Brazier.
Jesse Brazier. He was the drummer in the Eddie Randall Band.

Right.
Okay. So he hired you to sing and play the bass.

Right. Yeah, and so I thought it was a great asset to me because the sound of money was good at that time, you know, very good considering and he worked everywhere, all over the city, all over Missouri, all over Illinois; nearly every town in Missouri and Illinois.
Now did you all ever do any uh . . . any uh . . . you know, traveling from the riverfront; you know, go from town to town on the boats and stuff?

No. We never did. I never did get the chance to play the boats because they had a couple of bands in St. Louis that were just stationary bands on the boats. And that was Fate Marable's Band, and Dewey Jackson, and they had it sewed up every year, you know.

You all traveled by . . .

By car.

By car or whatever.

So we, uh, and other things Eddie used to do which was great experience for me, we done a lot of radio work too; we done a lot of radio work. We were on the finest stations around this part of the country. Station WEW.

Yeah, right.

And, uh, I got a lot of exposure like that and in the summertime we'd leave town and go up in like Iowa, Wisconsin or New York and Sotis Point in New York, Rochester, New York, Syracuse, New York; and we'd go up there on these what do you call em; um . . . resorts and we had regular jobs up there, and we'd go up there and stay the whole summer, you know.

Oh, yeah.

We'd come back and we'd be pretty fat.

Oh yeah yeah.

Anyway he always had his band dress immaculate. We had about three or four uniforms you know, it was a great thing and then I got a lot of experience out of that. So from then on we finally come back to St. Louis and then one year I wanted to venture out further.

Uh-huh.

So I quit Eddie's Band and I started back workin' at the Halstead's Club in Collinsville, and then after about a year or so, I think it was about 1942 that I left E. St. Louis and went to Springfield, Ill. I had an offer up there and I went up there on a job and so I stayed in Springfield about five years and in the meantime I had bands of my own there. Springfield was really jumpin' at that time. There wasn't anything but musicians in town you know. There was a lot of places to work.

Right.

Well, later on we left; I left Springfield. I got an offer to go to California to join the Four Clefs out of Springfield that traveled quite a bit and they were a name group so I went out on the coast to work for them and I stayed out there about a year until we came back and played on our off. We had about three weeks off during our travelin' time, we took a week for travelin' time and then we'd come on back to Springfield and we-started workin' in the club there . . .

Uh-huh.

. . . for the two weeks we were going to be off before we went back to California to open up the job again. So eventually I got homesick and everything. The money was great, more money than I ever made in my life, and so I just wanted to be back home. So I came on back to Springfield in, uh, that was after the war. In 1946 I came back to Springfield. Things were pretty dull then but I just had to play, so I couldn't stand that town so I come

on back to St. Louis, so I came on back to St. Louis and formed my own group and went right back in this club with uh, Pickett.
Uh huh.

No, it wasn't with Pickett then. I formed a group.
You had your own group.

Yeah. I had guys like Floyd Mailer in there, and Sammy Malone.
Organ player.

Yeah and Lee Howard on tenor and we had Jimmy; no that wasn't Jimmy, that was Misaib and Hibby Hardy.
Uh-huh.

Right.
I notice you got a few pictures of Lionel Hampton. Was it like at the time they would come through?

Yes, they were playin' a show at the Fox Theatre. They had big bands comin' at the Fox during that time, and he came to St. Louis and he heard we were playin' the Castle Ballroom so they all come down to the Castle Ballroom. Lionel, Jess Stacy, Ziggy Ellman, all the bunch and Benny and they'd wanna come in to, to see if they could sit in because at that time there was a lot of jam sessions goin' on. Musicians would get familiar with each other just by; you know; that was a good way to communicate. I mean all these jam sessions, you know, find out what guys could do and they could find out what you could do and we had a great time. We had a lot of things like that. I know during the time that I was in St. Louis and I worked with Ben Thigpen we had such a; guys comin' in on our job like Jimmy Forrest and, uh, Jimmy Forrest and, uh Joe Kid Amans? and Chris Woods and "Little Man" (Charles Wright) you know and you'd have quite a ball, man, you know.
Uh-huh. And I'm sure those were what you call the "do thing" days of musicians that were really trying to do their thing at that time, and I'm sure they were rewarding years. You know that you got a chance to meet . . .

Oh yes, man, it was a great life for me because I've always cherished music and I'm still active in the game, you know . . .
Right.

I went out playin' with different groups. I'm workin' with a group now; Chuck Tillman, yeah, and his quartet.
Is that the name of the group you're working with now? Chuck Tillman.

Chuck Tillman, yeah.
All right. At the present time where are you working now, George?

I don't have anything steady, I'm just free-lancin' mostly.
Whenever you're called; your last gig with Chuck and the group you work with now, was; do you know what club it was at?

We worked at Noah's Ark.
I see. Okay.

Yeah, we were out there and then uh, and then we had a few transcriptions. I played with him on . . . Of course I get a chance to work with more groups cause a lot of guys is callin' me you know.
Right.

And I stay pretty busy.
And that's just because you learned your instrument well, and you got with some of the greats and you did a good job; that's why you're always . . .

Oh yeah, well you get that name you know; either one way or the other; if you're not dependable the less gigs you'll get, if you're dependable and you go on a job to work and do a good job well, you know you can always get a call, you know. I found that out during my lifetime in music, you know.
Right. We're going to find out some info about George's brother another time, and we're going to end this one and at this time this has been an interview with Mr. George Brazier, Sr. on a Saturday afternoon, January 9, 1982. With George and Jimmy, we'll sign this off.

Jesse Leroy Brazier Born March 17, 1909, St. Louis, Mo., died May 14, 1981, St. Louis, Mo.

Jesse Leroy Brazier is the older brother of George Brazier (bassist and vocalist).

Jesse was a member of Eddie Randall's Band as was his younger brother, George. Jesse was called "drummer man" and was a top-notch performer in the field of music. He traveled extensively with Eddie Randall, especially to New York where he was always well-received in night clubs and the spacious Harlem Country Club.

Jesse had four brothers: George, Clyde, Harold and Roland Brazier, all of East St. Louis, Illinois.

Olive Brown Vocalist, drummer/Born August 20, 1922, St. Louis, Mo., died April 1981, St. Louis, Mo.

Olive Brown's mother was a ragtime pianist and the family moved to Detroit, Michigan, when Olive was three months old. She was raised in Detroit, but made frequent trips back to St. Louis. She sang at Kennerly Sanctified Temple in St. Louis in 1927. She left home to work outside music from 1936 to 1941. In the late '30s she worked with Todd Roades Orchestra in the Blues in the Night revue in Detroit.

From 1963 to 1967, Buck Clayton's group worked at Toronto's Colonial Tavern, known as a jazz mecca in those days. The management decided a vocalist would be a valuable asset and the world was treated to Olive Brown's vibrant voice. That critical audience was a mixed one—Canadian, European, and American—with their reserve, enthusiasm and indifference, and they decided that a new, worthwhile performer had arrived.

A Canadian critic, Patrick Scott, crowned her with a title, "New Empress of the Blues." Olive went to the local record shops in search of Bessie Smith records to broaden her repertoire and shape up her new image.

During these good years Olive worked the high spots and the low spots: The Silver Dollar, the Westover and Warwick hotels, the Town Tavern, Cav-A Bob, Golden Nugget, and the Colonial. She had a volatile personality and therefore had her ups and downs. She crossed swords with the Toronto Symphony at Massey Hall and came up a winner with a dazzling rendition of "Summertime."

Then Olive was on the move again, back to her country's ghettos, and a brief reunion with Don Ewell in Detroit.

Although her life began in St. Louis, she regarded Detroit as her home since her childhood years were spent there, but she was on the road at age fourteen, leaving her home behind her. Her life was anything but glamorous. It transversed from low-life clubs, to illness, to a missed movie role as Billie Holliday in 1958, to being out of work in New York. Things brightened when she sang for a performers' party at the Apollo Theater, for in the audience was Earl Warren, one-time lead alto player for Count Basie's Band, who was then a musical director. He was instrumental in getting Olive her gig with Buck Clayton, which led her to her first real recording session that produced the record "Olive Brown and Her Blues Chasers."

She was a combination of Bessie Smith and Ethel Waters with an echo of Billie Holliday. Her earthy smoothness makes her singing both real, authentic and great. Hers is the type of voice that attracts, hypnotizes and holds you forever in its spell. It is a constant voice; it was then, it is now. A classic.

A partial listing of her club dates and concerts follows.

1941   Club Zombi, Detroit.
1943   Champion Bar, Detroit.
1943   Uncle Tom's Plantation Club, Detroit, with Earl Bostic Orchestra.
1943   Smalls Paradise with Cecil Scott, New York, N.Y.
1943   El Grotto Room, Pershing Hotel, Chicago, Ill.
1944–1947   Club Three Sixes with Teddy Buckner Orchestra.
1945   T.J. Fowler Band in Paul William's Huckle-Buck Revue Lee's Sensation, Detroit, Mich.
1946   Royal Gardens Club with Gene Ammons, Flint, Mich.
1948   Recorded on Our World label, Nashville, Tenn.
Early '50s   Casbah Club with Jackie Wilson, Detroit, Mich.
Mid '50s   Club Moonglow, Buffalo, N.Y.
1958   William's Bar, Buffalo, N.Y.
1960   Sun Valley Motor Hotel, Harlingen, Texas.
1960   Holiday Inn, Mission, Texas.
1960   House of Steaks, Houston, Texas.
1960   Sho Biz Restaurant, Houston, Texas.

1960 Connies on Lenox, New York, N.Y.

1963 Olive moved to Toronto, Canada.

1963 Canadian National Exhibition, Toronto, Canada.

1963–1967 Colonial Tavern, Toronto, Canada.

1964 Westover Hotel, Toronto, Canada.

1964 Warwick Hotel, Toronto, Canada.

1964 Recorded with Hallie Ingram, Blues Spectacle label, Toronto, Canada.

1964 Appeared on *A La Carte Show*, CBC-TV, Toronto, Canada.

1964 On *Festival Presents the Blues*, CBC-TV, Toronto, Canada.

1964 Waverly Hotel, Toronto, Canada.

1965 Recorded on Spivey label, Brooklyn, N.Y. (date not verified).

1965 Town Tavern, Toronto, Canada.

1965 Ryerson Concert, Toronto, Canada.

1965–1968 Golden Nugget, Toronto, Canada.

1965 Penny Farthing, Toronto, Canada.

1965 Club 76, Toronto, Canada.

1965 Le Caberett, Toronto, Canada.

1966 Local club dates in Kansas City, Missouri.

1967–1968 Cab-A-Bob Club, Toronto, Canada.

1967 Ford Hotel with Cy McLean's Trio, Toronto, Canada.

1968 Town Tavern, Toronto, Canada.

1968 Massey Hall with Henry Cuesta Sextet/Toronto Symphony Orchestra, Toronto, Canada.

1968 Ragtime Society Concert, Toronto, Canada.

1968 Bakers Keyboard Lounge with Don Ewell, Detroit, Mich.

1970–1973 *Goldenrod/Admiral* Streckfuss riverboats, St. Louis, Mo.

1971 Blues/Jazz Festival, Memphis, Tenn.

1972 Cotton Festival, Memphis, Tenn.

1973 Chicago Roadhouse Restaurant, Detroit, Mich.

1973 Detroit Hot Jazz Society Concert with Gabriel Brothers Band, Detroit, Mich.

1973 Recorded JPT label with Blues Chasers, Detroit, Mich.

1973 Hotel Pontchartrain with New McKinney's Cotton Pickers, Detroit, Mich.

1973 Rod's Outdoor Theater with Teddy Wilson, Cool Valley, Texas.

1973 Coliseum with Lee Castle's Dorsey Band, Austin, Texas.

1973 Municipal Auditorium with Knocky Parker, Kerrville, Texas.

1973 St. Louis Ragtime Festival, St. Louis, Mo.

1973 Evansville Jazz Festival, Evansville, Ind.

1973 Big Horn Festival with St. Louis All-Stars, Mundelein, Ill.

1974 Cafe Nostalgique, Detroit, Mich.

1974 Highland Park Community College, Detroit, Mich.

1974 Ragtime Festival, Kerrville, Texas.

1974 Carnegie Hall with New McKinney's Cotton Pickers, New York, N.Y.

1975– Gave college concerts through South and Midwest.

George "Bubba" Buckner III Drummer/Born 1928, St. Louis, Mo.

Bubba was the son of George Buckner, who was the son of Joe

Buckner's grandfather, Owen Buckner. (Bubba was not a brother to Milt or Ted as has mistakenly been printed in other works.)

He now resides in Los Angeles, California, and is still working as a drummer at the time of this writing.

Joe Buckner Piano/Born June 4, 1924, St. Louis, Mo./Interviewed by Jimmy Jones and Lyn Cunningham.

Let's start with where you were born and how you became inspired to play the piano.

I was born June 4, 1924, I think sometime around two in the morning.
That's precise.

That's what they tell me. My mother was a singer.
What was her name?

At that time her name was Lola House. My father was a piano player. His name was Huston Buckner. He studied in Kentucky.

I started playing at eight years old. I was sitting in front of the keys and he was telling me what to hit and what not to hit.
From scratch.

My father had intended to give my brothers music lessons too, but while we'd be playin' they'd be dancin', so he decided they'd be better dancers than they would be players. We made our first gig with him.
Tell me about the crates, Joe.

All right, you took an egg crate that's heavy, see, and turned it so the tall part would be up and take cans like Karo or Top Most, or anything, take the labels off them and paint them and then he would nail it to the sides of those crates, then he would take a stick, put it right in the middle, take a pie pan or any kind of top, put it on top and make a cymbal out of it and then we'd go around to different taverns and make the gigs, just for the tips.
I see.

Dad could play about anything you could name. So since he knew Pine Top we played Boogie Woogie. I'd play the tin cans and my brothers would do the buck dancin'. At the end of the night sometimes we'd bring home fifteen or twenty dollars.
Now is that where the "Pine Top Boogie" came into being?

Pine Top wrote it, Tommy Dorsey, Harry James and all of them started puttin' out the "One O'clock Jump," all that originated from Pine Top.
I see.

And that was the motion of walkin' the bass with your left hand.
Right.

I think it's twelve on blues, but Pine Top made it up. My father said the tempo was so fast it was impossible to see that left hand.
Your father was a surveyor, right?

He surveyed all of Lickenwell Street right here in St. Louis. My grandfather was a farmer. He worked for a fellow called Billy Ferguson, and they worked him for years and years. I was eleven years old when my father died. Just before he died he called me to his bed and told me to look after my two brothers and my mother. One of my brother's names was Deador, the other Owen. That cut my schooling short. I scrubbed steps, sold wood, vegetables and at the age of sixteen I worked for Okie Doke Potato Chip Company.

I remember that company.

From the time my father died I started playing in church pretty regular. I enjoyed it, but as you know in church you have to have the feel for it. I've known my wife since we were about thirteen years old. The first thing she ever said about me was, "Who is that little skinny boy with the big head?" and I never thought I'd end up marryin' her. I really was underweight. I went to Turner school until I got out of the eighth grade. I didn't go anymore because I was workin'. I got married at the age of eighteen and went into service, in the Army. I was in the sixth wave to hit Normandy Beach. I have five Battle Stars and a letter from the President, President Roosevelt, and a Silver Star. I got wounded. I also boxed before I went into service. Fought for Golden Glove tournaments here and lost in the finals. I had three knockouts and one decision.

I got discharged November 27, 1945. My first job out of service was at Scullens. I stayed there about five months. Due to a near fatal accident there I quit and went back to playing music. Me and Pete Haney, a saxophonist, and Clarence Taylor. Didn't have a bass player. We played the Golden Fox and all around and at that time I met Joe Smith.

The Mighty Joe Smith.

Yes, the Mighty Joe Smith. He said you have to be in the Local, or else you don't have any protection. At that time the local was on Delmar and he put me in it. The first job he gave me was over at the Rio on Jefferson and Market.

Oh, yes.

March Deckwitie, Charles Lawrence, myself and Joe Smith; Joe Smith was the leader. We were doin' "Body and Soul." Now "Body and Soul" has always messed me up, still messes me up lots of times. Joe Smith had a way of poppin' you on your fingers with the sticks if you made a mistake. Rather than get hit with those sticks, when I got to certain passages in "Body and Soul," I just wouldn't play it. I'd just stop and let the bass and the saxophone do the playin' and when it came back to where I knew it, I would play it.

So I stayed with Joe for . . . I don't know how long. I stayed because we were playing at the Three Bees, right next to the Roosevelt Theater. Then I played with Horsecollar for about two years. I was still in my early twenties.

Top: Joe Buckner on piano. *Opposite:* As he appeared in a promotional shot.

I also played baseball. I played in the National in the U.S. League. I played with the Boston Blues. Made two hundred fifty dollars a month. The Kansas City Monarchs saw me and they wanted me, so I joined with them. Now me and Satchel Paige used to sit in spring training. He would play the guitar and I would play the piano.

Oh, he was a musician too?

He was also a vegetarian, he didn't eat any meat. And he would walk two or three miles every morning and at bedtime. I outreached my arm and hurt it and Cleveland wouldn't accept me.

After that period I applied myself to the music field and joined Tommy Dean's group. This was in the fifties. We recorded for Vee-Jays Recording Company. The songs were "Evenin' Times," "How Can I Let You Go?,"

"One More Mile" and "Deanie Boy." They say we stayed first on the charts about twenty weeks. We sold almost a million copies in Europe.
Was that of "Evening Time"?
Yes. Since it was the same record it went on A and B sides. In the U.S. it was about 150,000 copies short of a million. Personally I only made three hundred dollars out of the thing, and I was still walkin' around with holes in my shoes.
In other words they were rippin' you off. . .
Rippin' off good! Managing, marketing and distribution are the main things you have to have to sell records.

After that we toured from Milwaukee to Chicago and headed South for the whole circuit, all the way around through Texas. In Texas we met the Midnighters with James Brown. Then we went to California. In San Francisco we met Count Basie and had a chance to play on the same card, then we went to Seattle, Washington.

When we got back to Chicago, they had three secretaries you had to get through to talk to the same man we used to walk in the front door and talk to. They'd made a lot of money off of us! That was the time Jimmy Forrest was cuttin' in Chicago, but "Night Train" hadn't hit yet and I saw them jump down his throat when he asked for 300 dollars. And now it's one of the top records of all times. It's still sellin'.
That's right. And all of these are St. Louis products.
Any bands that's worthwhile, that you see, has somebody from St. Louis in it.

So I came back and played at the Ramada North for nine months, no . . . the nine months was the Hilton by the Airport.
And what we're really about in this research is to let people know that we have superstars that are not known. At least we'll let them know that we've got 'em, always will have them, and it's never too late.
It's a funny thing about the black musicians, they go into a place that is down, no crowd, build the place up, and once you've built it up, out you go. Then they want something new. Why try something new when you're making money with something you had all the time? Not all places are like this but the majority are. So they try something new, and the minute the bottom falls out, they call you up and say, "How about comin' on back?" So the whole thing starts all over again. It's an uphill battle all the way. All the time, rebuild.
He uses you up like the song says. Then he says, I want to try something else.
Right. But I will say the majority of black musicians got their roots from the church. We had to have something to hold onto, and that's what we held onto. It's faith. Now this is not all black musicians, it's white too. Musicians just have a hard way to go, period.

Milton "Milt" Buckner Piano, organ, vibes, arranger/Born July 10, 1915, St. Louis, Mo., died July 27, 1977, Chicago, Ill.

He was orphaned at the age of nine and he and his brother, Ted, were raised in Detroit, Michigan. He received his musical education from his uncle, John Tobias, a trombonist.

In 1930 he did some of his first arrangements for Earl Walton's Band. During the time he was attending the Detroit Institute of Arts he played with the Harlem Aristocrats, Mose Burke, and the Dixie Whangdoodles over a period of two years. Later on he played and arranged for McKinney's Cotton Pickers and he worked mainly in Detroit throughout the 1930s. He played with Jimmy Raschelle, Howard Bunts, Lanky Bowman, and Don Cox.

In 1941 he joined Lionel Hampton as an assistant director and staff arranger. He remained with Lionel until 1948, when he left to form the Milt Buckner Sextet, which he built into a big band. He did rejoin Lionel Hampton in 1950 and remained there until 1952.

After this period he made a specialty of playing his Hammond organ, featuring his own highly successful trio. He made tours of Europe during the late 1960s; in fact, during 1969 he spent several months in Europe with drummer Jo Jones. In 1971 he toured Europe again.

Theodore Guy "Ted" Buckner Alto sax/Born December 14, 1913, St. Louis, Mo., died August 12, 1976, Detroit, Mich.

Ted Buckner played in Detroit, Michigan, during the 1930s. He then went with Jimmy Lunceford from the late 1930s until 1943. He led his own group in and around Detroit and toured with a band led by Todd Rhodes. He co-led a big band in Detroit with the brother of sax player Ernie Wilkins, whose name was Jimmy Wilkins, the trombonist. He toured France with Sam Price in 1975, but his main job was studio work. He worked in studios with the studio bands as musical sound background for films and professional singers. His musical tapes were sent from one studio to the other all over the United States.

He was Milton Buckner's brother. He and his brother were orphaned at an early age and both were Owen Buckner's brothers. Owen Buckner was not a musician but he was Joe Buckner's grandfather.

Lynn Carol *see* **Carol Shoop**

Theodore "Wingie" Carpenter Trumpet, vocalist/Born April 15, 1898, St. Louis, Mo., died July 8, 1975, New York, N.Y.

Theodore Carpenter was born April 15, 1898, in St. Louis, Missouri. Early in his teens he was involved in an accident, and as a result his left arm had to be amputated. The amputation was performed by a surgeon who was the uncle of Doc Cheatham. Henceforth, his name became "Wingie."

In his early twenties he took up the trumpet and by 1920 was playing with carnivals and medicine shows around the country. In 1929 he toured with Herbert's Minstrel Band. Following that period he settled in Cincinnati, Ohio, where he worked with Zack Whyte, Clarence Paige, Wes Helvey and Speed Webb in 1926.

In 1927 he played in residency with Eugene Primus in Buffalo, N.Y. Also from late 1926 to 1928 he was with the Whitman Sister's Show under the direction of pianist Troy Snapp and His Band. In 1930 he was featured with Smiling Billy Steward's Celery City Serenaders in Florida, and a band led by Bill Lacey.

During this period he toured with Jesse Stowe, Dick Bunch and Jack Ellis. He settled in New York, working with Skeets Tolbert and Fritz Weston. He led his own small band from 1939 to 1960. He had long residencies at the Black Cat, Tony Pastor's, New Capitol, and the Yeah Man in New York City. He continued to lead his own band and play dance dates through the 1960s.

Gerald C. "Jerry" Cherry Bassist/Born January 19, 1929, St. Louis, Mo./Interviewed by Jimmy Jones and Lyn Cunningham.
Jerry, it's nice talking to you. How are you doing today?

Oh, about average.

And your full name is Gerald C. Cherry. Jerry is a stage name? Where were you born, Jerry?

St. Louis, Missouri City Hospital.

What year was that?

January 19, 1929.

All right, now what were your parents' names?

My mother's name was Ruth. My father I never did see, they were separated when I was very young. His name was Homer, but I was never associated with him.

Your early childhood was with the grandparents?

Just my grandmother.

And her name?

Ida McDowell.

Where did you go to grade school?

Down on 7th and Barron where they used to run the old hearse wagon by with the horses hooked to it. Then after six years I went to Madison School down near 7th and Hickory.

That's a high school?

No, grade school. I went to McKinley High School.

When did you start with the bass, Jerry?

I started in Okinawa. I joined the Air Force when I was about 18.

This was right out of high school?

Gerald C. "Jerry" Cherry

More or less, in fact I left about two weeks before graduation.
I see.

But I got over to Okinawa and a typhoon hit the island and there was a special service building up above us on the hill. The weather station blew away at about 180 miles an hour, and it hit that special service building and they kept instruments up there and everything and a bass came flying down and landed in our barracks yard. It broke the neck off the bass, and the bridge of it and everything, so I ran out into the typhoon and brought it back and threw it under my bunk and finally I repaired it. I didn't know nothing about it, the sound post — I threw that away, because I figured the top would stay up by itself. And so, that was my first repair job. I put two bolts through the neck and left them there and I wore all the cuffs off my shirts. It didn't occur to me to cut them off, isn't that dumb?

A bunch of country boys came by and said, "Are you a bass player?" I said no. I didn't even know how to tune it or which way it goes. They said, "Well, we'll show you, hey can you keep time?" I said, oh yeah! They said, "We'll give you ten bucks a night if you'll play with us, and we'll show you how to tune it." So I went out and played that first job with 'em and I hit one right note. And I knew it. So everytime, I'd wait for that note to come around, and I'd dive on that sucker! Pretty soon I realized there was a pattern to all this madness. You know, the country boys will give you an education. Finally I figured out if I could make ten bucks a night and not know anything, maybe if I learned a little something, I could make fifteen. But I stayed with those people about six months and we had a trio together doing all of Nat King Cole's stuff.

I met a guitar player from Clovis, New Mexico and there was a, one of those dudes there was an accordian player, waiting to get out on that section 8, and we were the only two guys who would have anything to do with it, you know.
Yeah.

Great accordian player, so we started this trio. We were doing all the Nat Cole stuff, Doris Day, you know. Then we came back to the states and I played with another country band. And then there was a place up on the hill in Cheyenne, Wyoming. The Palomino Club. This was about 1950. It was really a gas because they were playing all the good old jazz tunes and I was getting an education, but I never did study formally, but I studied.
You were a natural.

Well, what I did I'd turn the radio on, I didn't care whether it was in the cracks or what, but I played in tune, even though the bass wasn't in tune at the recording, because you never know how fast it's going or how slow it's going, but I would sit there and play anything or everything that came. I just listened to the tunes and played and I developed to the point where when something went in the ears it came out the hands. I don't recommend that for the average person but at that time I worked with what I had to work with. It paid off for me, because I never did study. But as far as young people are concerned they should go all the way. They should get in there and go for the concerts, where they have the facilities, and if they've got anything in their heads, they can go to the top.

When did you meet Herb? (Herb Drury)

I met Herb in about 1955 or 1956. He had just got out of the Air Force. I substituted for a guy who lived over there in French Village in East St. Louis. I walked in, I didn't know Herb, he didn't know me, but the first note we hit together, we hit together and from then on it was a case of everything coming together. We had no conversation about it, we just looked at each other and we just shook our heads. Herb and I have never had a dissenting word. We've been together for 28 years. Phil Halsey, our first drummer, was with us for 11 years.

Isn't that beautiful? Were you in the recording sets Herb did?

All of them. We actually made 3 records. One of them was "Jazz on the Right Track," in the early '60s. "Keep Your Sunny Side Up," "It'll Scare You to Death." If we ever do another album, we'll probably just do it ourself.

Are you working at the Daniele Hotel now, in Clayton?

Yes, on Meramac.

Is there anything else you want to say in ending this interview?

I was real lucky, but it was never a planned thing, someone would come into town and all of a sudden you were on it. Just listen to everything, don't make a choice in between, try to know it all. If you have the knowledge of it you'll know where you fit and when the time comes, you'll be ready. If these young guys would get together and stay together, and not jump around all over from group to group, they would succeed and make a name for themselves.

Thank you for giving us this insight on Jerry Cherry and thank you so much for your time.

Forrest Crawford Tenor sax, clarinet/Born November 11, 1908, St. Louis, Mo.

Forrest Crawford was born in 1908 in St. Louis, Missouri (the month and day are unconfirmed). As far as can be ascertained, his first paid work was with the Joe Gills Band in 1934. In January of 1936 he moved from St. Louis to New York where he worked sporadically with various bands and participated in many recording sessions, including some with Bunny Berigan. In 1937 he developed tuberculosis and was forced to quit playing.

In 1939 he was sufficiently recovered to lead his own band and he returned to St. Louis where he worked at the Showboat Ballroom. Shortly after that he left full-time music and no further trace of his activities can be found.

Leonard "Ham" Davis Trumpet/Born July 4, 1905, St. Louis, Mo., died 1957, New York, N.Y.

In 1924 and 1925 Leonard "Ham" Davis played trumpet with the Odd Fellow Boy's Band in St. Louis, Missouri. Then he moved to New York. Below is a partial listing of his club, concert and recording dates.

> *1926*   With Charlie Skeets.
> *1927*   With Edgar Hayes at the Alhambra Theater.
> *1927–1928*   Worked with Arthur Gibbs Band in New York.
> *1929*   Recorded with Eddie Condon.
> *1928–1929*   With Charlie Johnson.
> *1930–1931*   With Elmer Snowden.
> *1931*   With Don Redman.
> *1932*   With Russell Wooding.
> *1933*   With Benny Carter.
> *1934–1935*   With Luis Russell.
> *October 1935—Spring 1937*   With Louis Armstrong's Orchestra.
> *1937–1938*   Rejoined Edgar Hayes and made trip to Europe.
> *Fall 1938–Spring 1939*   Worked in "Blackbirds" show in New York.
> *1939–1940*   Gigged in New York and worked with Sidney Bechet's nine piece band at Mimo's in March of 1940.
> *1940*   Worked with Edgar Hayes and joined Maurice Hubbard's band.
> *1943*   With George James Band.
> *Late 1940s*   Worked off and on in Alberto Socarras' band.

After this he left full-time music but continued to gig whenever he could until his death in 1957.

Miles Davis Trumpet/Born May 25, 1926, Alton, Ill.

Unlike most of St. Louis' jazz musicians, Miles Davis came from a family with money. He was born in Alton, Illinois, in 1926, but his family moved to East St. Louis, Illinois, while he was still a small baby.

His mother and father encouraged him to be a musician. His mother wanted him to play violin, but his father had him pegged for a trumpet player and presented him with one for his thirteenth birthday. He received private instruction from a St. Louisan who was Duke Ellington's lead trumpet player, Harold "Shorty" Baker. But Miles was impressed by Clark Terry, another trumpet player from St. Louis, who also played with Duke Ellington's Band.

At age sixteen Miles was playing with Eddie Randle and his Blue Devils.

Sonny Stitt came to St. Louis with Tiny Bradshaw's Band and offered Miles a trumpet chair at sixty dollars a week, but Miles' mother refused to let him play until he finished high school. When Billy Eckstein's band came to St. Louis, Miles was ready, and after playing with him for two weeks he knew he had to go to New York. Two members of that band were Dizzy Gillespie and Charlie Parker. They had a profound effect on Miles.

Miles' father enrolled him in the Juilliard School of Music in New York. He searched for Charlie Parker, and finding him, became his roommate. Charlie was hooked on the needle, and this association cost Miles in more ways than one.

Parker did help Miles musically in return. Miles listened and learned because Parker never talked music, no one rehearsed, it was strictly on-the-job training. On recording dates, most of the material was new, never rehearsed.

Miles left Juilliard to go with Charlie Parker. Miles wanted to quit every night, he was so frustrated trying to play improvisation and develop his own style at the same time. He couldn't play like Armstrong, he couldn't play like Gillespie. He played in the middle register, he just couldn't hear that high and he had a dependency on lyricism.

He remained in a state of development through the '50s, '60s and '70s. He made a series of albums, and those albums document his progress. He has emerged as the most influential modern jazz trumpet since Dizzy Gillespie, both in nightclubs and on records. He is noted for his soft, rich, intensely personal tone. Lyrical jazz.

His health and habits definitely slowed him down to a near halt in mid-career. In 1949 Miles became a heroin addict. By 1954 he was cleaned up and had made records all through this period.

Miles had nodes removed from his vocal chords and this left him with a voice much hoarser than Louis Armstrong's, and he speaks in a rough whisper.

A car crash in 1972 put another stop to his activity. Both his legs were broken. This nearly made him a recluse.

"Agharta," recorded in Japan in 1975, was his last album of new material for five years. During this time he was recuperating from a hip transplant.

Then, through the encouragement of his new wife, Cicely Tyson, he reemerged in 1981 with a new album and concert appearances. Many old supporters were disappointed by his new pop cliches, including some vocals. A partial listing of his work follows:

1957	Miles Ahead	1969	In a Silent Way
1958	Porgy and Bess	1970	Bitches Brew
1959	Sketches of Spain, Kind	1972	On the Corner
	of Blue	1974	Get Up with It
1962	Quiet Nights	1975	Agharta

1978	Water Babies	1982	We Want Miles
1981	The Man with the Horn	1983	Star People

Miles records exclusively for Columbia Records. His last appearance in St. Louis was at the Kiel Opera House on Friday, October 13, 1981.

William "Billy" Davis, Jr. Vocalist/Born June 26, 1940, St. Louis, Mo.

Billy Davis was one of the charter members of The Fifth Dimension, and a cousin of LeMonte McLemore.

In 1969 Billy was married to Marilyn McCoo, who along with LeMonte McLemore formed the original group in the mid-sixties in Los Angeles, California. That original group was called The Hi Fi's. Marilyn and LeMonte recruited Floyd Butler and Harry Elston for that group and eventually formed a group of their own, after they left The Hi Fi's, called The Friends of Distinction.

Billy Davis was one of the replacements, along with Florence LaRue and Ron Townson. The group's name was then changed to The Versatiles.

Marc Gordon, a Los Angeles record executive turned agent, agreed to handle their careers. He got them a contract with Johnny Rivers' Soul City label and they made a minor hit called "I'll Be Loving You Forever," and changed the group's name to The Fifth Dimension.

With the unknown writers Jim Webb and Laura Nyro this group hit the top. In 1970 they switched to the Bell label and in 1975 were signed by ABC Records.

In 1976 Billy Davis and Marilyn McCoo left the group for solo careers, and Billy was replaced by Daniel Beard. Billy and Marilyn made records together and separately. In 1980 they split up and Marilyn McCoo co-hosted the TV show *Solid Gold*.

Calvin Dillard Saxophone, organ, banjo/Born October 16, 1911, Little Rock, Ark./Interviewed by Jimmy Jones.

We are getting ready to interview a man who has his own club in the St. Louis area. The first thing I should find out is, who I'm interviewing. What's your name?

Calvin Dillard.

Mr. Calvin Dillard. Okay, Calvin, first of all I guess we should find out where and when you were born.

Little Rock, Arkansas on October 16, 1911.

What were your mother and father's names?

My mother's name was Esther Webb Dillard, and my father's name was Luke Dillard.

And where were they born?

Little Rock, Arkansas.

Little Rock. That's my home town. When did you come to St. Louis?

My dad brought me when I was five years old.

Then you probably attended grade and high school here?

Yes. The first school I started to was El Overture down on Papan. 2612 Papan.

That was a grade school.

Yeah. We all went to secondary, that was Marshall, and then I went to Sumner High.

What was the first experience you had in music, Calvin?

Well, when I was five years old I could play all the church songs. My people were religious and we had an organ and I'd climb up on the stool and I could play all the church songs that they sang. That was the beginning. And I've always loved music all my life and my people were religious and they kept me in church.

I know about that. Was it sax all the time or when did you first have the experience with the saxophone?

Well, the saxophone. . . I don't exactly recall the year but my first instrument was a banjo and my teacher's name was Harris and she had a studio on Sarah Street (St. Louis).

That was your first teacher?

Right.

Do you remember her first name?

I can't quite recall her first name.

Did she have a house or . . .

No, she had a studio between Sarah and Fairfox.

How old were you then?

About sixteen or seventeen.

That puts you in an age for high school band.

I didn't play in the high school band, but I used to play all the high school parties.

You got the good gigs.

Yeah, I got the good part, yeah. We had a ten piece band going to school then and we used to play all the afternoon parties that they had in school.

I see. Did you have a name for that group?

The Rhythm Aces. The same as my group now, Calvin Dillard and his Rhythm Aces. The first leader of that group was Bob Johnson, he was a trumpet player.

Was he from St. Louis?

Yeah, he was a St. Louis boy.

After high school when you were doing gigs, and I'm sure there were

Dillard (on saxophone) with "Pops" Porter on piano.

plenty of them, were there any other things you want to remember or talk about?

Well, uh . . . I went to Chicago, William Weldon, we called him "Casey Bill," he played an electrical saw and he made it sound just like a violin and he was really good at it.

William Weldon?

He wrote the "Outskirts of Town."

The song? Gonna move on the "Outskirts of Town"? That was his number?

Yeah, that's it.

And his name was William Weldon.

William Weldon. We called him "Casey Bill."

That was his nickname.

Yeah. There were three of us, Henry Singleton, he's a St. Louis boy, Mr. Weldon and myself. I played banjo then and Henry played guitar, and William Weldon played the saw. We decided we needed an instrument so I got the saxophone. I got it that Monday and that Friday night I played the gig.

That's what I call quick versatility.

I'm tellin' ya. *(They laugh.)* From then on I've been playin' saxophone.

That was after you had the experience with the young man who played the electrical saw? And after that?

Yeah. My friends stayed there in Chicago, but I left and came back home and I stayed home a couple of years and then I went out to Los Angeles, California. First time I went to L.A. I hoboed out there.

That was in those years when you had to get around the best you could.

That's right, because you had no money.

Let me ask you this about your first paid gig. I asked a lot of guys and the pay was pretty low in those days.

Oh, yeah. I had a gig at the Wunderbar when I was stayin' in St. Louis and I made a dollar and a half a night, but see you could take a nights wages and pay your rent and still have fifty cents left. See what I mean? I really believe the value of money was better than it is now.

A dollar and a half a night. That was about the first paid gig that you had?

Right.

I think a lot of the men I interviewed talked about the Wunderbar.

We had Leo there and Jimmy Longstreet. We had Jeddie, quite a few guys.

Was this still the Dillard group?

No. In fact we didn't even call it a group, we just went to work. We didn't go under a certain name, we just went to work. Martin Boze was one of my school friends and he was one of the boys in the band. Martin Boze, Robert Johnson, Buford Haddocks, he played bass, Julius Wright and Bunky Park. They were in the band. And also the Johnson fellows, they lived out in Elmo Park. Tony was the youngest boy and he was quite a trumpet player. He had on little short pants, we used to take him to the job and set him up there in his short pants and he'd blow, boy! And sometimes he'd go to sleep and we'd have to wake him up and he'd wake up and blow.

Wake up and keep on blowin', huh?

Robert Corner, you remember him? And Alex Shells. Sometimes Martin Boze, he was the main drummer, but sometimes he'd be gone and we'd use Alex Shells.

Did you do a lot of traveling, play with any big names?

I only played a big name once, that was Earl Hines out in Los Angeles. I traveled with some bands. I recall them as pretty good bands, Jimmy Dimwittie, and Kettlelips Hacket. Kettlelips Hacket's band had Lawrence Dimwittie, he plays bass, you know, and Charlie Fox, Hughie Well. There were four guys from St. Louis, and the rest of them were from Indiana and Virginia. Jimmy Dimwittie was Lawrence's brother so he had the band and we traveled all over down south, all through Florida, and we played gigs. Once we were on a kick and we were following Count Basie. And we'd get the gravy. Count Basie had the best band but we'd get the gravy. We was the biggest clowns and we played pretty good too, see? The Count remarked once, "Why do you all have to follow us all the time?"

I guess in traveling you had quite a few experiences. What is one of the most weird experiences that you remember?

When we were travelin' with Jimmy Dimwittie's band we used to spell each other, take turns driving. We gave Charlie Fox the wheel that night and Charlie kept hollering for somebody to take it so he could sleep, and we didn't pay him no mind, and he run over in the middle of a big muddy field, that mud was seven or eight inches deep and we had to wait until next morning for a tow truck to come pull us out of the mud. That was really a tough experience in my estimation.

That would be frightening.

Yeah.

After doing some traveling I'm sure your home base was finally St. Louis.

Yeah, it was.

Tell me something about your St. Louis experiences. In fact, something about the club you own here in St. Louis. Now that took quite a bit of patience and money, I would imagine.

Yes.

How about that club? Where's it located anyway?

It's at 4422 Martin Luther King in St. Louis, Missouri. I had a terrible time trying to get things together. I had five or six different places, and always something happens that messes up the deal. Now, the club before this, a guy bought the building and wanted my part, so I got out of there and this is the place I got. Now of all the places I think this is the best one.

What do you think it takes to make a musician? Everyone has a different theory.

Well sometimes the guys that's got some money can go to the schools and study music. But guys like me, I made myself a musician. I didn't have no money, but I got the foundation together and after I got that foundation together, I studied. I arrange most of my pieces that I play. I took music out in California so I could arrange it. Now I can write down what's in my mind without the instrument.

Now for any young musician who would be reading this, what would be your advice?

The main thing is to get the fundamentals. The fundamentals are the main thing. Then you go from there. You have to practice, you have to study. Learn your instrument.

And I'm sure that Mrs. Dillard has been an inspiration.

Yes, she has.

Behind every guy that does anything at all, whether it's good or bad, there has to be somebody that's with him, that's in his corner.

That's right, my wife has been in my corner right along, all the time. And anything I do she'll fall right in there with me. Sometimes she don't like it, but she's right there with me just the same. Sometimes she don't like what is happenin', but if I like it she'll come on in and go along with me.

And that's really good. Is there anything else we should talk about, Calvin? As far as Mr. Dillard is concerned?

I have several pieces of music. I think I have about thirty-two numbers.

Thirty-two original songs that you have written?

Yes, but I've been working so trying to get these things together I haven't had time to really go through it.

Do you want to mention the one you have a copyright on?

This thing is, "Thanks For Nothin."

That's written, arranged and owned by Mr. Calvin Dillard of St. Louis, Missouri.

Yeah, it's really a beautiful number. In the minor key.

Anything else we should mention?

In California I played for some of the nice clubs. I played the Morocco, Club Alabam; I played the San Pedro Club. We stayed there almost three years. Then we played down at the Morrison Hotel on Fifth Street; we played there for about a year and a half. We played at the Navoo which is on Sixth Street. We played there six months. We had several places. I took my band from there to Las Vegas, Nevada. We played the Cotton Club in Las Vegas two years.

A lot of musicians have Las Vegas ambitions.

Well I had one of the richest reasons in the world. I don't know whether he still remembers me, but he used to come over and keep me up every night after he got off the strip. Sammy Davis. He used to come over there and I'd play piano while he beat the drums, 'cause he liked to beat those drums. He used to like to sing and everything like that, and he used to keep me up every night. After my band had got off I'd have to stay there with him.

Sammy Davis Jr.

We had quite a ball. We also had a tour with Olive Brown. Do you remember Olive Brown?
Yes.

Well, we had a college circuit, we toured the colleges. We went to Nebraska, Kansas City, Missouri in 1976 and 1977.
All of these are good memories.

Yes, I don't regret a bit of my life.

Hurbert T. "Herb" Drury Piano/Born November 10, 1928, East St. Louis, Ill.

Herb's mother was Mabel Claire Keyton Drury and father was Welton Joseph Drury.

They were not musicians. His mother, however, had two brothers who were musicians. Their names were Howard and Earl Keyton. They had a band together, with Howard playing alto and tenor sax and Earl playing the clarinet.

Herb attended grade school in East St. Louis on the corner of Erving and Monroe streets. He went to Rock High School and East St. Louis Senior High in East St. Louis.

He attended the St. Louis School of Music and Washington University, and graduated from the Institute of Music with a Masters' and B.A. in music.

Mr. Drury has played with no big bands but has made two recordings, "Jazz on the Right Track" and "Keep Your Sunny Side Up." Both are out of print at the present time.

Herb teaches at University of Missouri at St. Louis and teaches private students at his studio.

His advice to younger musicians: "Get as good as you can get, work hard and you have to love it. Don't have illusions that you have to get rich."

Cheryl Ann Dueren (Ann LaRue) Pianist, vocalist/Born October 20, 1950, Florissant, Mo./Interviewed by Jimmy Jones and Lyn Cunningham.

Mother: Dorothy Ann Cook, born St. Louis, Mo., April 1, 1918, still living. Father: Joseph F. Peters III, born St. Louis, Mo., May 19, 1919, still living.

Schooling: Sacred Heart Grade School, Florissant, Mo.; St. Thomas Aquinas High School, Florissant, Mo.; Southwest Missouri State College, Springfield, Mo. (3 years); Florissant Valley Community College, Florissant, Mo. (one semester). (Has had no musical training in school.)
This is Jimmy Jones in the home of Miss Ann LaRue on 10/16/83 about 3:25 on a Sunday afternoon, a dreary Sunday afternoon.

Herb Drury

Four days from my birthday.

Four days from her birthday. (They laugh.) *We're getting an interview from Ann and hopefully we'll be able to use it in the research book we are compiling. How are you, Ann?*

Tired. This is morning time for me.

Lyn Cunningham is with us also, my partner. We're going to feed some questions to you and I think she's already started asking about birthdates and mom and pop, and whatever, right?

Right.

Okay Ann, I think you can just start telling us about your musical training and when and where.

I think my musical training started in this basement with my father. He used to play piano all the time. When I was about three years old he used to sit me on his lap right in front of the piano and he'd play, "Somebody Loves You." Do you remember that old tune?
Yeah, I've got it.

And as soon as I started playing, he never played again. I would just kinda mess around and tinkle with the keys, tune, the notes...
And his name?

Joseph Peters.
Joseph Peters.

...and uh, when I was in grade school I joined the church choir, of course. I sang in the church choir every day. I went to church six days a week. Five days in school, Monday through Friday, and on Sunday I'd sing in the church choir. So that's where I kinda got my start as far as singing, and my mother and I used to do dishes together and she'd teach me all the old standards and all the Mitch Miller stuff and I'd sing harmonies and she'd sing lead and when I was in about third grade or fourth grade, I started taking piano lessons. So I really didn't have any formal training other than being in the church choir, learning from the nuns the theory of the piano, just enough to get me going, because I'd never planned on being a professional musician. I studied sixteen years to be a dancer.
Would you believe that?

I studied five days a week and I taught for four or five years as an assistant to my teacher and I had never planned on being a musician. Never. It was something I really enjoyed to do, it was something I could take frustration out with. It was just a hobby. Playing piano was just a hobby and singing was something you could get out of one hour of school with because you had to go over to church and sing.
Right!

For weddings and funeral masses and you got a chocolate candy bar if you sang in the choir for that day so it was really something just as a hobby and I really ... my real professional job was when I was fifteen and it lasted three months. It was weekends at _____ Louies Lounge at Alton Illinois. Do you remember Louies?
Yeah, I've heard about it.

I worked with two other girls as a three vocalist backup trio for this four piece band. I don't even remember their name. I remember working at Louies though and Cindy and Sandy Baradino, their father would drive us over there on Friday nights, we'd do the gig, we'd come back and we'd each get fifteen dollars a piece and I just thought that was great. Then my mother and father decided that wasn't very good for me to be doing at fifteen and we played one job in Gaslight Square before it went down, at Pepsi A-Go-Go.

Cheryl Ann Dueren, professionally known as Ann LaRue.

Oh, yeah.

We did one job there and the manager found out that we were under age and he fired the band and we only worked one night. Fired the band and that was it and that was the end of my professional career until 1971.

Do you remember the name of the street that this club (Pepsi A-Go-Go) was on?

Next to Whiskey A-Go-Go.

That was in Gaslight Square.

Main drag. Gaslight main drag.

There was only one street there in Gaslight Square.

Uh huh. And we used to sing out in Jackson Park. That was about three months. I guess that was the summer inbetween my freshman and sophomore year. I was fifteen years old. So it was 1965, no, I guess it was 1966. Cause I was already fifteen when I started freshman year.

Now in your study, in your musical learning, is there any specific names that you want to mention as inspiration or people that have maybe helped you besides your mom and pop?

I never received any major help until I was in my twenties. I think that the person that helped me the most was my dancing instructor, Delores Rehling. She really, really kinda said, you know, you can do it. Well I was studying to be a dancer, I wasn't studying to be a musician, but dancing, music and entertaining all kind of mingle within one another...

The Arts.

...So she really gave me a lot of confidence to be on stage.

How do you spell your dancing teacher's last name?

REHLING. Delores Rehling. She used to have the studio, which is very ironic, right next to where my recording studio is now. Her dance studio was at 440 St. Francis and my recording studio is at 430 St. Francis (Florissant, Missouri). So here I am twenty years later right next door to where I spent my whole childhood. But she, I guess, was the most responsible for me deciding to be in the entertainment field because I received no help from any of the men I was involved with in bands up until 1975 when I met my husband Karl. Up to that time I received no positive input at all. All I received was negative input.

And by the way, his name is Karl?

Karl with a K Dueren.

Dueren and he's a bass player.

And as I was in my early twenties when I became a vocalist, I was away at college. I was away at college and my father was sending me fifteen dollars a week for spending money and I needed more money so I could party because I went to college to get away from home. I didn't go to college to study or to study music. I just went, you know, 'cause that's what you do, and uh, I always sang. I was always singing. I never thought I could make money at it. It was just something that was fun, you get paid for havin' fun and I was hangin' 'round with some musicians from college and I'd go and sing for free with anybody I could sing with and somebody offered me a job. And I thought, why not? Why not do it? That was in 1970 and I wasn't getting paid. I didn't get paid professionally until 1971. It just kinda snowballed and the next thing I know I was a member of a band. A regular member of a regular band and made eighteen dollars apiece a night. It was terrible. They found out I played keyboards and I really wasn't a keyboard player, I just played and the leader of the band bought a piano and said, now you're going to be a piano player and I was just in shock. "Why I can't play in a band." "Sure you can." So I just, it just started happening.

Do you remember the name of the band?

Yeah. Now I gotta say that guy did help me a little bit. His name was Chris Albert and he went by the name of Chico.

Was that his band, Chicos?

Let's see, what was it called? We were called Shorty Dunn. I don't even know why we were called that. We worked weekends and a lot of private parties and fraternity blasts, beer blasts where the crowd is a pretty wild crowd, hangin' from the rafters, getting pretty wild on beer. Now he did have a positive attitude towards me, but most of the musicians I worked with at that time said well, you're just a girl. At that time I didn't think I had enough to offer to ever say anything. I didn't realize the reason I was in the band was I was the selling item. You got a girl in the band and you sell the band. Regardless of your talent, if you're any good, if you're ugly, if you can sing or not, you're a calling card because you're a woman. I finally realized in 1975 when I met my husband that I might have a little bit of talent that I could start using and start becoming better at and I stopped working for other people. I doubled my salary within one month after I met Karl. He said you should quit working for other people. You should start working for yourself. I said I can't work for myself, I don't know what to do. Well sure you do, you know what to do, just do it. That's how I met him. I'd hired him as a bass player. A guy that I'd been working with named Glen Riceleck, he was an excellent jazz guitarist, but he really didn't know how to sell a band to make money. He knew how to put together a band for jazz, but you can't make money at jazz in 1975 in Saint Louis if you're not Herb Drury.

That's right.

So Karl had lived across the street from him when they were little kids, two miles from this house and Glen had dated a couple of my girlfriends when . . . this was . . . it was real odd how this all happened, he said well, I know a bass player. Let's have him come and work with us, so we auditioned him and the next thing I knew the band Glen had put together did not work out. It was a disaster. It was a good band but we couldn't play dance music, so Karl and I stayed together, and we hired a drummer, we rehearsed five days with Randy Risch, the original LaRue and the Flames. After five days I got us an audition at Ruebens and he hired us for forty-five days. Risch used to play in a Greek band here in St. Louis and the next thing you know, we didn't even have enough material to do the job. I figured we just needed an audition to see how we would react under pressure and he hired us for forty-eight weeks. We had to come back home and learn some new songs. We did long versions of songs those days.

Yeah. Well naturally.

We opened the Moorings up there on Clayton Road, Ruebens on Olive, Ruebens in Florissant, and Ruebens on Manchester and that was my first attempt at my own band. With the help of Karl. He was pretty much the brains of it and I was the diplomat, I could sell it. See, here's what you have to do, you talk to these people and tell them how much money you want, because he's not a diplomat, I have the gift of gab, he doesn't. And I've been working very steadily since then.

In interviewing everyone Ann, we always want to try to get our feelings to someone who is going to read this . . . in other words if this book is in a library or college and some young kid is reading it, maybe they're reading the story about Ann LaRue, and in your own words how would you advise a young musician or potential musician, what would you advise them to do musically?

I know one thing, people won't help you, you have to help yourself, realistically speaking, there are people along the way that might support you financially or emotionally, equipment-wise, whatever, but for the most part you have to do it yourself. Some musicians can go to school and learn everything they need to know. Some musicians can go to school and not learn a thing. I know one thing, school doesn't teach you how to get a job. Fortunately for me I was just in places at the right time. I learned how to approach music as a business, rather than as an art. For a long time before 1975, I think that was my breaking point, where Karl said to me, this is not all fun, this is a business. And I'd just thought you got up and played really good and you sang and everything was taken care of for you, and that's not true. Maybe 25 percent is really the music, 50 percent is the way you look and the way you carry yourself, and the clothes you wear and the makeup you put on, and 25 percent is kinda bull. It's kinda just talk, so a musician that's in school that feels like they're the only one that's suffering is natural. There are some musicians that don't have to pay dues. They are just so talented. God's gift. It's a gift from God. It just happens to them. But 99 percent are not God-gifted talented. I have a talent here and a talent there and I use what I have to make it work for me. You have to just pursue. Persistence. If you knock on a hundred doors, one person might talk to you.

If you're not going to go out and pursue your job, your art, your craft, they're not going to knock on your door. They're not going to know you're out there at 903 St. Catherine. You have to go out and make people know who you are. I'm not the best keyboard player in town but I can entertain people. But I know some musicians that can blow me away that can't get jobs, and why is that? Because they haven't mastered the business of music. So, it's just not scales and notes and learning how to play, it's a combination of many things. Being able to sell yourself, being able to budget your money. So that you can buy your equipment, you have to have good equipment and if you're a woman you have to have clothes and you have to understand how to use makeup. I never used makeup before I met my husband. He said, my God, cut your hair, get rid of your glasses, put on some contacts, you got to fix yourself up here. Why does anyone want to come and see you if you sound the same as the person next door, and she's beautiful? They're going to go see her even if you're just as good. So there's tricks.

I want to support myself by playing music, and since I'm not the best piano player by far, and I'm not the best vocalist, I have to make the talent that I have work for me.

Karl II. Dueren Bass/Born May 20, 1953, St. Louis, Mo./Interviewed by Jimmy Jones and Lyn Cunningham.
We're interviewing a young man that's a bassist, and what's your full name, Karl?
Karl Henry Dueren.
And what's your mother and father's name, Karl?
Henry and Joan.
And were they St. Louis born?
Yes.
And were they musically inclined?
My mother was a fair pianist. My father can sing. He used to sing when he was a kid. My grandmother played for the symphony when she was younger.
What was her name?
Hiawatha Lee. I don't know what her real maiden name was because she was an Indian. She's an old, senile lady now and she just started slipping away this year. She's eighty, and her big thing, what she did, her first husband Calvin, he died of tuberculosis. You know back then it took forever to die. She had to quit pretty much serious piano and go play for the silent movies, and play in bars and taverns to make some money for my mom who was the only kid that they had until she got married again, then she had a son and another daughter. She played those kind of speakeasys and saloons to make money so they could have some food.
(Karl's wife) Didn't she tell us once she played behind chicken wire?

Oh yeah. I played behind chicken wire.
Now you were born . . . ?
I was born here in St. Louis.
Birthdate?
May 20, 1953.
Okay. Your grade school and high school?
I went to two different high schools. I went to school in California. I left home when I was seventeen. I went to Walker elementary school. I went to Hazelwood High here and then I went to school in Orange County [California].
Okay. What was your first experience with the music?
It was so early I used to get grounded from the instrument. When I'd mess up my dad would say, okay that's it, put it away. I'd get it out at night anyway.
I started when I was three or four.
I was about nine or ten.
What was the first instrument Karl?
A guitar. A $29.95 special. My parents weren't . . . There was six kids in my family. The first three of us were not as well off as my three younger. My one brother and my two little sisters. By then my father's business had become very profitable. I lived in a small house with six kids. My one brother and two little sisters when they lived at home lived in a great big house, it went totally in the other direction then. My father finally becomes semi-successful. I guess.
What does he do?
He owns a printing company. Arrow Printing.
Okay. What was your first experience with the bass that you're doing now?
Oh, I was about twelve years old, I didn't have a bass guitar, it was an old 6 finger electronic guitar and a guy across the street, it was an old guy you know, he was into jazz and stuff when I was a little kid and I just got in with him and he said maybe we can help you out here . . .
Do you remember his name?
Glen, no, I don't remember his last name, he was just a neighbor.
Yeah, okay. Did you have any important band or places that you played with that you want to mention?
No, I don't want to get into that.
What was the first paid job you ever had?
Oh, a contest.
What kind of contest?
It was a talent contest. M.S. put it on. We were twelve years old. The oldest kid I think was twelve. The youngest guy was ten. We had a four piece group. The singer was ten.
(He laughs.) *Oh, that's neat.*

We were all munchkins, really. And we won the contest. I think that's when I got the bug there, because we won fifty dollars.
Fifty dollars apiece?
Oh, no. We were lucky to even get paid.
And how many of you were there?
Four guys.
Four guys, well that was pretty good.
Yeah. Well two of the guys are still playing music, myself and one other guy. He's an excellent drummer.
To think, fifty dollars did it.
Yeah, that's a thought. *(He laughs.)*
Do you remember some of the places that you played?
I was in almost every bar in St. Louis at one time or another.
Any big names?
I played with some big name people but I'm not gonna...
Okay.
I played with some people that were number one at one time or another.
Uh huh.
That's like all the rest of our people, they're all the same way, modest.
It's no biggy.
Do you want to mention your business? What you're doing now? I know this is primarily number one now, isn't it?
Yeah.
That's what I thought. 'Cause you're investing so much time in it.
Yeah, I've written a couple of songs, but I can't afford to play with my own toys.
Yeah, I know.
It's terrible, I waited years to get this and then I still can't play with it. It turned out to be ironic. I did when I was first wiring it up. It took a few months to wire it up, because it was wire by number, you know?
Do you have any advice for any person or young person who will read this book? Any experience that you had, advise them something to do or not to do?
Oh, I can't give advice, I'm not qualified. *(They laugh.)* Definitely not qualified.
Okay, but you know it's not a piece of cake?
Oh, no. It's the neatest job and at the same time it's the one that will break your heart more than anything.
That's good. That's a good comment...
That's good.
...a very good comment because it's true. Anyway Karl, do we have your permission to use what you have told us in our research book?

Sure, I don't care.
Okay.

Horace Eubanks Clarinet, saxes/Born June 15, 1900, St. Louis, Mo.

After working with Jelly Roll Morton in Vancouver, Canada, in the late 1920s, Horace moved to Chicago, Illinois, and worked with Doc Watson's Band. He then returned to St. Louis where he worked with Charlie Creath. Following is a partial listing of his work.

1925   Charlie Creath, St. Louis, Mo.
1927   "Dixie Strutters," Chicago, Ill.
1928   Worked with violinist Wilson Robinson, Chicago, Ill.
1929   With Benny Peyton in Europe.
1931   With G. Compton in Europe.
1931   Willie Lewis, Europe.
1934   Returned to United States and joined Carroll Dickerson in Chicago, Illinois.
1935   With Zutty Singleton's Band until late 1935 in Chicago, Ill.
1936   Moved back to St. Louis, Mo. and worked for Fate Marable and Charlie Creath.

At this point in his life he suffered a severe illness and spent some years in the Missouri State Mental Hospital in the 1950s.

James Robert "Jimmy" Forrest Tenor saxophone/Born January 24, 1920, St. Louis, Mo., died August 26, 1980, Grand Rapids, Mich.

Whatever unique quality Jimmy Forrest had, he kept until the day he died. It was a pushing, pulsing force within him that kept your ears glued to that tenor sax and once hearing it it was always recognizable in his constant work. He was, in short, one of the greatest musicians of his time, a consistent force that never let down despite his problems and misjudgments. He had plenty of these. Taking into consideration that he was a leading talent in major black bands for over a decade with nothing at all to show his presence there is, to say the least, ironic.

James Robert "Jimmy" Forrest was born in St. Louis on January 24, 1920. His mother, Eva Forrest, was also a musician and had her own group, Eva Forrest's Stompers. By the time he was twelve he was a member of his mother's band. In summers, he worked on the Mississippi riverboats with Fate Marable and others.

He attended Sumner High School in St. Louis. Here he was known as an athlete, not a musician. He lettered in track, baseball and football.

After finishing high school he went to his music full-time. He joined Don Albert and then the Jay McShann Band. He did not record with McShann, but he had a chair next to Charlie "Bird" Parker and learned

much from him. It is said that when they played together most of the applause went to Jimmy.

In 1942 Jimmy replaced Al Sears in the Andy Kirk Band. Al left to join
Duke Ellington. This was the first major move for Jimmy Forrest.

In Kirk's Band, which was doing well, were Mary Lou Williams (who
left), Dick Wilson, Kirk's main soloist (who died), and such notables as
Howard McGhee ("McGhee Special"), Fats Navarro, John Young, Lavern
Baker and Ben Thigpen, a dynamic rhythm section. The band had a Decca
record contract.

America was at war, as was James C. Petrillo's Musicians Union. There
were no commercial recordings by the Kirk Band until late 1943. Those
recordings were never issued or reissued. The never issued included seven
of eleven sides that Jimmy made with the Kirk Band. There is in existence,
however, one album by the Kirk Band taken from radio broadcasts, giving
us our first glimpse of Forrest as a tenor player on record. Not all tenor sax
on that album is Jimmy, for it was a three tenor sax band.

In 1947 Kirk broke up the band and moved on to California. Jimmy
came back to St. Louis and worked for two years, changing with the times.

In 1949 Al Sears left Duke Ellington. A sax chair was open and Charlie
Rouse was in it a short time. Jimmy Hamilton played a lot of tenor but he
preferred clarinet, so when Jimmy Forrest joined that summer, things were
rather up in the air. Jimmy made one recording session with Ellington and
as Jimmy's luck ran, the one tune with a Forrest solo wasn't issued until after
Duke Ellington's death. There is an album of airchecks by Ellington that
does feature Jimmy Forrest solos, "St. Louis Blues" and "It Don't Mean a
Thing."

In 1950 Jimmy was back in St. Louis working with his own combos.

In November of 1951 Jimmy took his band to Chicago to record for a
new label, United. Roosevelt Sykes, Robert Nighthawk, Tab Smith, and
Tiny Grimes recorded for United. Here they had the use of the best sound
studio in Chicago. Jimmy did four sides in one day. The first one was "Bolo
Blues." The flip side turned out to be "Night Train." The Forrest luck
had struck again: Two hit records on one record. This time two and two
made one.

The second hit was to come a few months later. It was called, "Hey,
Mrs. Jones."

By now Jimmy had a drug problem and the years between 1953 and
1956 require no explanation musically. In 1957 Jimmy was on his way up
again. In late 1958 he formed a partnership with Sweets Edison which
lasted a long time and became a showcase for Jimmy. From 1958 to 1962
was the period of his greatest recorded work.

The Edison group recorded for Verve and Roulette. Verve was great
for Jimmy's solos.

He recorded for Enrica, Time, and Bethlehem and signed with Prestige in 1960. He made five exceptional LP's under his own name. Jimmy had recorded for Delmark, but these albums were not issued until years later.

In 1961 Sweets began backing Joe Williams. Joe and Jimmy did two LP's together and appeared at the Newport Jazz Festival. They were joined by Coleman Hawkins and Roy Eldridge in a jam session that closed the Festival. That set belonged totally to Jimmy.

After that, Prestige dropped Jimmy and Joe Williams left Sweets.

Jimmy moved to California and worked Los Angeles night clubs. During this period he suffered two minor heart attacks and could not be as active as he had been. Again he went unrecorded for nine years.

An old friend, tenor sax man Eddie "Lockjaw" Davis from the Andy Kirk days, was Basie's tenor sax player whenever he wanted to be, and for as long as he wanted to be. Lockjaw was prone to take vacations whenever he felt the urge, so Jimmy was recommended as his replacement and soon that replacement became permanent and Jimmy found a home.

Forrest and Al Grey were the spark plugs of Count Basie's Band during the mid-seventies and the summer of 1977. This duo split from the band and worked together from that time on.

Jimmy and his wife Betty lived in Grand Rapids, Michigan, where Al and Jimmy made their last tapes, and where Jimmy died of a liver ailment on August 26, 1980.

Charles W. Fox Piano, dancer/Born April 28, 1921, St. Louis, Mo./ Handwritten interview, 1983.

Born April 28, 1921 in St. Louis, Missouri to Mary E. and Sylvester Fox, being one of ten children. My mother played guitar, my father played mandolin.

I began my career as a dancer or hoofer. At the age of ten, I directed my attention to the piano, while recuperating from a broken leg received playing football.

At age 13, I began playing with various jazz groups and big bands in St. Louis.

I made tours with Len Bowden's 18 piece band in 1936; Kid (Lipps) Hackett's Band; and worked with Ernie Field's Band out of Tulsa, Oklahoma in 1941 and '42.

In 1943, I was drafted into the Army Air Force, where I was placed in special service as a pianist and part-time bass fiddler. I was discharged in 1946. I then started working with Jimmy Forrest, and later worked with Stuff Smith for two years.

Among the jazz greats that I worked with throughout my career, included Charlie Barnett, Ben Webster, Charlie Parker, and Dexter Gordon. I recorded with Dexter Gordon.

I lived and worked in New York for about ten years, commuting to St. Louis.

In 1979, I toured Europe with Clark Terry's Big Band. Later that year, I toured with Clark Terry's quintet and Joe Williams, in 12 countries in east and west Africa.

I now work locally in St. Louis, Missouri and commute to New York working with Clark Terry and his Jolly Giants.

Raymond Gay Piano/Born April 18, 1909, St. Louis, Mo., died 1986, St. Louis, Mo./Interviewed by Jimmy Jones.
Raymond, state your name and where you were born and how you started playing music.
Well I was born in 1909.
Here in St. Louis?
My mother used to always tell me on twenty-second and Franklin, between Franklin and Delmar streets. Everytime we used to pass there she'd say, this is the house you were born in. Of course it's tore down now.
It used to be Easton Ave., now it's Martin Luther King.
And Delmar, yeah.
How long have you been playing music, Raymond?
Well, let's see. Oh, I'd say ever since about 1930.
All right, do you remember what inspired you to start playing?
Well my father used to play a little bit of guitar, he didn't read much but . . .
What was his name?
Selvidge Gay.
So you actually had kind of a musical background in the family?
Well, yes. I always liked music. My mother wanted to be a violin player. She liked a violin. I never did like one myself, they're too squeaky or something. That sound used to go all through me.
So you chose the piano then.
I really started on an old mandolin we had around the house. Dad taught me how to finger it a little bit. I got so I could play four or five numbers on it. Dad would get behind me on the guitar and boy we'd have a little session there.
Father and son, huh?
Yeah, and it kept on. I had a cousin named Dan Mickey and he played piano. He played by ear, and after awhile my mother bought a piano, a player piano. But you could work the keys when that roll was goin'. My cousin would come over and play the piano and I'd stand behind him and watch. After he had gone I would try to pick out the tune with one finger. My mother she'd watch me around there for awhile, and then she'd say, what you gonna do? Why don't you learn to play the violin? We had this

Raymond Gay

little debate on that. She said, so you want to play the piano? I told her I'd like to take lessons. Afterwards she got me a music teacher. His name was John Boler.

Was he from St. Louis too?

Yeah, he was from St. Louis. I think the lessons were fifty cents an hour then. I took lessons from him for about eight or nine years. I got so I got pretty good. I just took it up to entertain myself and I used to give little concerts at the church, you know? I never thought of becoming a professional. Some of the boys in the neighborhood had a little band and they found out I could play a little bit, so they commenced to call me for little jobs. Do you remember Vianthony Taylor?

Raymond Gay (center)

Vianthony Taylor?

You heard of him. He used to be at the DuBoise Hotel over there. So I had some sessions over there, little parties and things. Some of the older guys wouldn't hardly let me set in with the band because I wasn't good enough. That used to hurt my feelings when they'd make me get up and all like that, but I was just determined I was gonna do it. I'd come home and I'd cry, and I'd say some of these days I'm going to make you guys glad to play with me.

Yes.

Well I just kept monkeyin' around like that and finally it did happen. Anyhow I kept playin' those little parties, and it got so I couldn't get up in the morning to go to school. My mother got onto me about it. She told me to get in there and practice and then go to school. She'd go to work in the morning, and instead of me gettin' up I'd go back to sleep and

I commenced missing school, you know? But the boys kept callin' me for those parties, and I was making a little money. Then I lost some school books and I was scared to go back to school because I knew I would have to pay for them. Then mom found out about the whole thing, missing books, missing days, all that stuff. Finally I just got out of school. I really don't remember if they expelled me or not. But I'd go out and make some money and take it home and give it to mama. As long as the money was coming in she kinda went along with the program a little bit.

What were they paying you for a job then?

Well, let's see. I think you'd make between a dollar and two dollars a night.

Isn't that something?

Yeah. Down at Jim McMahons, on Market Street. A place called Radio Inn. I worked there for four or five years. Then Jim opened up a place upstairs called, The Four Roses. That was in 1932 or 1933. That's before they paved Market Street, it had cobblestones then. I fooled around that area for five or six years. They had Jazzland, Six-O Lounge, Dublin Village, and that place where the funny boys hung out, I can't remember the name of that.

Yeah, I used to see those guys after the show, they dressed up like girls.

That was prohibition. They wouldn't sell whiskey then, they drank this alcohol and water that somebody made. Joe Crouch had a joint and a lady had one across the street, but I forget the name of it. Bobbie Merrill was the boss of the band down at the Dublin Village. They had a little ole floor show. Don't know what happened, but Bobbie Merrill left from there after two or three years, and the man asked me to take over the band. I worked there for eight or nine years at the Dublin Village. I worked for about two years at the Backstage and the Downtowner.

Then I commenced workin' with some main bands. Do you remember Mose Wally?

He was one of the big names at that time.

Yeah, and he played a guitar. He had a five or six piece band and he said I could play with them. In the daytime he ran a cleaners, at night he played places like the Chase and all the main joints. Sometimes we played down on the *St. Paul* boat on the Mississippi River.

Now, the St. Paul, *was that the boat that used to travel down the river from St. Louis to other towns?*

They used to leave at night from the levee at the foot of Washington Ave. and go up to Alton or someplace. It was about a two or three hour run. I never did play regular there, I just filled in. From then on I got with Albert King.

Blue Boy King.

When Albert King started going out of town, I had a day job and I couldn't keep up with him. I was working six days a week and seven nights a week. I worked over in East St. Louis at the False Club for Mary. I was really breakin' my back. That was around 1955–56 I think.

Around 1959 I went down to Waynesville, Missouri, played at Fort Leonard Wood, in all those joints they had up there for the soldiers. Then I worked all over St. Louis. There used to be a lot of joints on Olive Street. Do you remember that Vandeventer?

Yes, that was almost a Gaslight Square . . .

. . . worked all around in there and just drifted from place to place.

You got your own group here in the city.

Yeah I finally got me a group here in the city. Used to call it Raymond Gay's Sharps and Flats. I worked on Kings Highway and Page for two or three years with Willie Fagen and finally he quit there. I took the band over and worked it for five years. It's kinda rough gettin' things together like that, but I had it. I never did get to go out of town too much, being with my mother, she wouldn't hardly let me. There was just her and I and she didn't want to . . . Jimmy Lundsford came through here and he wanted to carry me off . . . I had chances . . .

Now he was a big name.

My mother just didn't like for me to go out of town, she would always tell me no. I had a lot of offers to leave town. Sometimes I'd even have my suitcase packed and she'd start cryin' and telling me that there was only her and me, don't go. That's how I always backed down. I'd have to call them up long distance and tell them not to meet me at the train. I went to Chicago once. The girl that I married she was up there. I'd just go up for a couple of months, not with a big band or anything, just fool around from joint to joint. Now I'm gettin' kinda old, so I don't do too much goin' out of town, you know. When you got responsibilities, you got a house and things, you can't afford to do that.

In those days and right now you never could make enough money to do some of the things you really wanted to do.

That's right, that's right.

That's the life of a musician. It's an art, it's a skill, and this is what we're really hoping to project because of the people not really supporting the art and skill of a musician.

Live music, musician or something . . .

You really can't get mad at these people but you just want them to support your thing.

It's a profession. But I don't know, a lot of musicians have run it down so, like rock and things comin' in and the boys they . . . you couldn't make no livin' off of it. We've got good musicians in St. Louis.

Some of the best.

Maybe it's a good thing I couldn't leave. I'd probably went off, got

into some of that fast life in New York or somewhere and I'd be dead now.
You never know.
I was never used to that fast life and them parties and things.
Currently you're doing weddings and things.
Yes. Mostly I take private engagements like Six Flags, the Chase Hotel and things like that. I went to Memphis, Tennessee here a couple of years ago, with Willie.
How was that?
It was real nice. Now Willie Fagen has a bus tour that goes to New Orleans. I've always wanted to go there. I've read so much about it, Mardi Gras. Some good musicians came from there too, but I've never had a chance to get there. I've always wanted to go there all my life. If it's the last thing I do, if I live long enough, that's where I want to go, 'cause I've heard so much talk about it all my life. Do you smoke, Jimmy?
No, I used to, but I quit.
I wish I could quit.
Thank you for the interview Raymond, we have enjoyed it. I think our time was well spent on this.
Yeah, I think this is a good idea you have too.

Frank George Goessler Trumpet, piano, arranger and copyist/Born July 13, 1955, St. Louis, Mo./Telephone interview by Lyn Cunningham.
Frank was born on July 13, 1955 in St. Louis, Missouri. His mother's name is Betty (Davies) Goessler—born St. Louis, Missouri, and his father's name is Frank George Goessler Sr. Neither one were musicians.
Frank attended grade school at Woodward Elementary, high school at Cleveland High, and college at the University of Missouri at St. Louis (UMSL). There he had two years of traditional theory. Then attended Berklee College of Music in Boston, Massachusetts for two years.
The man who had the most influence on his career was Ed Levinsky, the high school band director at Cleveland High.
Frank studied jazz theory and contemporary music at Berklee College of Music. He studied trumpet with Ralph Hollowell in St. Louis and with Malcomn McDuffee at UMSL. Greg Hopkins, Wes Hensel, and Gary Guzzio were his teachers at Berklee.
Frank's first paid job was in 1969 at Bayless High School with a band called the Monarchs. He made $10.00.
Recordings and Commercials:

> Recording with Bob Kuban Brass, a 45 called "Big Red" and on the flip side, "Big Red Fight Song."
> McDonald's commercial.

Central Hardware commercial.
Sulard Market commercial (radio).

Frank Goessler was still playing with Bob Kuban as of 1985. The advice Frank shares with younger musicians: "Don't close yourself off to any aspect of the business. You'll make more openings for yourself.

Clarence "Sonny Hamp" Hamilton Drummer, dancer/Born October 6, 1928, St. Louis, Mo./Interviewed by Jimmy Jones.

Sonny, tell me something about your parents, your mother and father, where they were born if you can remember.

I think I can get all of that. I know mom and dad were both from Mississippi.

Do you remember what part of Mississippi?

My mother was from Greenville, Mississippi. My father was from Natchez, Mississippi.

Do you remember the year?

Well. . .

This goes back a little bit further. OK, how about your birthdate and place? Your name first of all is Sonny Hamp, right?

Well, you want the real name?

The real one.

You want the real one. Clarence Hamilton.

Clarence Hamilton.

Real name Clarence.

And birthdate is?

October 6, 1928.

Do you remember the place that you were born?

On Twelfth Street, I believe; about 1300 on Twelfth Street. Downtown St. Louis, Missouri.

Where did you start to school; grade school? Do you remember that?

Oh, yes I can remember that. Desolane. Desolane, (sic) downtown on Hadley Street. Early thirties.

Ok. Are your mother and father deceased?

Yes.

Do you remember the year they passed away, Sonny?

Yes. My father just passed away. Not *just* passed away. He passed in 1968 and my mother passed in 1937.

Were they here when they passed away?

Yes, they were both right here.

In St. Louis. All right. Now to get back to the grade school. You went to grade school downtown.

Yeah, then I come on out after we migrated.

Yeah. And did you go to high school here also? Do you remember the name of the school?

Dunbar, the school I graduated from. I went there twice in my life in my grade. I went to Turner open high school. It was sorta like handicaps. I was sorta underweight. And that's where I first met John Chapman, God bless the day. Then I went back to Dunbar and I graduated from Dunbar. *Now, in your years in high school were there any people that you would want to mention that were inspirational? In your deciding what you wanted to do musically? Or did you just kinda fall into it yourself?*

Well, Jimmy, I had it all through my life, you know. Like early. I can remember back when I was about three years old. My oldest brother, Morgan Hamilton, he played the piano . . .
Oh, did he?

And I can say this here and have a great amount of feeling about it; I used to hear that live sound at least three times a month and I'll never forget it. My brother was on piano and a drummer who was playin' regular trap drums, named Eddie, and had a bass guitar player, I guess it was a bass guitar then; No, it really wasn't like it is now but he played it and his name was Woodrow and we used to hear them play; quite naturally we'd hear it because we had the piano in our house. One of those big upright pianos, you know?
Right.

We used to hear men play it like Fats Waller. I had it comin' up pretty good, you know. I had another brother that played very well, as a matter of fact he's a very good friend of the Nelsons; the late Oliver Nelson and Tina and Eugene Nelson and his name was Joseph.
Brother's name Joseph? OK.

Yeah. Like I say, I heard it through my life and at this time now up into high school, dancing was really on my mind.
Oh, you were a dancer first?

Yeah. I was one of the rhythm hoofers.
I see. You were with a show or a team?

Like I say, I was one of the hoofers. There were two of us; Owen Buckner. Do you know the piano player, Joe Buckner? His brother.
Joe Buckner's brother was your other partner?

That's right. He was my partner. Right.
I see. On the dance team.

They called him "Duce."
His nickname was "Duce"?

Right, and we danced at Western Waiters, Riviera . . .
These are clubs, right?

Right.
The Western Waiters' Club and the Riviera?

Yeah, and like in school there was a recreation house, Carver House on Belle in St. Louis. The kids in our neighborhood were very musically equipped. Our clubs and things like that. We had a small club and Charles Gilbert and I were in the same club and we had a dance team; like a troup, like; because this is another person who was very influential in my life was Mr. Levi. I couldn't think of his last name to save my life, but he helped us produce a show.

Do you remember the name of the show?

The *Music Makers.*

The Music Makers?

That's right, and there were about a dozen of us boys and girls and our own band. Man, I was playin' on milk crates and boxes and Charles Toples brought a jug. Van Hare was playin' on a tub with a string. This is the truth, J.J. I'm tellin' you the truth, man. And Gil was playin' trumpet. He was the bugle man in the band. Charles Gilbert. And I had a dance kick. Oh, man we were fallin' off a log and kickin' 'em high, can-cannin' and it was just beautiful. We was twelve and thirteen years old, now just before. Now we was just going into high school, you know what I mean?

Yeah.

And so that dance thing just stayed with me, you know, up to I'd say about into the latter years that I was in the high school. 'Cause we had beautiful teachers over there at that instruction thing. Mr. Henderson and Miss Green. They were very good. They tried, you couldn't help but get it from them.

Right. Now at this point, Sonny, when you were doing the shows and that; were they really giving you any money? Or were you just doing it because you liked it, or experience, or what?

Yeah, I hear that. Well we had an agent. Smilin' Bob Palmer.

Palmer.

Yeah, Bob Palmer. He was a nice fellow. He would give us a few bucks, you know what I mean. We weren't really on a big payroll or something like that. He'd throw us out fifteen, ten or twenty dollars or something like that, you know, and it was good enough for us at that time. And I'm not trying to sound off or anything but that was a little money to us, you know.

And at the time, fifteen or twenty bucks was a lot of bread.

Uh huh. And then we were getting out and meetin' people too and, like I say, it was just gettin' to know people; that experience; 'cause I started runnin' into musicians and things then too.

Uh-huh.

You know like Tommy Give and fellows like that. Ed Wynn down to Western Waiters, you know; Austin Wright, the late Austin Wright. It was all very good. With a little money.

Right, right. I'm sure this was going into high school days and since you were surrounded with music and show-business stuff, like that it really kind of gave you an inspiration to move forward into music.

Oh yes. Yes.

And in your high school days I'm sure you continued on in some type of music.

Oh, yes.

At what point did you continue on dancing in high school?

No, no. I . . . Right into high school I started getting interested in drums because this new music they called "Be-bop" was just comin' in and I don't know. . . I heard that man Charlie Pozo play that conga drum. That was my first instrument.

Fascinated you, huh?

I played that. When I left high school I was workin' different places, but when I first started playing any kind of music, that was my first instrument.

And you played the conga drum until you started on the drums?

Right.

At what time, do you remember when you first set down to a set of drums?

Well, I think it was around . . . to say to play, you know what I mean . . . to set down behind a set of drums to play, was around 1947.

Uh huh.

Because there were fellows around like the late John Chapman, pianist, and the late Ace Coleman and Melvin Green, and we had a group with Charles Williams on trombone; very good trombonist; and we had our dancers with us too, like Shawn McGon. We had him and we had dancers like Liz and Vera that was chorus girls for Riviera and stuff like that, and that helped me in music too.

At that time the Riviera was some kind of a place. I think that was the place in this area, wasn't it?

Oh yes.

Right. And then moving on past high school, did you have . . . do you remember the first really good paid job that you had that you want to talk about, Sonny?

Well, I had so many before I got to where I'd call makin' the big money. Like I say, I used to work around the city with little bands like Jimmy Dolittle, Channa Brown. Now those cats, like Jimmy Dolittle, he'd make a little money because he didn't work in the city. He worked all around Wentzville, Herculeon, Missouri, and places like that, and he had a small band like six or seven pieces 'cause I remember some of the fellows that used to be with him, you know what I mean? And we'd make a little money. The first big money I really made was when Fats Dudley, Ollie Dudley; he come from Peoria here; and he took myself, Hershel Habates and John Chapman,

piano. We went to work at the Open Door gambling casino, East Perkins, Illinois.
East Perkins?
Yes East Perkins. East Peoria, they call it really.
Oh yeah. Okay, okay.
And we was makin' big money up there, and after that job closed, well we just went to work right there in Peoria. Workin' for Brice Collins, a very nice powerful young man up there, you know. Had a nice hotel. Matter of fact, his wife was Margaret Cook, Mr. James Cook's daughter. So that was good for me too, knowin' people and workin' for Brice Collins. We got a chance to meet all the better musicians because when they'd get off, we played 'til three or four in the morning, they'd come there and any kind and all kind of musicians would come there. Man, I got the thrill of my life when "Memphis Slim" come in there, man.
Right.
I had another good experience, if I may say it, with Fats group. John Chapman, the piano player, had to come back to St. Louis and Laura Crosby took his place at the piano; she a big sister of Isarel Crosby, the bass player, that used to be around here so long. Laura Crosby. Very good. She's from Chicago and I met her and worked with her quite a few times later on up in Chicago, but that was where the turn come in for me because they had good musicians come in there. You know PeeWee that used to be with Chris Woods? He was workin' up there. He used to be one of our mentors. I loved him. He showed me a lot too.
How about big name people, Sonny? Big name groups? Did you ever have an encounter with big name groups. That you want to mention?
Well... Okay. Yes, I can. Let's see, in 1950 I went from Peoria to the army. No, 1951. I'm sorry. While I was in the army I met Buddy Montomery, traveled west with Montomery the first time. Matter of fact, we was takin' bits of training; bivouac and giggin' at the same time in Johnson City, Kansas. After I come out of the army I was here for a while and there was a friend of mine, we were in the army together, and he found out where I was playin'. I was playin' pretty good then, and he was gettin' a few things and points from me; his name was Mobart Ami, and he was a very good friend of Amah Jamal and at this time I think Ray Crawford was Amah's guitar player. I don't know if he was leaving the group or going to be gone for awhile or something like that, so Amah and Mobart . . . they copied each other quite a bit, you know, and he was telling me about how he would work something up for me; you know what I mean; and I said, yeah we'd do that then because Chicago was just like home to me. All my mother's people was up there, you know?
Right, right.
So I left (for Chicago). When I did go up to Chicago Amah had formed

this trio there, you know what I mean? It was Iserals group; Iseral Crosby, I think his name was; a drummer so I didn't get a chance to do that, but I went with Tiny Davis. Tiny Davis' Sweethearts of Rhythm.
Uh huh.

And she had a place up there workin' near northside down in the Loop and you know, makin' the good money. And sometimes I would get a chance to get Mondays with Johnny Griffin at the Morocco Hotel. In the Morocco Hotel on Thirty-ninth St. Well, everybody came through there like Wilbur Ware, Dewey Christin, Eddie Harris, John Gilmore, Cliff Jordan, those people. So that was about my biggest thing in Chicago. Then I come back home, (to St. Louis). I was workin' with Don Cunningham. He had a Latin group. At the Crystal Palace, down in Gaslight Square, we were workin' there and we were doin' shows for Dick Gregory, Phyllis Diller, Smothers Brothers, and I can't really think of all them, man; you know.
There were so many name people.

In that one spot, you know what I mean? And Professor Windell Corey too. I had my own group, the Sonny Hamp Trio, with John Chapman and John Mixon on bass. There were two Johns and one Sonny.
Yeah.

We had a good time. I think you might have heard of that group, didn't you?
Yeah, oh yeah.

Okay. Then I split for awhile. Let's see, where did I go this time? I think I went . . . yeah . . . I went up in Ohio. The reason I went up there I got married. I was workin' with Regenald Evans, a trumpet player. He had a position at Wright Patterson Airforce Base out there, I believe. He was something like an agent. Man, we were workin' in Springfield, Dayton, Cincinnati, and places like that, and I got a chance to meet and play with the great tenor saxophonist, Joe Henderson. His younger brother, Leon Henderson, was a very good reed man, so I stayed up there for awhile then I come back home and I think my first big gig comin' back home was myself, Charlie Fox on piano, and John Mitchell on bass with Jimmy Witherspoon. I think that was about 1964. Then about 1967, I said man, well here we go; I say Dakotas Dayton, Jimmy Smith, Della Reese, Al Hibler, Sonny Stitt, Spanky Wilson . . .
These are all people that you played with?

Yes. Well . . . okay. I'm hung up right now for a minute. I played in the Playboy Club for awhile with Brook Benton. I almost forgot that.
Was that the one on Delmar?

Lindell.
Oh, Lindell. Okay.

Let's see. I know there's something I'm leaving out. I'm really sorry about that. There was something I really wanted to tell you; talk about it; you know what I mean?

I can always insert it, you know, when we write this up because we can't get it all.

Okay. Then I went to New York about 1973 or '74. I had the most beautiful experiences I ever had. I got to work with Richard Otto, the violinist, and his wife Sarah.

They were husband and wife?

Yes. You remember that?

Right. And they were from New York?

Right, but they had recorded well up into the 1950s. Do you remember that?

Yeah.

All of the great standards. Love songs, ballads . . .

Right.

So, I got a chance to work with him in New York up around 125th St. Lochamel Supper Club. Very good. Joyce Stupps, a pianist up there; he's a beautiful fellow, man. Like Tommy Flanagan, you know. He's done a lot of things with Ella (Fitzgerald), Sarah (Vaughan); things like that, you know. That was a good group. But I went to New York with a thing in my mind to get out and make some money first, and then you know how I mean; explore or whatever. So I got a chance to get with Bill Dogget and that was taking us in and out of New York, you know what I mean. I never did get a chance to come back here. The closest I got back this way was South Bend, Indiana, but that's when I had my attack. After that, the itinerary was . . . oh, six months ahead. Like I had my attack in 1975 . . . well, the early part of 1976 . . . and that slowed me down so I just come on back into Manhattan, what they say? Go to roost or something like that?

Yeah, yeah.

And, uh, and so I got a chance to go back to work with Richard again. I couldn't put it down, Jimmy. I was terribly sick, man. I was bent all over, you know, I was just messed up and God is good to me now.

Yeah.

So, uh, I got a chance to; the last part of the time I was up in New York I worked with Richard and lived down in Chinatown with some of my St. Louis homies. They gonna make sure that I do it right.

Yeah.

I did that until I said let me drag my tail on out of here and go on home. So then I come home and I'm gettin' pretty well now. I done some things since I been home. I just can't think who I done it with.

Right, right. Now about recordings, Sonny. I'm sure that in your musical career there has been somebody that you want to make mention of that you recorded something. Did you ever do any recording?

I did some with Bill and I did some with John Hicks.

John Hicks. Okay. John Hicks, the piano player?

Yes, our boy.

Okay, a St. Louisan. Now do you remember; did they record here or in New York or where?

New York with Bill.

Do you remember what label up there?

I do, but I just can't think of it.

How about John Hicks?

(Continuing on his own train of thought) If I could remember the name of it. It's right over here on Locust. See, now it's kinda coming to me. I did some recording in 1978 with Charisma and Technosonic.

Yeah, that's out in (St. Louis) the county.

Out in Brentwood, yeah. I did some with Oliver Sands, and that's about it.

Now how about . . . I know your hopes of the future is to keep on wailin', Sonny.

That's right; you know that.

And, uh, whenever that phone rings and somebody lets you know that there's a job, you're ready to go.

Like right now. When I was talkin' to you the other night about working, I was serious.

Sure. Now, is your biggest interest in life still music?

Yeah, J.J. You know that.

Did we get all the things down, Sonny, that you wanted to mention?

One thing I meant to talk on a minute. I know you know this fella, Jimmy McKlennon.

Oh, yeah. The late Jimmy McKlennon. Fantastic piano player!

That's right. He had a place in the early 1960s called the Mellow Cellar.

Yes, yes, yes. I remember that. The Mellow Cellar.

Well, that place, to me, was the starting point for a lot of musicians. As a matter of fact I went in there and got a little sharper sometimes. Everybody that was up to par in the city would come through there. The late Bob Grafton was there, and Jimmy Forrest and Oliver; all of 'em whenever they'd come in town, they'd stop and see that place. You know, Jimmy (McKlennon) was already polished, but he never did get a chance to play because of the fact of cookin' that barbeque. He'd be upset sometimes because he'd want to come out there and play, but he couldn't leave because of . . . (the barbeque)

Jimmy did some things in musical arranging for me.

I miss him very much. You know, we had a little club about 1962. There was five of us. Charles Gilbert was president, Buck Gabney, trombone

player. And myself and Bill Shorten, piano player late. The late Bill Shorten.
We had a place called the Time Locker. It was like a coffee house during
that time. We sold nothing but beverages. Coffee, pastries and Kosher food,
and we did very good on that. Some people didn't want us to have it because
they got us out of there. One time we turned around, man, and we caught
a guy trying to put some pot down on the floor. We hit him pretty good then
they sent the police in there to see if we were selling liquor and stuff like
that. So's that's some of the bad things that happen to you when you're trying to do it, we didn't need to have anything like that because we were doin'
good with what we had. He come in there one night I know—a little saxophone player. He was a sly little fellow. He wore white gloves, you know
what I mean, quite natural man, you don't know what you might get into
now-a-days. You don't know how strong some of the people are. When he'd
get off work over on the south side, he'd drag a couple of people over
there—mainly women, you know what I mean?
Yeah, right.
   Oh man, they spotted him out for what's that charge they try to do? For
harboring prostitutes? Oh man, they tried to raid us one night. It's like you
say, you got the good things and bad things going at one time, they just keep
hoppin' on us so much that we just had to, just . . .
Let 'em have it.
   Yeah.
*But I tell you, I know that there was some bad times and good times in every
musician. Every person's life and we've covered quite a few important people
in your career. Is there any other dates and places or times that you want
to mention?*
   Not right off-hand. Now while I was overseas I had a band over there.
I rigged up an organ and stuff, and I was playin' organ over there.
Really?
   Scat singin'. Makin' money, man. Had five pieces. Bass player out of
New York; a real authentic Puerto Rican. Man them guys was good, you
know? They was playin' Conga drums and that was a good part of my life.
I was over there in a bad neighborhood, though. Then, too, one of the bad
things that happened to me; when I went to the St. Louis Institute of Music;
and when I got to book three, they let me start going to my advance. My
teacher was Roy Duemochi . . . I get so tired of saying late; the late Roy
Duemochi. He has a brother here that's playing trumpet nowadays. Thomas
Duemochi. But I had been going to school, I had been playin' so long at this
time, Jimmy, I wanted to go out so I could find out what I was doing; you
know, technically. I was playin' it by ear to death, so I had a chance to do
it by being in this G.I. thing, so I went. I enrolled and I was going to school
and things was goin' fine. I was going to the Kruger School of Music; that's
where the studio was. You know, old Gaslight Square? Right on Boyle and

Olive. Right up the street from the Crystal Palace. And it was a good school and boy; he passed me. He passed on me and that kinda turned me around, you know. Well, it wasn't too long after that that I went up to Chicago, so I was hangin' out with drummers up there like Wilbur Campbell, Durell Anderson, Bob House; you know, studying and practicing together and stuff like that. Staying in good company.

Sonny, are you still planning, thinking about doing some big things musically if the opportunity ever presents itself? I'm sure you are.

I'm definitely ready.

Maybe possibly someday you might do some musical arrangements on your own.

Yep.

Oh, one thing before we close, I know you by Sonny Hamp. Now when we first started the interview you told me your name was what?

Clarence Hamilton.

Now where did the name Sonny Hamp come from?

Well, mom and dad called me Sonny until they got ready to get to me, then they called me Clarence. But they drafted the Hamp name. I guess it come through the time I was dancin' and gettin' ready to play drums, or thinking about playin' drums. Lionel Hampton was already all over me and when this tune come out, "Hamps Boogie Woogie," Hamp was doin' the boogie and I think that's where it come from. About in the early 1940 things, because my school teacher used to say; Sonny Hamp. They wouldn't say just one name. They just called it Sonny Hamp, and I just had it and I liked it.

That's when it became attached to you?

I was in my teens, early teens and like I say, I was so hung up on Lionel Hampton I was hung up on him because half the time he looked like he was jumpin' up and down dancin' so much and beating the devil out of the drums, you know what I mean, and I just figured they put that handle on me and I liked it.

I know everybody has a . . . like Gene Washington in E. St. Louis . . . now he's got a nickname of "Stumpy." Everybody calls him Stumpy. I don't know why, but that's one of his nicknames, you know? I was just wondering. I was just curious, and thought we ought to insert that.

Since I had it for twenty years, huh?

I really didn't know the real name. Okay. I guess if there's not anything else we can mention, I think we'll close this interview and it's really been a pleasure to visit your home, and hopefully now that I know where you're at, we'll be pretty close together, and we'll probably visit each other a little more. I want to thank you for the time and the effort, and taking this time to talk to me and tell me about the great Sonny Hamp.

It's all my pleasure, J.J. All mine.

John "Bugs" Hamilton Trumpet/Born March 8, 1911, St. Louis, Mo., died August 15, 1947, St. Louis, Mo.

John Hamilton was born in St. Louis on March 8, 1911. At age 19 he went to New York where he played in a band led by trombonist Billy Kato in 1930 and 1931 and briefly performed with Chick Webb's Band. In 1935 he was with Kaiser Marshall's Band at the Ubangi Club in New York. In late 1935 he was with Bobby Neal.

The longest stint for him was with Fats Waller from 1938 until 1942, and his last one was with Eddie South's Band during the summer of 1943. He contracted tuberculosis that year and his condition increasingly worsened until his death on August 15, 1947, in St. Louis.

Arville S. Harris Saxes, clarinet/Born December 1904, St. Louis, Mo., died July 1954, New York, N.Y.

Arville was the uncle of LeRoy Harris, Jr., and brother to LeRoy W. Harris, Sr., and Jennie Harris. Arville played on the riverboats in St. Louis in the 1920s, with Hershal Brassfield's Band in 1921, and with Bill Brown and the Brownies through 1925 to 1928.

He made recordings for Clarence Williams in the 1920s and joined Cab Calloway's Band in 1931, and stayed with Cab until 1935. During this period he made a trip to Europe with Cab Calloway. He was with Jack Butler in 1935. Between 1935 and 1937 he worked regularly for LeRoy Smith, and from 1937 to 1939 with Claude Hopkins and pianist Maurice Rocco.

Arville led his own band in New York at the Majestic Ballroom during the last 10 years of his life. He died of a heart attack in July 1954 in New York City.

Ben Harris Drummer/Born July 14, 1924, St. Louis, Mo./Interviewed by Jimmy Jones.
Now let's get some information on you, Mr. Harris.

Okay, well, my name is Ben Harris. I was born in St. Louis, Missouri on July 14, 1924.
When did you first start getting interested in music, Ben?

During my early years I lived downtown in the Jefferson-Pine area. About three blocks away was a Catholic Church and I joined the Boy Scouts there. They showed an interest in developing the drum and bugle corps, so our leader happened to be a drummer by the name of Stokes, who I didn't know at the time was Chauncy's dad.
Oh, really?

Yeah, do you remember Chauncy?
Yes.

Anyway Stokes played drums and piano, so he was playin' the piano down there one day and they had some drum sticks layin' around and I just

Ben Harris

Left to right: **Sonny Little, Elaine Donahue, Ben Harris and Joe Buckner.**

picked them up and started keepin' a little time. He gave them to me, I brought 'em on home and the gift was given by the Catholics, they got me interested. The drum and bugle corps never really got off the ground, but during the interim I moved out on Cook, the 4000 block, and the interest had begun to build. I started making boxes, and tin cans and stuff like that, just puttin' a little homemade set together, so I could play in the daytime. Livin' behind me, right across the alley, was Ralph Golenham. He came to my house where we always had a piano, and I was beatin' with him, you know? Elijah Shaw lived up the street about four doors. I passed by there lots of times and I would hear him practicing. I really never confronted him or anything, about taking any lessons. That must have been about a year before I graduated from Cole.

You were a teenager.

When I left there I went to Sumner High School. Naturally they needed drummers for the football games and stuff and I was playing well enough then to go into the band. I went right into the Senior band, but I hadn't done any serious studying. You know I wasn't able to read a note as big as a house, this type of thing. You know the band masters really didn't press too much, but there were certain things they wanted you to do and this was all that was necessary. In the meantime, during this time, there was a guy living in Kinloch named Alonzo Smith, so naturally with the high school situation being what it was at this time, they had to come all the way into the city to go to school.

Right.

Well, Tony Smith, Marion Miller and I all went to school together.

Marion Miller, the piano player at the Godfather?

Right.

The Mr. Marion Miller.

But what you probably don't know is, that Marion Miller used to tap dance.

I sure didn't.

He's a pretty good dancer. That wasn't long ago.

All right.

In fact after being in high school we formed a dance band.

Now who was in that dance band?

At that time there was a trombone player by the name of William Seals. He played with the Count (Basie) and also with George Hudson. There was Arvell Shaw, he's a tuba player, but he went into the Navy and started playin' string bass. Well, Arvell Shaw went with Louis Armstrong when Louis came through here.

We called him Orville Harris but his name was Arvell Shaw.

(tape stopped here)

We were talking about Mabelle's brother, right?

Well we hadn't really got into it, but Maybelle's brother is Leman Boler. He had a band, the one with Joe Foster. Then you had John Moore, his dad owned the High Wires right here at Vandeventer and Finney.

Okay, that was the place they jammed at.

They used to have the blue Monday's jam sessions. All the musicians used to come through town and go up there after everything closed, I mean we'd be there until five or six in the morning.

Do you ever think they'll get that back again?

No, I doubt it. Oh, some of the guys are tryin' it, Calvin Dillard is tryin' it, and Bob Moore.

Who else was in that band?

A fellow by the name of Milton Whidden, but he died at an early age.

I see.

Milton left here and went to the Julliard School of Music, then he came back here and worked for the Post Office. He still tried to play music because his heart really wasn't in the post office, but his folks wanted him to stay home.

So this was the group that was formed between 1939 and 1943? Mr. Godfather the II will be in it.

Oh, yeah. We're talkin' about Marion Miller, right? No, he was just a dancer. At that time I didn't even know he played piano. After we formed the big band we used to play the Wire Circus and they were on the show as tap dancers.

In 1943 you were in the Marine Corps, weren't you? Did you do any special service while you were in there?

On my transcript for service the information that I played was on there, so it was like no choice deal, you're in the band, you know?

Yeah.

In fact that's when I met Johnny Johnson.

Really? Was he in that bunch?

Yeah, but Johnny wasn't playing in the band, he was in the gun battery. I also met a guy named Joe Wilder, a trumpet player. A few years back he played in Doc Severinson's band. In fact I'm trying to think if he was playin' before Clark Taylor got this job. We did play when the U.S.O. sent shows overseas. We played for Betty Hutton when she came through there, unrehearsed. We'd had to go out in the lagoon and unload the officer's whiskey so there wasn't time for a rehearsal. So it was cold turkey all the way. We were on the Marshall Islands. The main island was Eniwitok, so the main base was there but they had gun batteries ten to fifteen miles away on the smaller islands in order to defend the whole network. So we went from the main base to the little islands with the dance band to entertain there.

Naturally.

Once in awhile we would play for the officer's club. After the war was over, Johnny (Johnson) went his own way, so I didn't run into Johnny again until years later when he was playing with Chuck Berry. After I came out in 1946, the first thing I did was go down to the old musicians hall and I joined the Local. Local 197. I saw and met a lot of musicians there. Brother Joe Smith, Jimmy Davis, Fred Goodman, Jimmy Spears, his daughter Vivian Spears (she played piano with Jimmy Forrest for awhile), John Lindsay, a piano player who we called, "Layem Straight."

During this time there was a big band formed, wasn't there?

Yeah, that was the Negro Symphony.

Who were some of the people in that orchestra?

Willie Fagen, a trumpet player, Bigsby, Blight, a trumpet man, Leta Ward and Amanda Ambrose, piano.

Who was your conductor?

A fellow by the name of Leedon, he came from Canada.

How many pieces were in the concert band?

There were about seventy pieces. Winfield Baker played trombone, Elijah Shaw and his brother Alex Shaw were in the drum section, Harry Blight on trumpet and Harry Windell.

Did you do anything after that big band thing?

No, I went to work at the Post Office, and I enrolled in the Ludwig House of Music.

I'm sure the money you made in music was unbelievable.

Oh man, I've played some fifty cent gigs.

I know.

Four hours, fifty cents. A dollar, dollar and a half, two dollars . . . that's big money! The living part was out, you couldn't make no living off that.

There just wasn't any money.

No. A five dollar thing man, that was like being rich!

Well you know when the phone rings and it's a job, you're free, you're right on top of it.

That's right, yeah. I'm ready!

This has been a live interview with Mr. Benjamin Harris, a St. Louis drummer, and it's really a pleasure having this conversation and interview with Mr. and Mrs. Harris and we are going to close this interview at this point. Thank you Ben.

LeRoy Harris, Jr. Alto-clarinet, flute, oboe, vocalist/Born February 12, 1916, St. Louis, Mo.

LeRoy is the son of LeRoy Harris, Sr., and a nephew of Jimmie and Arville Harris. He took violin lessons from his Uncle Jimmie between 1923 and 1927. In 1929 he took up sax and clarinet. He worked with Chuck Finney and his band in 1930, and later in the same year moved to Chicago with Burns Campbell. He played with Ray Nance from 1932 to 1936, with Eddie Coles in 1937, and with Earl Hines from 1938 to 1943.

He served in the U.S. Navy Band from late 1943 to 1944.

During the late 40s and mid-50s he played with Bill Martin, Bill Dogget, Ben Thigpen, Four Tons of Rhythm and Earl Hines. LeRoy was back in St. Louis with Archie Burnside between 1957 and 1969 and was with pianist Eddie Johnson's Trio in St. Louis from 1960 to 1971.

LeRoy W. Harris, Sr. Banjo, guitar, flute/Born February 1895, St. Louis, died March 1969, St. Louis county.

Father of LeRoy W. Harris, Jr., and brother to Arville S. Harris (sax and clarinet), and Jimmie Harris (violinist and music teacher).

LeRoy played on the riverboats in the 1920s. No other information is available on LeRoy W. Harris, Sr.

Ernie Hays Organ, piano, music teacher, recording artist/Born 1935, St. Louis.

Ernie Hays was born and raised in St. Louis. At age eight he took his first piano lesson. By age 13 he was playing professionally on the organ, piano, sousaphone and string bass. Ernie attended several colleges but never earned a music degree. Years later, however, he did graduate from Washington University with a bachelor's degree in industrial management. This opened new fields of employment: engineering, broadcasting, music teacher, recording artist, Navy man and deputy sheriff, among others. But music has always been his first love and he returned to it time and time again to support his family.

In 1971 he auditioned for the job at Busch Stadium and got it. There he performs for millions of people every year. When you attend a baseball game at St. Louis, it's Ernie Hays who plays the National Anthem, and the seventh inning stretch music.

Catherine Henderson Singer, dancer, impersonator/Born June 23, 1909, St. Louis, Mo.

Catherine's father's name was Griffin Henderson. Her mother's name was Kitty Gibbons. Following are some important dates in Catherine's career:

> *1912* Toured with Josephine Gassman and her Pickaninnies (working as pick).
> *1915–1917* Toured with Josephine Gassman Phina and Company Show working theaters in Australia/Tasmania/New Zealand.
> *1917–1921* Continued with Josephine troupe as singer, dancer and impersonator on Albee and Keith circuits across the U.S.
> *1921* Settled in New York, N.Y. to attend local schools.
> *Mid-20s* Brief tours on vaudeville circuit as single (or with Eva Taylor) Theater gigs in New York, N.Y. and Youngstown, Ohio and other cities. Occasionally substituted for Eva Taylor on local radio shows in New York, N.Y.
> *1926* Brief appearance in a revue at the New Douglas Theater, New York, N.Y.
> *1927* With Eva Taylor in show "Bottomland," Savoy Theater, Atlantic City, New Jersey.
> *1927* Princess Theater, New York, N.Y.
> *1920s* Worked for Clarence William's Music Publishing Company, New York, N.Y.
> *1928* Worked with Kathleen Kirwood Underground Theater, Greenwich Village, New York, N.Y.

> *1928*   Recorded QRS/Paramount labels, Long Island City, N.Y.
> *1929*   Appeared in musical, "Keep Shufflin'," Pearl Theater, Philadelphia, Pa.
> *1931*   Appeared on "Careless Love" Show, WEAF-radio NBC, New York, N.Y.
> *1933*   Appeared with Eva Taylor in "Folks from Dixie" NBC-radio, New York, N.Y.
> *1940s*   With Sylvester Wolfson Orchestra in residency at Joe and Rose Beer Garden, Queens, N.Y.
> *1944*   Moved back to St. Louis, Mo. Inactive in music after that.

Eva Taylor was her aunt and she used the pseudonym "Catherine Henderson." She is no relation to Rosa or Fletcher Henderson. Catherine was billed as "Only Me," and she was influenced by her aunt, Eva Taylor.

Otis "Lightnin' Slim" V. Hicks Guitar/Born March 13, 1913, St. Louis, Mo., died July 27, 1974, Detroit, Mich.

Otis Hicks was born and raised on a farm in St. Louis County. At an early age he was interested in music and his father taught him guitar.

While still young the family of six moved to St. Francisville, Louisiana.

At age 13 he dropped out of school, playing music full-time, and continued working outside of music through the thirties.

He learned some music from his brother, Layfield Hicks, and sat in with local country bands playing dances, country suppers and picnics through the '30s and '40s. Then he moved to Baton Rouge, Louisiana, where he worked with small combos in back street joints.

> *1946*   Worked with Big Papa's Band at Johnny's Cafe in Baton Rouge, La.
> *1948*   Worked with Schoolboy Cleve in local clubs and on radio shows in Baton Rouge, La. on into the '50s.
> *Late 1950*   Recorded on Feature label, Crowley, La.
> *1954*   Recorded on Ace label, Jackson, Miss., worked with Slim Harpo.
> *1955*   Recorded on Excello label, Crowley, La.
> *1955–1966*   Formed his own band and did country gigs, working with Whispering Smith in the Baton Rouge area.
> *1960–1962*   He moved to Detroit where he worked house parties in that area.
> *1965*   Worked local clubs with Slim Harpo in Chicago, Ill.
> *1967*   With Slim Harpo at The Scene in New York, N.Y.
> *1968*   Grand Ballroom in Detroit, Mich.
> *1970*   University of Chicago Folk Festival.
> *1971*   Recorded on Excello label, Sheffield, Ala.
> *1971*   Worked the Blues Festival in Ann Arbor, Maine.
> *1972*   Toured England and Europe.
> *1972*   Recorded for Blue Horizon label in London, England.
> *1972*   Marquee Club, London, England.
> *1972*   Worked alone at Concord Club, Southhampton, England.

1972 Jazz Festival, Montreux, Switzerland.
1973 Toured with American Blues Legends in concert, TV and radio dates through England and Europe.
1973 Worked local concert in Windsow, Canada
1973 Recorded for Big Bear-Polydor label, London, England.

In late 1973 he entered Henry Ford Hospital in Detroit, where he died of cancer. He is buried in Oak Hill Cemetery in Pontiac, Michigan.

He is reported to have been "one of the truly great, unspoiled bluesmen of the post war era." — *Detroit News,* July 27, 1974.

Charles W. Hill, Sr. Trumpet, vocalist/Born October 29, 1915, Blytheville, Ark./Interviewed by Jimmy Jones.
Charles, what is your full name?
Charles W. Hill.
And your parents' names?
Maggie Hill and Albert Hill.
Do you remember their birthdays?
No, I don't.
But they were originally from Blytheville, Arkansas?
Right.
And then your family moved to Cairo, Illinois?
Yes.
And where did you finish school?
I finished at Vashon in St. Louis.
Were any of your family musically inclined?
I had an uncle who was a trombone player. His name was Wiley Brown. I had another uncle who was a piano player, his name was Dave Hill, and of course my father was a piano player.
When did you become interested in music?
In grade school I played drums and then I switched to trumpet. Then I returned to Sikeston and attended the Business College of Sikeston. I organized my first group in 1936. I worked in the Hillcrest for five years. That club's owner was Walter Kinnard. Later I picked up a radio program KWOC (Keep Watching Our City) in Poplar Bluff, Missouri. I had my own thirty minute program three times a week, Monday, Wednesday and Friday.
And after that?
After that we went on the road. We did stints with the All American Shows (or Royal).
Any other name bands you want to mention during the '50s, '60s, or '70s?
Well I did a little stint with Joe Keys and Cootie Williams at the Apollo in New York. After that I brought Charles Hill and his Rhythm Kings back

Charlie Hill, Sr., in 1982.

Hill at the beginning of his trumpet-playing career in 1936.

to St. Louis. We did a lot of organizations, community centers and clubs. My son is also a musician and I fronted his group and he also played in a group with me.

And his name?

Charles, Hill, Jr. That group was called The Swingin' Limitations. He was backed by Chick Finney, the piano player.

Are you now semi-retired, Charles? Do you still play?

Yes, I still play.

And your dream in music was to have been . . .

A good trumpet man and a vocalist, and that's just what I've been.

Did you ever make any recordings?

I recorded with a group from Popular Bluff, it was out of WDIA in Memphis, Tennessee.

But you're still by the phone available for dates when that phone rings.

I tell ya', I'm tellin' you I am. Jimmy, I used to play for a dollar and a half a night back in the '30s. I remember that . . .

Is there anything else you'd like to add before we close this interview?

Well I could add that I knew guys like Fate Marable, and I had a chance to hang around with him.

All right Charles, we'll close on that. Thank you.

It's been very enjoyable having this interview with you, I just wish I could remember more.

Jimmy Hinds Bass, drums, piano/Born January 9, 1950, St. Louis, Mo./Interviewed by Jimmy Jones and Lyn Cunningham.

Jim, what's your full name?

James Hinds. No middle name.

I think that's pretty self-explanatory. And birthdate?

I was born in 1950. January 9, 1950.

Where?

At Homer G. Phillips Hospital in St. Louis, Missouri.

And wives, children, that sort of thing?

Oh, goodness! I been married, I better not mess this up, eight years now and my wife is Emma Jean Hinds. I have four kids, John, Jamie, Jennifer and Jamel.

Are any of these musicians?

No, not yet. John shows an interest in piano. I think he may turn out to be a pianist.

How about your mother and father?

Bessie Hinds and Leon Hinds.

And where were they born?

Clifftonville, Mississippi.

I remember that name from somewhere. And their birthdays?

Mom's was June 25th, I don't remember what year. Daddy's is October 17, 1925, I think.

What were their occupations?

I don't know what Daddy was doing when he got his first job up here. He had several jobs. When he and Mama came up here they had two children, but for some reason Mama went back to Mississippi, so that kinda left Daddy up here looking for things to do. I don't think anyone got the straight of what he did. But he wound up running the garage over at the Chase for a good while and he's retired.

Any of your brothers or sisters musicians?

No, but I have a little sister who plays piano. She won't get serious, she's good, but she won't buckle down to it.

What are their names?

The musical ones?

Yes.

That's Doris Hinds and Leonard Hinds. There were eight of us.

Just two out of eight?

Yeah.

Are your mother and father still living?

Yes, they're still with us.

Do you remember anything about your grandparents?

Yeah, yeah. All four were sharecroppers.

In what state?

Mississippi. In Clifftonville.

And their names?

My mother's mother, Martha Sanders and her father was Ed Saunders. My daddy's father was Pete Hinds and my daddy's mother's name was Sweet. We called her grandma Sweet. We saw her a little less than the other grandparents.

At what age did you become interested in music, Jimmy?

In 1958 we got a stereo with two speakers. My sister got it for my parents. They loved music. We lived two blocks from Joel's Music Shop on Easton and Sarah and Mom would send us down there for Brook Benton and Dinah Washington records and that stuff was really jumping off the speakers. I was fascinated with sound at a very early age, but I couldn't get my hands on an instrument. At twelve I kinda thought it would be music.

Who influenced your interest in music?

Sterling Parker, my sister's husband. He had a barbecue house and he played jazz for his customers. I was jazz oriented at a very early age. As a musician's kind of music.

When did you first choose the instrument that you play?

I played drums first, I still play some drums. I play song-writer's

Jimmy Hinds with his group, Mañana.

piano or arrangers piano. But drums and bass are my principal instruments.

How much did you get paid for your first job?

Seven dollars and fifty cents. As a singer. The musicians got twelve dollars and fifty cents and God knows what went into the manager's pocket.

Yeah, right.

We worked the east side heavily, a lot of colleges, a lot of private dates, and certain organizations would drag us up to Fenton. We did very well in the early '60s. Then I took up bass and that landed me up in Gaslight Square and into a house band in Lennon House in East St. Louis with Richard Landsfield and the Magnificent Seven. I've always played with older cats. I think I was seventeen when I was working there. A house was the kind of place you played if you felt you counted for something.

Yes, at that time. Who did you study with down through the years?

Every year Oliver Nelson would bring a three month seminar to Washington University. I caught him two years in a row. I thought I was one of the hottest little players in town on bass. Then he asked me to tell him what I was doing, and I couldn't. He said well, that's what we're going to buckle down on.

He wanted you to know what you were doing and why you were doing it.

After that I went on the road with Bobby "Blues" Bland. I got drafted into service in 1969. I think I got the rest of my musical training in there.

Jimmy Hinds

I think we all got a little bit.
    They hit me with military police, but I wound up as a musician. I found out if I wanted to play bass in service with a twenty-one piece stage band I'd have to take the courses at the U.S. Naval Institute of Music. That's one of the highest musical institutes. It was really good for me.
Have you ever written any music?
    Contemporary writings for vocal groups and I'm into record production. I worked with Oliver [Sains] extensively on his albums. You can find a couple of compositions of mine on some of his older albums.
What's the name of the club where you're working now?
    I'm at Gene Lynns on Whittier and Lindell. Also the Moose Lounge at Pope and Carter Streets.
What are your plans for the future?
    I don't plan to stop playing, but producing will be the major thing.
You also teach, don't you?
    Yes, I teach music at Casa, the St. Louis School and Conservatory for the Arts located on Washington and Compton Aves.

What are some of the basic fundamentals the young people should have if they expect to be professional?

First getting a basic love for people, you've got to like people because music is an extension of you. Everything is done in levels, you master one and move on to the next level. Every step you make should be a sure step. Listen, you can't listen enough, and remember the instrument is a slave to you.

Thank you so much for your time and patience in giving us this interview.

David Edward Hines Trumpet, piano, flügelhorn/Born July 18, 1942, St. Louis, Mo.

David's mother's name was Anna L. Roman Gaten Hines and she was born in Baton Rouge, Louisiana, on April 18, 1907. His father's name was Edison Hines and he was born in Indianola, Mississippi, on November 22, 1919; neither one of them were musicians. David attended grade school at Cote Brilliante, and high school at Sumner High. David's musical education is as follows:

1961   St. Louis Institute of Music.
1964   Southern Illinois University.
1965   Chicago Conservatory of Music, B.A.
1966   Lincoln University, Jefferson City, Missouri.
1978   Washington University, St. Louis, Missouri.

David Hines' work experiences are indeed impressive. From 1960 to 1984 he was busy.

1960   Gospel Chorus pianist at the Central Baptist Church.
1962   Gaslight Square.
1963   Ike and Tina Turner Revue, U.S. and Europe.
1965   Albert King Blues Band—Midwest Tour (trumpet), T-Bone Walker Blues Band—Chicago Tour (trumpet), Little Milton Campbell, Midwest Tour (trumpet).
1968   Ike and Tina Turner Revue, U.S. and European Tour.
1969   Jazz soloist/trumpet with the Woody Herman Band.
1970   With the Ray Charles Orchestra as Jazz soloist/trumpet.
1972   American Theater Orchestra playing trumpet.
1972–1975   Performed with the Saint Louis Muny Opera Orchestra on trumpet.
1976   Arranger/conductor on the St. Louis production of *The Wiz*.
1977   Jazz solo at the Contemporary Music Festival with George Russell. Also arranger/conductor and lead trumpet for the Persona Players—Black Images.
1978   Toured U.S., Europe and Canada as lead and jazz trumpet.
1978–1981   With American Theater Orchestra. *The Wiz*/trumpet,

Eubie/trumpet, *Timbuctu*/trumpet, *Ain't Misbehavin'*/jazz and lead trumpet, *Lost in the Stars*/trumpet.

1982 Westport Playhouse: "The Magic of Black Music"/jazz soloist/ trumpet and piano (February and April), Phyllis Diller in Concert/ jazz trumpet.

1980–1983 St. Louis Conservatory of Music—David Hines Ensemble, Lena Horne/Fox Theater/trumpet. Television: David Hines Ensemble—*Mid-Day A.M.*—KSD-TV Channel 5; Talk Show Guest—*Mid-Day News*—KTVI-TV Channel 2; Talk Show Guest—*Proud*—KPLR-TV Channel 11; Jazz with David and Donna—KETC-TC Channel 9; Nominated for Emmy for contribution and ability on trumpet.

Teaching:

1973–1982 St. Louis Board of Education, Neighborhood Youth Core; Ferguson-Florissant R-2 School District; Community of Schools for the Arts (CASA); St. Louis Conservatory of Music; St. Louis College of Pharmacy; Honors Music Program—St. Louis, and Public Schools.

Organizations:

1982 President, Arts & Letters Commission, University City; Chairman, Instrumental Division—Clarence Hayden Wilson Music Guild; Member, Musical Association of St. Louis Local 2-197.

July 1984 World's Fair in New Orleans, Louisiana; eight jazz concerts for the senior citizens of St. Louis at O'Fallon Park at the "Boat House."

When David Hines was asked what advice he would pass on to younger musicians coming up in the profession he replied, "Be serious, and work hard. Know and be honest with yourself and about your talent."

David has practiced what he advises, for when one mentions jazz in St. Louis, David Hines comes instantly to mind. He is a jazz great.

Dewey Jackson Trumpet/Born June 21, 1900, St. Louis, Mo.

Dewey Jackson was born in St. Louis at the turn of the century. He was one of St. Louis' early jazz greats. He played with the Odd Fellow's Band, an organization sponsored by The Odd Fellows in his early teens. This was the first musical instruction he had ever had. His first professional job was with Tommy Evan's Band at age sixteen, on Pine near Union Station in St. Louis. He was with George Reynolds' Keystone Band for about a year. It was located in the Keystone Cafe on Compton and Lawton in St. Louis operated by Charlie Mills. In May 1919 he joined Charlie Creath on the riverboat, *J.S.*, and old tub subject to breakdowns. Following are some highlights in his career:

1920–1923   Led his own band, the Golden Melody Band.

1924   With Fate Marable on the SS *Capital*, a steamer.

1926   Moved to New York, spent four months with violinist Andrew Preer at the Cotton Club.

1927   Went to New Orleans and rejoined Fate Marable on the SS *St. Paul.*

1927–1929   Led his own band and had occasional gigs with Fate Marable.

1932   Led his own band at the Castle Ballroom, St. Louis.

1934   Rejoined Charlie Creath.

1936   Working in a band jointly led by Charlie Creath and Fate Marable.

1937   Led his own Musical Ambassadors on the riverboats in summer and played local ballrooms in winter.

Until 1941 he continued to play the riverboats then left full-time music to operate a hotel, but began to play again in 1950.

1950   With Singleton Palmer's Band.

1951   With Don Ewell's Trio.

1950s–1960s   Led own band and played a few dates until the late 1960s.

He played at the Humming Bird on Lucas Avenue in St. Louis.

Dewey had a four piece band, a six piece band, and finally a ten piece band (eight members from St. Louis, two from New Orleans) which he called The St. Louis Peacock Charleston Orchestra, later renamed The New Orleans Cotton Pickers. The uniforms for that group were fancy satin coveralls.

He looked upon Louis Armstrong as his idol.

Percy E. James, Jr. Bongo-Conga Drums/Born March 6, 1929, St. Louis, Mo./Interviewed by Jimmy Jones.

First of all Percy, what were your mother and father's names?

My father's name was Percy James, Sr.

And your mother?

Ada Mae James.

Do you remember their birth dates and places?

My father was born in 1900, in January.

And that was where?

Tennesaw, Alabama.

And your mother?

Mom was born in Beatrice, Alabama.

How about your other relatives? Were they musically inclined?

I had a brother and a sister.

And your brother's name?

Jessie James.

All right! And what was your sister's name?

Shirley James.

Are they still active in music today?

My sister is deceased. My brother is an administrator and a teacher in an elementary school now. He didn't pursue music.

Where is he teaching?

St. Trinidad's School in St. Louis.

Are you the youngest James?

Yes, I am the baby.

What grade school did you attend?

At Dunbar, then I got transferred to Duval.

And how about high school?

Vashon, our rival.

At what point did you become interested in music?

I was influenced by all the things that happened around me. Jazz musicians, gang fighting, playground mouth music, the jitterbug dancing at night on the street, mocking the white boys on the inside. I went through that period of getting into singing. We had brothers who could sing like Billy Eckstine, sing like anybody and you would sit and listen to them. Then I fell in love with the dance period, the big band period, and we went to the Castle Ballroom and I was hearing the big band every Tuesday night and throughout my whole life.

The first college I went to was Tennessee State. They've got a heck of a music department there. This was where I had the first chance to see a pair of bongos and it just thrilled me to be close to the instrument. From there I dropped out of Tennessee State and went to Lincoln University, another good music department. My training actually started on the campus at Lincoln. I was frightened at my first rehearsal, because I didn't know nothing about music. I walked in, they stopped the music and the leader said, here's the bongo player I was telling you about. I didn't know nothing about no bongos except that I liked them. I sat down and they played the first piece. I didn't know what I was doin' but I was doin' it.

But your mind and your ear told you.

It's in time, in time. Your timing is the ultimate, no matter what you're doing. I worked with the big bands for about five years.

Then I came out and worked with Jimmy Houston, George Hudson, and I got with Jimmy Forrest for seven years. I was trained by the master. I've been an international musician for thirty-three years. I go back to the original Nighttrain. I covered the jazz period thoroughly. We could outclass the white musicians because we had smaller groups and no budget. Nobody would pay for this kind of thing with big bands. Even right now you can't work a big band.

Do you remember your first paid job?

I always got paid. I got paid on campus. That's how I made my hustle. You know back in the early thirties we did a lot of creative things. We were closer to our native state. We did a lot of things with materials. One of the guys could really play trumpet, his father bought him a trumpet. Now all the rest of the guys wanted to play instruments and they fashioned instruments out of, I don't know what kind of materials, but they really looked like a saxophone, trombone, drums . . . and one of the musicians was so fabulous. His name was Emmick. They called him Sy, he could play drums, sing and play piano at the same time. He was a down musician.

At what point did you connect up with Tres Bien?

Well, I'm the originator. I brought the group together.

That's what I thought. Do you remember how you got them together? They made such a great giant of a name. They're still here now, even though you guys are separated. Tres Bien still lives.

And we've done a lot of things together here lately too. The group first came into conception in 1954. First, Jeter Thompson and I came together with the bass player, Van Osdale. It was the Van Osdale Trio. We worked together from 1953. We used several bass players, but we ended up with Hawkins, Al St. James and Jeter Thompson.

Do you have any idea how many albums or records you guys really did do? (Tres Bien)

About fourteen or fifteen, I guess.

That's a safe guess.

It was the most recorded group in the midwest, as a group, you know.

And all of St. Louis birth.

I went to the Apollo six times. The Apollo Theater in New York. I've got my credentials. I played the Howard Theater, The Riviera. Dick Gregory is one of the biggest influences in my life, one of the most beautiful brothers I've ever come in contact with. He is real.

If I had to talk about my career per se, I had so much experience because all the older fellows were very hip. This is a drummers' town. This is where I was most accepted and I was never a jungle player, I'm a jazz musician. This is a musical town.

It is that. Hopefully if the things we are trying to do come into the hands of the right people, they can hear where people have come from and what they're about, and what they want to do. Hopefully those avenues will open.

We are a nation of people too lazy to do for ourself. Avenues are open. We just need leadership in this town.

The only thing I didn't mention was that I recorded with Oliver Nelson. The Tres Bien featured Jimmy Forrest, Chris Woods, Oliver Nelson, Willie Akins, and Freddie Washington. We had 'em all in our group, and I got some things on tape with Oliver Nelson that really would amaze you. We also did a live recording session with Theolonius Monk. I think it was Decca that really recorded Monk, but they recorded a session and gave us

the tapes. I think we should consider a re-release, or release because they have good sound quality and everything.
That would be a tribute too. That should be.
To work with a guy like Monk for two weeks is an experience in itself.
Thank you so much for the interview Percy, I think you have paid your dues and then some.
You're sure welcome, Jimmy.

James L. Jeter Alto sax/Born 1904, St. Louis, Mo., died 1980, St. Louis, Mo.
Years ago, one of the top black bands around was led by Alphonso Trent who played out of Arkansas and Texas. Out of that band came two talented musicians named James L. Jeter and Hayes Pillars.
They formed the Jeter-Pillars Orchestra, widely known as the band that captivated St. Louis and the Southwest for years. At one time this band supplied the music for radio 's "Fitch Bandwagon Show." The Jeter-Pillars Orchestra produced some top musicians: Walter Page, Sid Catlett, Floyd Smith, Jimmy Blanton, Kenny Clarke, Charlie Christian, Teddy Buckner, and Chester Lane.
At the time big bands lost their popularity, and demand for live performances dropped, the Jeter-Pillars Orchestra disbanded. James Jeter became a representative for Anheuser-Busch in St. Louis, and when he died at age 77, another era of music went into the history books.
Jeter and Pillars were achievers; these two gentlemen accomplished a great deal in the music world.

Edith North Johnson Piano, vocalist/Born 1905, St. Louis, Mo.
Edith was born and raised in the St. Louis metropolitan area. Her mother's name was Hattie North. During the 1920s and 1930s she worked in Jessie Johnson's DeLuxe Music Shop in St. Louis, Missouri. Following are some important dates in her career:

1928   Recorded on QRS label, Long Island, N.Y.
1929   Recorded on Paramount label, Richmond, Ind.; and Grafton, Wisc.
1929   Recorded Okeh label, Chicago, Ill.
1929   Recorded Vocalion label, Kansas City, Mo.
1929   Recorded with Oliver Cobb's Rhythm Kings on the Brunswick label, Chicago.
1930–1940   Worked mostly outside music except for private party work in St. Louis.
1950   Owned and operated DeLuxe Restaurant, St. Louis.

Eddie Johnson

Edith married Jessie Johnson in 1928. He was the brother of James "Stump" Johnson. She worked under the name of her mother, Hattie North, on occasion and also Maybelle Johnson. (It is not known if her mother was also an entertainer.)

Edward "Eddie" Johnson Piano, band leader/Born March 8, 1912, East St. Louis, Ill.

Eddie Johnson was born in East St. Louis, Illinois and became interested in music at the very early age of ten. His cousin Florence Johnson was one of his first instructors.

He gained advanced knowledge and experience as a student at a music conservatory in New York City. Eddie Johnson was one of the most aggressive music makers in the Middle West.

He revived riverboat jazz of yesteryear in a two-hour concert at the University of Missouri–St. Louis campus on November 19, 1971, which attracted a record attendance. His six gentlemen of music were drummer Martin

Luther McKay of Count Basie fame; Ralph Williams, vocalist and guitarist formerly with the Ink Spots and Orioles; Bill Martin, a trumpet stylist; Cliff Batchman, saxophonist; Eugene Thomas on bass who worked with the Earl (Fatha) Hines, and Della Reese.

Eddie credits his success of four decades to many, especially the late Jessie J. Johnson, one of the world's greatest dance band and entertainment promoters. Through the guidance of Jessie J. Johnson, Eddie says both his new band and the late Oliver Cobb's Orchestra skyrocketed with concerts, ballroom dances and nightclubs.

Eddie played several riverboat excursions, including the *Avalon* and the *St. Paul*, another stepping stone for the new St. Louis Crackerjack Orchestra, the nucleus of the late Oliver Cobb's twelve piece orchestra. He opened the Club Plantation in 1931 featuring Tab Smith, a brilliant saxophonist, arranger and vocalist. They played most of the dance halls in and out of the St. Louis area.

The Eddie Johnson Trio members are: Goldie Johnson, piano, LeRoy Harris, sax and vocalist, and Eugene Thomas, bass.

Members of his first jazz group were the Martin twins, Freddie and Walter, on alto saxophones; Ernest (Chick) Franklin on tenor sax; Singleton Palmer, trumpet; James Telephy, trumpet; and Winfield Baker on trombone. In the rhythm section were Lester (Sparib) Nicholar, drums; Benny Jackson, vocalist and banjo; and Sidney Todd, tuba.

He has recorded, played one-nighters and steady engagements in major cities including Kansas City (Missouri), Chicago, Milwaukee, Detroit, Pittsburgh, and Louisville.

Eddie heads the E.L.J. Recording Company in University City, and books the Eddie Johnson Orchestra, plus all kinds of entertainment for conventions, ballrooms, theater, and night clubs.

Following are some highlights of his career:

1929   Joined Oliver Cobb's Orchestra.
1930   Took over the orchestra when Oliver died, it became KMOX Staff Orchestra.
1931   On road from Chicago to all points on the East Coast.
1932   Played Greystone Ballroom, Detroit (taking McKinney Cotton Picker's place).
1932   Opened Club Plantation in St. Louis.
1932   Reopened Greystone Ballroom with the Mills Brothers' first appearance in St. Louis (1932) with the Eddie Johnson Orchestra.
1933–1936   Jessie Johnson back orchestra with such name bands as Earl Hinds, Duke Ellington, Fletcher Henderson, Don Redman. Toured with Fats Waller out of Cincinnati, Ohio.
1936–1937   Played at Black Cat Club with Larry Steele Show in Detroit.

1938–1939   St. Louis, worked on the steamer *Idlewild* and dance dates.
1940–1945   Played around St. Louis, East Side Harlem Club.

Top musicians that played with Eddie Johnson:

Tab Smith   Harold Arnold
Harold Baker   Floyd Smith
Francis Widsby   Wendell Marshall
Singleton Palmer & his band: Milton Fletcher
a. Robert Carter   Eugene Porter
b. Bennie Stark   Lester Nichols
c. LeRoy Harris   Jimmy Forrest
d. Ben Thigpen

Floyd "Candy" Johnson Saxophone/Born Madison, Ill., 1922, died
June 28, 1981, Framingham, Mass./Candy's aunt and uncle, Mary and
Johnny Gaskin, interviewed by Jimmy Jones.
*We're going to find out some personal information about Candy's mother and
father. Mary, can you tell me something about Candy's mother and father?
What were their names?*
   The mother was Ethel Johnson.
Ethel Johnson.
   She also played piano, she was good on piano and Candy's father was
my brother, which was Floyd Johnson.
And were they residents...
   They were residents of Madison, Illinois . . . and Candy also attended
grade school over there.
Was Candy born over there?
   Yes, he was born [there].
They attended grade school in Madison, you say?
   Yes . . . the Dunbar grade school.
*And were there any other relatives they didn't mention in the articles? What
were their names? His other relatives' names?*
   Well, his daughter, Carol Johnson.
Carol Johnson.
   Carol Johnson and should I mention that one he adopted?
   Did you want the wives' names?
   Just a minute Johnny, they did enough about the wives.
That's all right.
   What was that child's name?
   Pam?
   Pamela Johnson and then my sister Linell Wheeler, that's Kenny's
other aunt, see I'm Mary *Jackson* and she's Linell Wheeler, see?
I see, and you play a little piano too, don't you?

Musically Yours
Candy Johnson

"Candy" Johnson

I used to. I used to think I knew how. *(She laughs.)*
All right. (They laugh.) *Now, Candy Johnson was born in Madison, Illinois and he went to school . . .*

He went to Dunbar, I don't know if he went to grade school in East St. Louis, I'm not sure about that, oh yeah, he come over here and lived with my mother and go home on the weekends you know and then I think he went to, what school did he go to over here? I think he went to Sumner. I don't think he . . .

To high school?

No. I don't think he went to grade school . . .

He won a scholarship in basketball in one of the schools.

Yeah, but that was in college . . .

But that was in high school and then he go to college . . .

I know that, Johnny, that I know but I'm trying to think of what school did he go to over here, it must have been maybe Sumner, it had to be Sumner because he eventually went to the army or something.

He was in service.

And he got out of the army because they thought he had a bad heart or something, but anyway he, oh well you ask me some more questions.

But anyway, I am sure that when he was first getting into music the first instrument, was that a type of a fiddle?

First it was a violin and he told his mother, first he told his mother he wanted a violin and his mother got him a violin, he was a little boy then, and he thought now that's just kinda sissy, I don't think then he had drums, his mother got him a drum after that, then he got tired of the drum and he wanted a saxophone. I think when he started the saxophone is when he went to the army. I think that's when he got into this business, when he got really into saxophone so I don't know if he, 'cause I didn't even know he had taken lessons or something, I think when he went to the army that's when he, uh, went someplace and had lessons. I didn't even know he had lessons . . . I said you know Candy played and he never had any lessons but he did. I didn't know that, see? But a lot of stuff he just made hisself and he just put in there what he wanted to, see?

Right. And the article will tell who he played with and . . .

That's right, the article, that's in there. Right, uh huh, uh huh.

Does the article also mention when he was born?

Yes, it does. I think it does.

Yes. It does.

I'll get it. I'm sure it does.

I'm sure it mentions . . .

I want to get a little bit about Mr. Gaskin, also because since he was related to Candy, some of his relatives were famous musicians also. Will you name them for me?

Quincy Jones. Quincy was born here in St. Louis and his mother's name was Sarah, Sarah Jones.

She lives in California now.

No, she lives in Seattle.

Seattle, Washington.

I see.

Quincy have two more brothers.

Are they St. Louisans?

No I don't know where they are right now, but his mother's in Seattle and his mother was a musician. She played three or four different instruments. She played the piano and he had an aunt, she played for a church here. The Church of God and Christ located now right here on Compton and Page and she played the piano until she passed a few years ago.

And what was her name?

Amelia Bell. She married one of the Bells. Herman Bell.

I see, I see. You know I didn't know Quincy Jones was a St. Louisan.

Yeah. Oh, yeah he was definitely until a few years ago but his mother moved to Seattle when he was small though.

All of his sisters were . . . those were his aunts though, they are all dead except Mable and Sarah are the only two livin'. That's his mother Sarah and Mable was an aunt.

His mother, there were about four or five girls of them and four boys, about nine or ten all together in the family.

But Quincy Jones was and still is a big name.

I know it, I know it.

I just saw him on television two or three weeks ago.

He writes some music for shows on the television and all that stuff.

You know St. Louis has been quite a producer of a lot of big name people.

That's right.

Quite a producer, so I'm going to get a lot of information off the article that you let me use and I'm going to close the tape right now if there's not any other information I should hear.

I think that's enough.

James "Stump" Johnson Piano/Born 1905, St. Louis, Mo., died 1972, St. Louis, Mo.

James "Stump" Johnson was a self-taught pianist and as a youth played in the local bawdy houses in St. Louis. Here are some important dates in his career:

1929 Recorded on QRS label, Long Island, New York.
1929 Recorded on Brunswick label, Chicago.
1929 Recorded for Paramount label, Richmond, Indiana.

1929 Recorded for Okeh label, Chicago.
1930 Recorded on Paramount label, in Grafton, Wisconsin.
1930 Recorded on Victor label, Dallas, Texas, and had club dates in St. Louis.
1932 Recorded on Bluebird label, Chicago.
1933 Back to St. Louis after mid-thirties and into the '50s and in the late '50s was in business with Edith North operating the DeLuxe Restaurant in St. Louis City while continuing to gig sporadically through the '60s. Inactive in the late '60s due to bad health, but did record again in 1970.
1970 Recorded for Euphonic label in St. Louis, Missouri.
1970 Recorded soundtrack for VK film, *Blues Like Showers of Rain.*

His nickname "Stumpy" came from the fact that he was a very short, stocky man. Probably his most remembered song was "You Buzzard You."

John Clyde "Johnnie" Johnson Piano/Born 1922, St. Louis, Mo.

Johnnie Johnson started playing the piano at age seven. It was in the middle of the depression era, and no one would have guessed then that he would become one of the most respected musicians of early rock and roll or that he would be the leader of the Johnnie Johnson Trio, a unique group.

Johnnie hired Chuck Berry as a replacement for an ill saxophone player one night in St. Louis. Chuck Berry made a tape and took it to Vee Jay Records in Chicago. They turned it down and he went to Chess Records in the same area. They in turn liked it and Johnnie, Chuck and the group made a live recording of it. It was called "Maybelline" and on the flip side was "Wee Wee Hours." From then on it was Chuck Berry all the way.

The Johnnie Johnson Trio was changed to the Chuck Berry Trio. Johnnie said, "I could never sing anyway, I was just a piano player." Johnnie seemed to get lost in the shadow of Chuck Berry, but actually he was the support behind the man. It just depends on how you look at it.

Johnnie Johnson has been true to his art and turns to the greatest stars for his own personal listening pleasure. He is reported to have said he would "run through hell to get to Oscar Peterson," his favorite piano player, and then there was Earl Garner, his other favorite, now deceased.

He's done a session with Rod Stewart, performing "White Women and Black Stockings" and "Don't Lie to Me."

Johnnie still resides in St. Louis and the Johnnie Johnson Trio still takes the stage four nights a week, and he often sits in with other local bands on his nights off.

These authors were pleased to meet again and be entertained by Johnnie Johnson at Henry VIIIth on Lindberg Boulevard in St. Louis County in

October 1985, where he was playing piano for a Chuck Berry Concert. One more time . . .

Johnnie Johnson is still out there, he's still refining his art and spreading the joy.

Frank Joseph "Pappy" Kloben Tenor sax, clarinet, flute, all woodwinds, private teacher/Telephone interview by Lyn Cunningham.

Frank Kloben was born in St. Louis, Missouri on November 28, 1939. His mother's name is Naomi (Cole) Kloben, born in Chillicothe, Missouri, and his father's name is Frank Joseph Kloben, Sr., born in St. Louis. Frank's mother sang during the 1930s, and his father loved dancing and music and used to go on the *St. Paul* and the *President* to see and listen to his favorites, Louis Armstrong and Jack Teagarden.

Frank started on the clarinet at age eleven. He studied privately with Mr. Cramer and John Bergeron. From age 14 to 18 he studied with John Littich on clarinet. Then he began on tenor sax, also with John Littich, then baritone sax, alto sax, then back to tenor sax. He was 25 years old at this time.

He attended Shenandoah grade school, McKinley High School, went to college at the University of Maryland, University of Southern California, Meramec, and finished at the University of Missouri at St. Louis.

His first paying job was with the Walter Medcalf Sextet. He was paid $10.00 for the job. He started with Bob Kuban in 1973 and played for seven years aboard *The Admiral* with him, from 1973 to 1980. He worked for Johnny Polzin, Nick Musci, Larry Mantese, Bonnie Ross, Dick Renna. He was tenor sax man with all these groups. He had his own group from 1962 to 1964 with his brother, John Kloben. It was a pop and jazz group called The Frank Kloben Quartet. He also played the football St. Louis Cardinal games for 12 years, and the Miss Universe Pageant Ball.

Frank made a recording with the Meramec Community Jazz Lab Band, and a recording with Bob Kuban's Brass. His advice to younger musicians: "Learn every facet of the business, your instrument and all the instruments if possible, so you can double, because nowadays you have to be versatile. Always have a neat appearance."

Mike Krenski Electric bass, writer, sousaphone/Interviewed by Lyn Cunningham.

Mike Krenski was born in St. Louis, Missouri on March 18, 1944. His mother's name is Vedas McClure Krenski, and his father's name is John C. Krenski; neither one is a musician.

Mike attended Walnut Park Elementary, Hazelwood High School, Parks College, St. Louis University, all in St. Louis. His first paying job was with a group formed in high school for which he was paid $5.00. The group was called the Mellow Tones and they played school dances, lounges, and weddings for five years.

Several cuts were made with the Mellow Tones, but none were released. Two promotional records, "Long Haired Music" and "The Guise," were represented by the William Morris Agency. Those were put out in the St. Louis area between 1967 and 1970. Mike wrote Bob Kuban's top hit, "The Cheater," and worked for him between 1962 and 1967.

Mike worked with Jake Jones Group between 1970 and 1973. It was a pop-rock and country-rock group.

Mike had a Piper Aircraft dealership between 1973 and 1980. He went to work at McDonnell-Douglas Aircraft in 1980, working on the cruise missile project, and as of 1985 he was still with them. Mike started writing music again in 1981 and is still working at that.

His advice to younger musicians is, "Get formal musical training, keyboard, theory, keeping main interest on your own instrument, but definitely study theory."

Bob Kuban Drummer/Born August 19, 1942, St. Louis, Mo./Interviewed by Jimmy Jones and Lyn Cunningham.
Bob, we'd like to get some information on your life. First of all, I want to start with your mother and father. Where were they born?

My father was born, he's been dead for almost 18 years now, but he was born on September 5, 1909, in Poland and then of course he and his family came to the United States from the old country. My mother was born in Omaha, Nebraska. She was born on September 6, 1913. Their birthdays were back to back.
Were there other children in your family?

Oh, yes. I have a sister Donna who is a couple of years younger than I am, and my brother Larry who is five years younger.
Are either one of them musicians?

No, I'm the only musician.
Now we're getting down to the nitty-gritty, Mr. Bob Kuban. Where were you born?

I was born right here in St. Louis, August 19, 1942. I'm 43 years old. I really didn't get into music until my sophomore or junior year in high school. I sorta dabbled with it a little bit but . . .
Where did you go to school?

I went to Riverview Gardens High School. I always wanted to be a drummer, but it was one of those things that no matter where you went they didn't need a drummer. Everybody wanted to be a drummer but I was always the last kid in line so I never got into anything. Then finally, I remember how I broke into it. One day they had an assembly and Chuck Berry came out to perform at our school and he was by himself and he was

The Band: *Top row, l-r:* **Dean Kresyman, Chris McCready, Karen Zelle, Bob Kuban, Bill Miller.** *Bottom row:* **Joe Shaddock, Frank Hloler, Jim Stevens, Dan Potter, Carl Makarewicz, Fred Goessler.**

playing guitar and he asked if anybody at school could play anything and they had a set of drums there. I'd never really played before but the guys picked me up and threw me up on stage and I played with Chuck Berry and he enjoyed it. That was in 1954.

In fact I'm a runner and I was running track. I'll bet I've run that track six thousand times. Anyway, I just went on from there. The music teacher saw me play and decided to put me in the high school band in my freshman year. I didn't play any professional gigs until my sophomore year. Then I started getting jobs.

Do you remember the first gig that you got paid for?

I played at a teen town over at Corpus Christi High School and got five bucks. Back then that seemed like all the money in the world.

In your teen years I'm sure there was a teacher who wanted to make Bob Kuban a musician.

Yes, Paul Koenig over at Riverview High School who has now retired. He kinda took me by the horns and I think he saw that I had some ability. Plus the other music teachers. Then they came up with the John Phillip Sousa award and I was the first person to receive that award at Riverview High School, and now it's an annual affair.

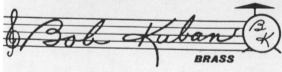

Publicity still for Bob Kuban Brass.

That was the beginning.

I went on to the Institute of Music at Washington University.

What is the biggest band you've ever played with or conducted?

The biggest group I ever conducted was the St. Louis Symphony Orchestra. I got to conduct that one night which was kind of neat.

That was an honor.

Oh, my God, was it! We performed "The Cheater" with the St. Louis Symphony at Kiel. We sorta launched this contemporary sound with the Symphony. That was something you never heard of until then. After that you saw the Beatles and all those different groups doing it.

Now about traveling with big name bands, Bob?

Oh yeah, we traveled quite a bit and did several TV shows, two *American Bandstands*, a telethon in St. Louis. Then they had us on a soap opera called *Never Too Young*.

I worked with you on that telethon.

Yeah. We did a Casey Kasem Show out in Los Angeles. That was when no one had ever heard of him back here. I told everyone back here that there was this DJ out in L.A. that was just dynamite. Of course Dick Clark is the big one now, but Casey's show was unique the way he pulled it off. "The Cheater" was the number one hit then and we traveled all up and down the West Coast.

Was this your band?

Yes. My band, Bob Kuban and the In Men.

Do you have a picture of that band?

Oh, yeah, sure. A lot of pictures.

I'll talk to you about that later. After doing tours and traveling, finally you come back home, and what's home been like since you came back?

Well I'll tell you what brought us back, Jim. At that time the Vietnam War was in full blaze and all of us were draft bait in the band. The kids today don't realize how easy they've got it. Back then you kept your grades up. You had a choice, pass the course or go to Vietnam. One of the two. I was a music teacher at Riverview High School after I got out of college, so that kept me out. But none of us could go on the road and stay out for any length of time. With a national seven top record we had a nine week tour booked in Australia, and couldn't go. We couldn't get our deferments. If we did get one, we went straight to Vietnam.

So basically from the beginning of your career you have been with your band.

Yes.

That's a great track record.

I started my band in 1960, 24 years. I was a very little kid.

I'm sure everyone in St. Louis and all over have heard about you. And that's what we're about. To let people know that we have the tops here in St. Louis and that some of the tops came from St. Louis. We're making that known in book form.

Sure.

We want the people of St. Louis to know that when they want a good musician, they don't have to send out of town to get one.

It's funny you said that, and you can print this, I just came from the Union Hall, I guess it's been a month now, I was down there and I requested an audience with the board, and it was for this exact thing. Why is there no recording in this town? Why is it the city of Nashville did 25 million dollars in master cuts last year while we did nothing? The city of Nashville is half the size of St. Louis. You can't tell me there are 25 million dollars worth of better musicians there than there are here. They said, we got to do what the book says, and I said to hell with the book. Nashville's not doing what the book says.

Now if you had any advice to give to the younger musicians, what would that be?

The first thing would be, stay away from this Mickey-Mouse stuff, like the drug thing and the alcohol thing thinking that this is part of it. This is definitely not part of it. I'm a business man first and then a musician. I like to feel that I'm both, but the one thing I won't tolerate is drugs or alcohol in any way shape or form. I find a guy like that, he's gone. That's just the way I am. So I'll tell them to look at it from a business standpoint. It's not easy, it's hard work and it doesn't happen overnight.

Everybody can't be a star.

Have you made any albums?

Oh, yes.

Do you have the names of them?

"Bob Kuban Brass" made in 1975, that was the latest, but because I had so much hassle with the Union, I decided I wasn't going to record in this town anymore, which is pretty sad. And "The Cheater Album" and the "Explosion Album." I have some stuff to record now but it will probably be recorded elsewhere because we just don't have the proper facilities here.

Thanks so much Bob, and we'll be talking to you for your pictures and leads of people to see real soon.

Tina LaCoste Pianist/Born April 11, 1929, St. Louis, Mo./Interviewed by Jimmy Jones.

We are here to interview Tina LaCoste, sister of the late Oliver Nelson. So, tell us a little about yourself Tina.

My name is Tina LaCoste and I'm a pianist. I've been playing piano since I was a child. I was blessed to be born to a musical family. My parents played. My mother played piano and my father played guitar. My grandparents played. My uncles . . . well as I say, my family is musical. Through

elementary school I used to play for programs, I didn't know what I was doing, but I was playing. I'd like to know how I sounded. And then through high school, I played with different bands at different functions.
Name bands too?

I played with, no, not any name bands. I once accompanied Al Hibler, the singer, when I was working with my brother's group, the late Oliver Nelson. I have accompanied many singers.
Yes.

When I started I was a beautician. I was working at a beauty shop and then Leonard Bolden, the mailman, on the route to the beauty shop, told me they needed piano players very badly at this musicians union. So I joined the union and I've been working ever since.
At that time it was Local 197, right?

That's right. And I worked with many, with many fine musicians. I worked with Jimmy Forrest, I worked with Singleton Palmer and a lot of the older musicians. I started with them and they taught me a lot by working with them, and John Carter, who was secretary of the Union, encouraged me to do a single because he thought I could do a single.

So I started out doing a single and that's what I've been doing all the time now. I'm currently doing a single but I worked at Brennans Restaurant in Ladue for nine and a half years. Before that I worked on Gaslight Square at the Port of St. Louis about three years and then on Central for a short while, and then I worked at the Crest House. I worked at Cheshire Inn, I'm currently working at Beaucaires. So as you can see, I've been very active. I play a lot of private parties.
Did you get your foundation from church music?

Yes, I played in Sunday School, Church choirs, yes.
I know that's where I did.

Yes, I started in Sunday School, playin' in Church.
Then you get the thing and you go from there.

My mother taught me a lot and I had private teachers.
What was your mother's name?

Lucille Nelson. She was never a professional, but she taught me and then she . . .
But since she was the foundation, I think we should mention her.

Oh, definitely!
You know, because she was Oliver's foundation, and she's your foundation.

Definitely, because she exposed us to classical music. Good music, and she made us learn to play it the right way, the correct way. She guided us. And I had one teacher, Bernice Spola who was instrumental, she was a teacher in the elementary school system also, but she was very important to my musical training.
Very good, very good. Thank you so very much, Tina.

Ann LaRue *see* **Cheryl Ann Dueren.**

"Lightnin' Slim" *see* **Otis V. Hicks.**

Otis "Sonny" Little Bass guitar/Born St. Louis, Mo., died May 31, 1986, St. Louis, Mo.
This is "Sonny" Little, a bass man. His name is Otis Little.
Everybody calls me Sonny professionally. Play bass. I have a private tutor. Play second bass with the St. Louis Symphony.
Really? I didn't know that.
Sure do.
If you can think of any name groups that you worked with . . .
Oh, yeah. I play contra bass, electric bass, cello, played with guys like Gene Amins, Sonny Stook. I played from Canada down through Mexico, played with quite a few name groups.
And how about some recordings?
I recall recording one time, and it never did get off the ground. When I was in Springfield, Missouri, I played some classics, country and western, buy my preference is jazz 'cause it's so creative.
Right.
I love to play it because it's our music, my music. But it takes an artist to play it. Really takes a sensitive type person to be able to feel it, and hear it, to improvise different melodies . . . it takes someone who knows what he's doing. Sometimes you have to be trained to do this, some people are just born naturally with it.
The gift.
Yes. In all my studies, all my endeavors I've found out that books are very good, the same as the exercise book, the same as any. Each artist has his own set of fingerings and I would say to the young bassists just starting, to somehow learn fingering, because eventually you'll come up with your own style. I've found sometimes that doesn't work the proper way to get to the place you want to go, it's how you're going to get there. Sometimes it's very awkward trying to move from one passage to another, ya know, according to how you let your inner ear take over. I've been playing for quite awhile with a lot of groups. Now I'm playing with "Pops" Porter, he plays the piano and sings, I play the bass and yodel.
You yodel?
As best I can!
In Highland, Illinois?
I'll go anywhere! We played Switesville, Illinois, Chicago, Illinois, Indiana, . . . we just made a duo out of it since it's so hard to keep a drummer, ya know.
Man, I know what you're talking about.

"Sonny" Little

But now if we can we try to find a drummer who knows whether he wants to stick or haul.
That will fit in to what you're doing?
Yes. The hard part is finding someone that's going to fit. We also have Charles Wright in our group, better known as, "Little Man," he plays one heck of a tenor, tenor saxophone.
Thank you for this short but informative interview, Sonny, maybe sometime we'll catch you later when you're not on the run.

Jimmy McCracklin Harmonica, piano/Born August 13, 1921, St. Louis, Mo.

Jimmy McCracklin was born and raised in St. Louis, Missouri. In the early 1940s he served in the United States Navy. After his release he settled in the Watts section of Los Angeles and worked as a professional boxer. His most popular songs were "Every Night and Every Day," "I Just Got to Know" and "You Know Who to Turn To." Following are some important dates in Jimmy's career:

1940   Studied some piano with J.D. Nicholson and recorded with his group on the Globe label in Los Angeles.
1945–1946   Worked in the Santa Barbara, California, area. Recorded on Excelsior label in Los Angeles.
1947   Recorded on Cavatone label, Oakland, California.
1948   Recorded on J and M Fulbright label, Oakland.
1949–1950   Recorded on Trilon label, Oakland, RPM Modern label, Oakland.
1951   Recorded on Springtime label in Los Angeles.
1952–1953   Recorded on Peacock label, Houston.
1953–1954   Recorded on Peacock label, Oakland.
1954–1955   Recorded on Modern-Crown label, Oakland, and Hollywood label, Oakland.
1956   Recorded on Irma label, worked the Savoy Club in Richmond, California.
1957   Appeared with Frankie Lee on American Bandstand ABC-TV (unconfirmed).
1957   Recorded on Checker label, Chicago.
1958–1959   Recorded on Mercury label, Chicago.
1962   Recorded on his own label (Art-Tone), Oakland, and toured with Eddie Boyd, working concerts.
1965   Formed own band and worked club dates in the South.
1965–1973   Owned the Continental Club in Oakland.
1971   Recorded on Stax label in California.
1973   KPIX-TV appearance San Francisco, University of California Extension Center.
1974   Joe's Melody Club, Vallejo, California, La Jolla Club, San Francisco, California.
1975   Blues Festival, San Francisco; recorded on Vanguard label, New

York City; Cassidy Hotel, Richmond, California; West Dakota Club, Berkeley, California; Singleton's, Houston.
1976 Eli's Mile High Club, San Francisco; Green Earth Cafe, San Francisco; KPFA-FM radio, Berkeley, California; WOW Hall, Eugene, Oregon.
1977 At Slats, San Francisco.

William "Red" McKenzie Vocalist, kazoo/Born October 14, 1899, St. Louis, Mo., died February 7, 1948, New York, N.Y.

When William McKenzie was a baby his parents moved to Washington, D.C. After both his parents died he moved back to St. Louis, Missouri.

With Jack Bland and Dick Slevin he formed a musical act later named The Mound City Blues Blowers. In 1922, with Gene Rodemich as band-leader, they made their recording debut in Chicago. They released their first recording, "Arkansas Blues," a best seller, and did a series of theater tours.

During the late 1920s Red McKenzie was active as a talent scout for recording companies, and was largely responsible for gaining recording contracts for Bix Beiderbecke, The Chicago Rhythm Kings, and The Spirits of Rhythm.

1923 From Atlantic City they went to London, England. Eddie Long also worked with them on that trip.
1925 Returned to U.S.A. and toured. Red led the group.
1932 Played long residencies in New York and Florida.
1932 Signed contract with Paul Whiteman and led his own band on recording sessions with other band leaders.
1933 Left Whiteman and reorganized his own band.
1935 Opened a club of his own on 52nd Street in New York, and the revived band made recordings under the name of The Mound City Blowers.
1937 After the death of his wife, Marie, he left New York and returned to St. Louis, Missouri.
1939 Returned to New York for a short residency at Kelly's, then returned to St. Louis.
1939–1944 Inactive in music, worked in St. Louis brewery.
1944 Worked the Eddie Condon Town Hall Concert in New York.

Red became ill while in New York and died of cirrhosis of the liver on February 7, 1948 in St. Clair's Hospital, New York City.

LeMonte McLemore Vocalist/Born September 17, 1940, St. Louis, Mo.

The Fifth Dimension was formed by LeMonte McLemore and Marilyn McCoo in the mid-sixties in Los Angeles, California. McLemore was a photographer for a Los Angeles fashion magazine. He and Marilyn decided to put their past gospel singing backgrounds to work in a group.

They recorded briefly as the Hi Fi's. LeMonte's cousin was Billy Davis. The second group, called The Versatiles, had the charter members of Florence La Rue, Ron Townson, Billy Davis, Marilyn McCoo, and LeMonte McLemore. They obtained a contract with Johnny River's Soul City label and achieved a minor hit called "I'll Be Loving You Forever" and changed their name to The Fifth Dimension.

Their first national hit in 1967 was called, "Go Where You Wanna Go," followed by "Another Day, Another Heartache." Their big breakthrough was a recording called "Up, Up and Away," which also launched the career of songwriter Jim Webb. Then, an unknown songwriter made her career with their "Stoned Soul Picnic," "Sweet Blindness," "Wedding Bell Blues," "Blowing Away," and "Save the Country."

In 1970 they switched to the Bell label and in 1975 were signed by ABC Records.

In 1976, when Billy Davis and Marilyn McCoo left the group, Billy was replaced by Daniel Beard.

The McPhersons Vocalists/Born St. Louis, Mo.

The McPhersons, Fedora, Andraine, Andreina, Juanita, and Roxanne, have been hailed by audiences as a talented entertainment group in concert and on television. They present the exciting blend of old and new tunes, ballads and upbeat discotheque, mixed with original songs and choreography.

Their concert tours have included Alaska, California, Korea, Taiwan and Australia.

The McPhersons are a family of overwhelming talent, recognized as top performers around the world.

Carl Makarewicz Trumpet, clarinet, flute, trombone, drums, elementary music teacher/Born April 16, 1959, St. Louis, Mo./Interviewed by Lyn Cunningham.

Carl Makarewicz was born in St. Louis on April 16, 1959. His mother is Genevieve (Forman) Makarewicz, and his father is Henry Martin Makarewicz, both born St. Louis. His father played trumpet and violin with Johnny Polzin in the 1930s. He still plays, but is a dentist now. Carl's father gave him his first lesson on the trumpet and always supported him.

Carl attended Good Shepherd Elementary in Ferguson, Missouri, high school at Rosary High in Spanish Lake, Missouri, and graduated from UMSL in 1982 with a degree in Musical Education. He now teaches fourth to eighth grade students in an elementary school.

His first paying job was with a grade school trio consisting of a drummer, a guitar player and himself. It paid $3.00 for the group. He was with his high school band and orchestra from 1974 to 1977 and the University of Missouri at St. Louis Jazz Band, 1978–1982. At age 16 and 17 he played wedding receptions for $20 a night and was with Joe Morello and The Pitts (a rock and roll group) for two years. He was 20 years old then and the group played in north county bars, and down on The Landing, between 1981 and 1982. He started with the Bob Kuban Brass in 1982 and as of 1985, was still with them.

Carl's advice to younger musicians is, "When you're young you must practice! Practice every day. I practice two or three hours. Have something to fall back on. Don't depend on music making your living totally. Be prepared to sweat."

Freddie Martin Saxophone, flute/Born July 1908, St. Louis, Mo./ Interviewed by Jimmy Jones.
I am in the home of Freddie Martin on this rainy Sunday afternoon, so Freddie tell me your name and where you were born.
My name is Freddie Martin and I was born in the city of St. Louis. I started music in school, junior high at Sumner School.
Any people you want to mention that were an inspiration to you?
Yes, there was, he's dead now. Clarence Harvey.
Was he a teacher in Sumner High School?
No he wasn't, he was a player.
He was a player? I see.
At that time Pres Wheeler was the principal. Clarence and Raymond Gay, we all came up together. I started playing piano, from there the saxophone, then the flute. I started playing about 1931. The first band I played with was Oliver Cobb.
Was he a St. Louisan?
Yeah. First of all he left and went on a Hollywood show, then we had the band, and we took the band into the city. The St. Louis Crackerjacks.
Oh, that means you worked with Eddie Johnson then?
No, Eddie Johnson worked with me.
Oh. Okay, all right.
Eddie Johnson came into the band and we put Eddie Johnson's name up in front because it was a nice name.
I see.
But he was the leader of the band. We had what is called an incorporated band. My twin brother, I guess you heard of him, he played saxophone.
What was his name?
Walter Martin. Walter H. Martin.
Did he play with you at that time?
Yeah, he played and there was Chick Franklin. We called him Chick,

Freddie Martin (left) and his St. Louis Crackerjacks.

but his name was Ernest Franklin. He played tenor sax. But before him, we had another fellow that was playin' with us, let's see what was that guy's name, Maynard? Well anyway he was in the band before the Chick come along.

What did he play?

He played tenor . . . I remember his name was Bradford Nichols. And then he went with Harvey Langford's Band.

Did you do any riverboat playing?

No, that was before my time. The first time we got on the *St. Paul*, Jessie Johnson took the Crackerjack Band on there. Fate Marable was on there, but we had the kick band, Jessie Johnson. What a band! At that time we had Al Baker, you see Winfield Baker was the manager of the band. That *was* Al Baker, you've heard of Al Baker the trumpet player?

Oh, yeah.

Played with Duke Ellington. I've got my picture with Duke. I played with Duke too.

Oh, okay, okay.

And Hal, it was Hal that played with us I mean, Winfield had two brothers and then we had a band, I guess it was about 1937. And then the band broke and we changed the band see? And then Chick Finney come into the band.

Chick Finney used to write for the Argus, didn't he?

Yeah, yeah, he was, well, I'd say he sat at the piano, he wasn't no hell of a piano player. We were playin' in Little Rock, Arkansas then with Winfield. It all started over ten dollars, you see everybody was supposed to make the same. Winfield had got ten dollars and we all spent it and we went to Chicago for the Labor Day. We used to go there every Labor Day, from the Hawaiian Club.
Where was the Hawaiian Club?
Here in St. Louis.
Oh, here in St. Louis.
They gave a dance there over Labor Day in Chicago. We'd leave on a Saturday night and come back Monday morning. First we made some recordings with Oliver Cobb. I got my book on it, you can see right here. I'll show you.
When we get ready to leave, I want to borrow a couple of your black and whites, you know?
You know I've had so much trouble with them doggone things, about guys bringin' 'em back. I think I got one here.
From that point on what were you in musically?
Well we played on up to about 1939. That was in the band. The band broke up. Then we started playing with individuals around here. When Terry Smith come to this town, we had a band, Terry come in our band, see?
And the name of that band was?
The St. Louis Crackerjacks. We went from here, we were that good, to the Graystone Ballroom in Detroit, and the band was so good we got a return engagement. That was the first time the band broke up. Eddie Johnson broke that band up because he wanted to be the leader and we wouldn't let him be the leader, so he broke the band up and kept the brass and we had but half the band, see? So that was the whole show on that. Now this is the band I used to have. Remember when you used to come over there where you was at? I had this band here.
Yeah. Right.
Now this is the band I recently had, this one here, but I had trouble with them guys, they wouldn't stay in the union, see?
But during the time I saw you over in Illinois, Tab (Smith) called you to work for him because he was ill.
Yeah, I worked for him, I always called him. Horsecollar and I done a whole lot of work together.
Yeah, Fred Lee.
Fred Lee and they had a little trouble over there, they kinda messed the band up.
Right.
And then they fool around and the singer he, they was cuttin' the band

out. I don't know if you was still there or not but he started to try to play drums, didn't he?

Yeah.

He tried to play drums and lost his job.

Yeah, I remember that!

He lost his job and then when Ted. . .

That was Al Henderson, wasn't it?

Yeah that was Al Henderson, see he thought he was a helluva drummer and he couldn't play nothin' on them drums, you know that.

Yeah.

Just a lick here and there. . .

Hunt and peck. . .

Yeah, hunt and peck and he was playin', and he was singin' he was a pretty good old singer. He was one of the best I heard around. Then I played the Plantation with Jeter Pillar.

Oh, yeah.

I got some pictures upstairs. I'll show you my pictures that I made with Duke (Ellington) and oh, God, I got a gang of pictures up there. I played with practically every band that came through St. Louis at the time of the war (World War II).

They would call you?

Yeah, they would call me. I played in Johnnie Hodges Place when they split the band. That's the reason they called me and Tab with every band in town.

You better believe it.

We'd hang up, see?

That's right, in fact you'd make Tab play when you come in to play.

Yeah, I'd make him play. In fact I told him wake up, he'd be asleep. In fact when I come in I'd wake him up 'cause I was gonna blow. You know I was gonna blow, and Horsecollar come in there. Wishbone was goin' too on highway 67, the Roundhouse, you know?

He got so sick he couldn't play the organ anymore so the man, you know I was still with him for a good while back there in the time of war when the bands started comin' through. All the bands come through here and there was the secretary of the union. When they'd come in there I was just hittin' 'em. I played it by ear. I played every night and after awhile I just said, I'm kickin' this off, I'm goin'. I played six weeks down at the Ambassador Theater with Duke Ellington. Six weeks.

Well Freddie I guess we've about covered it all. I cannot begin to thank you enough for the time you've spent giving me this interview.

Freddie Martin played with Duke Ellington in 1946. He's also played with Lucky Melliton, Cootie Williams, Ella Fitzgerald, Earl Fatha Hines and Tab Smith.

Richard Martin

Richard Martin Jazz, classical and rock guitarist/Born 1948, died October 6, 1984.

Richard Martin was born and reared in North St. Louis, Missouri. His mother was Juanita Martin, and his father the Reverend Gus Martin, pastor of the Martin Temple Church.

Richard began taking guitar lessons when he was nine years old. His mother often commented that he would rather play than eat. He was giving guitar lessons at the Ludwig Music store when he was 16 years old.

He performed in guest appearances with such stars as Buddy Rich, the Doobie Brothers, Gene Almonds, the "Mad Greek," Jimmy Smith, Jimmy McGriff and Richard "Groove" Holmes. He played with scores of musicians in the St. Louis area, including the Sound Merchants and with groups in other major cities.

Friends said he was better known in Europe than in the United States. In 1983 he toured 32 countries, and had performed before Queen Elizabeth II in London.

The last song he wrote was "Music in Prayer."

Emmett Mathews Saxes, vocalist/Born May 20, 1902, St. Louis, Missouri.

Early in his career Emmett Mathews worked with many bands in St. Louis and toured with Wilson Robinson's Bostonians.

He moved to New York in 1928 where he worked with pianist Irvin Puggsley's Hot Six and at the Alhambra Theater with Edgar Hayes. In 1930 he formed his own band while working with Bill Benford's band. He took this group to Chicago in 1931, but he returned to New York and joined bassist Charlie Turner's Arcadians. He was still playing with them when they became the accompanying group for Fats Waller.

During the 1930s he led his own band and made recordings which spotlighted his soprano sax and vocal talents, but he stayed with Fats Waller until 1937. After this period he formed his own band again and played theater dates in New York.

During the 1940s and 1950s he was a regular of the Red Caps with Steve Gibson, a vocal and instrumental combo. He then retired from full-time music.

James "Iron Head" Edward Mathews Pianist, drums/Born July 24, 1943, Gloster, Miss./Interviewed by Jimmy Jones.
The first thing I want to ask you about is your father and mother. What were their names?

Jesse Mathews and Francis Mathews.
And where were they born?

They were born in the state of Mississippi. The exact town, I just don't know right now.
We'll try to get their birthdays a little later on. Your full name is?

James Edward Mathews.
Nickname?

They call me "Iron."
When is your birthday?

July 24, 1943.
Your birthplace was Gloster, Mississippi?

That's right.
What was the name of your grade school?

Well, I went to a little school called St. Malachi. During that time it was located right there at Clark and Garrison [St. Louis].
This is what I was getting at. Mostly your childhood career was in St. Louis, even though you were born in Mississippi.

That's correct.
At what point did you start thinking about music, or was it a gift?

Ironically, I really became interested when I started there at St. Malachi grade school. They played music there about three days a week and rehearsed there in the school yard so I had an opportunity to really become exposed to a lot of music there, marching bands or what have you, and that was my first encounter with music. The drums.

Well let's back up a little bit to your mother and father. Did you want to get that in? When you were a small boy they had some kind of restaurant, or night club or something like that at home.

Right down in Grandville, they owned two big nightclubs down there.

And the name of the clubs?

Well, one of the clubs was named Club Desire, and there was another club. I don't quite remember the name, but both of them was in operation at the same time and I got a chance to be exposed to a lot of the old players, guys like "Sonny Boy" Williams, B.B. King, Little Milton and even Oliver Sands, Ike and Tina (Turner), and all those guys you know. Got a chance to see them and see them perform as a kid and that's one of the things that really inspired me. Also it was just a great time, you know?

In your career here in St. Louis, James, do you remember, can you go back and remember your first encounter with your first instrument?

The drum was my very first instrument, because that's what we heard mostly in the schoolyard. Drums and trumpet.

Yes.

So I really became interested in the drums there.

At what point did you switch over, or did you?

I switched from the drums to piano at the age of seven. I became exposed to a young man who had just entered college and he sat at the piano and he played. I will never forget this Steinway piano, and I just couldn't believe a piano could sound so beautiful. This was when I really became interested in the piano. Well, really I was always interested in piano because even when I was in grade school, I would play on the piano in kindergarten and I was always getting punished. My teacher would make me sit in the waste basket, or go to the cloak-room because I was always playing on the piano.

So that was your punishment.

That was my punishment.

At what point do you remember a specific teacher or name that inspired you to really continue on the piano?

At about age 14 I began to take piano lessons at Ludwig. During that time they were on Pine Street and my teacher's name was Mr. Jones. And that was the first formal piano lessons that I had. My two sisters were going to school and they were about nine and ten, and mother just couldn't afford to send all of us, so I got my training at 14 and 15.

Do you remember your first paying job?

The first paid job . . . I was 14. I played with a guy by the name of

James Mathews

Floyd. I can't think of Floyd's last name but he had a band around St. Louis, and the guys I played with during that time were Jerome, we called him "Scrooge," Raymond Eldridge, and Rick Bolen. We all performed and I'd say that was the first paying job that we had.

Do you remember the pay at that time?

I would say we got roughly about eight to ten dollars a man, and back during those days that was big, big money.

You can say that. We should mention some clubs where you played at an early age, if you can remember any.

One of the first gigs I had when I was in high school was at a club on

Goodfellow. I can't remember the name of the place but we played there during the time we were in high school and it was a gig that was paying four dollars a night and we enjoyed that. We did that on Friday and Saturday and I think we knew approximately four or five songs and it was kinda funny because the way we played 'em people never really recognized that, but that's all we knew. We played 'em blues, you know part of the night, slow and fast, then come back to our same old tunes three or four times.
That's amazing.

Yeah, that reminds me of a song they wrote called, "Faking Your Way All the Way to the Top."
Right! Did you know any big names at that time in your life? After the young part of your life did you work with any big name people?

Eddie Fisher, I know you heard of him, the guy who put out the record called "The Third Cut." He and I got together, did some traveling to Chicago, Detroit and played around locally and cut a couple of albums together.
Were those the only records you played on, James? Were they Eddie Fisher labels or do you remember the name of the record label?

Well the record that I recorded with Eddie was called, "Eddie Fisher and the Next 100 Years," and we also have another album out now, I cut I think two tracks on that one particular album, I can't recall the record, but it's out now. I also had a chance to play with several of the guys like Richard Willard Holms, Eddie Harris, they were just coming through town and we had a chance to play with them. That was quite an experience.
When you were starting your career are their any names you would want to mention that help you in what you are doing now?

Well, I think one of the most interesting musicians I've encountered was Johnny Mixon. He was quite an influence. Also Tommy Strough. Later on I met guys like the great pianist, Johnny Overhill, a young boy out of Detroit. I mean he is a fantastic player now, just signed with Columbia Records and he's doing great. The Jazz Clinic Workshop has been most inspiring. I worked with a piano player by the name of Jesse Wheatley, oh quite a few guys, but I think these would be the main men that influenced me as a pianist.
I know you are still working clubs, but what club are you working right at this point in time?

We are playing currently at Mr. B's Lounge at 3232 State Street in East St. Louis.
What is your hope for the future?

One of the goals I'd like to try and set for myself is to further my musical creative expression by continuing my education in music. I've thought by working at Berkley School and getting my degree, I'd like to get into composition and arranging. I understand that this is a great way for a man to advance as an artist.

As far as it concerns your music, I think we're covered. What advice would you give any young person reading this interview?

Be real with your music, you better be really real. I think one of the first things that we as people have to know is, we came from the Creator and eventually we will return to the Creator, so I always keep that in mind.

First, focus, priority one.

That's my priority one, yeah. I realize that's where my strength comes from. It's a God-given gift and I respect that. You can't give up, that's one of the main things. There are times when we have to be inspired through one another. We have to be uplifted, and I think we as musicians should always give credit where credit is due. Inspire one another. Sometimes we don't feel like it, but if we learn to get together and share ideas, I think we can grow, not only as a people, but as a society.

That's what life is, sharing things.

Yes, sharing, that's what it's all about.

We really appreciate the time and effort invested in what we're trying to do, and we're hoping that this interview will be inspiring to someone, somewhere, sometime.

We sure do. By the way, Jimmy, the reason they call me "Iron Head" is because in high school I was pretty reckless and ruddy, kind of a character, and playing football just became a part of me. I ran track with my head up, played football with my head down, so in football I was "Iron Head." Since I was athletically inclined, basically that's where the name stems from.

Thank you for this fine interview, Mr. James Mathews.

Louis Metcalf Drums, cornet, trumpet, vocal/Born February 28, 1905, St. Louis, Mo.

As a young boy Louis Metcalf played drums and then was taught cornet by P.G. Lankford in St. Louis. He played with Charlie Creath and Warnie Long's Kid Jazz Band, and was off to New York in 1923.

Confirmed highlights of his career include:

1923   Jimmy Cooper's Revue, New York, N.Y.
1924   With Willie "The Lion" Smith, Rhythm Club, New York.
1925   Joined Andrew Preer and the Cotton Club Syncopators with the Johnny Hudgins Variety Act and Elmer Snowden Band, New York.
1926   Charlie Johnson Band, New York.
1927   Duke Ellington, New York.
1928   Jelly Roll Morton, New York.
1929   Connies Inn Revue, Vernon Andrade's Orchestra.
1931–1935   Worked in Canada.
1935   With Fletcher Henderson, New York.

1935 Returned to St. Louis, played on the *SS St. Paul* riverboat with Dewey Jackson. In Chicago with Zutty Singleton Band, late 1935.

1936 Returned to New York and organized own band.

1937–1940 Ran own club in New York called Heatwave Club.

1945 Led own band in Philadelphia for short time.

1947 Moved to Canada and directed his own band until the 1950s.

1950 Briefly quit the music scene.

1951 Returned to New York and led his own small group playing several clubs, The Embers, Baby Grand, The Metropole, Howards, etc.

1960 Led own band at the Alabab until he fell ill.

1969 Recovered from illness and formed another small band.

Velma Middleton Vocalist/Born 1916, Holdensville, Okla., died February 11, 1961, Freetown, Africa.

Velma Middleton's family moved to St. Louis when Velma was a small baby. She grew up and attended school there, and sang in school plays. After growing up in St. Louis, Miss Middleton began writing lyrics and singing in local clubs and churches.

A few amateur triumphs convinced her to try her luck in New York.

In 1938 she sang in South America in the "Cotton Club Show" with Connie McLean's Orchestra.

Velma worked with Bill Robinson, the dancer and singer, and then joined Louis Armstrong and his band in 1942, and as his singer she toured the world with Mr. Armstrong until her death in 1961. She became ill on January 16, 1961, and collapsed on stage during a performance, while the trumpeter Louis Armstrong was on his African tour. The band left to fulfill other engagements after the vocalist was stricken. Velma Middleton died on February 11, 1961, at the age of 45 at the Sierra Leone Hospital in Freetown, Africa.

Bill Miller Guitar, drums, bass, writer/Born January 16, 1948, Newport, Arkansas/Phone interview by Lyn Cunningham.

Bill Miller's parents were Lucille (Byrd) Miller and Forrest G. Miller. Both played and sang with a country band in the 1950s in Newport, Arkansas. They had a chance to go into Red Foley's Ozark Jubilee but circumstances prevented it. His mother was a singer and his father played guitar and fiddle, and sang. They always held band practice at their home and Bill was exposed to music at a very early age. At age five Bill played his first note on the guitar. There was a song his mother and father did that required just one note at intervals and they let him play that one note every time it came around. His mother listened to the radio while she did her work in the house and Bill sat outside the kitchen window and sang along with Hank Williams, Elvis Presley, Jerry Lee Lewis and Little Richard.

Bill attended grade school up to the third grade in Walnut Park School in Newport, Arkansas. Then his family moved to St. Louis, where he finished grade school, junior and senior (Normandy) high school.

He bought his first guitar at age 12 and he is a self-taught musician.

The first group he was with was called The Jive Five in 1962 and 1963. The second was called The Highlights (1965), the third was a group called Daybreak (1972). The fourth was a show group band, Spirit of St. Louis, which was on the road from 1975 to 1979, covering Toronto and Montreal, Boston, Chicago, St. Cloud, Minnesota, Rochester, Minnesota, Des Moines, Iowa, Oklahoma City, Oklahoma, Florida, Lubbock, Ft. Worth, and Dallas, Texas and Little Rock, Arkansas.

Bill joined the Bob Kuban band in 1980 and was still with them in 1984.

When asked what his advice would be for the younger musicians coming up he stated, "First find your field of music and learn as much about your field as you can. Do an in-depth study of the professionals you admire and find out what it took to make them a success and what their appeal was to the public. And, study, study, study, practice, practice and most of all, don't give up! Develop endurance because the music business is no place for a faint heart. You may doubt yourself temporarily, but you will develop a gut feeling that will tell you you will succeed."

John Mixon Bass/Born July 17, 1927, St. Louis, Mo./Handwritten interview by John Mixon.

[I] started playing at age twenty-one in the Army. After leaving the Army I went to Ludwig School of Music for two years.

Studied with bassman from Boston, Massachusetts, Kenny Roberts. Stayed with Roberts for two years.

Started playing with Jimmy Forrest in 1951, stayed with Jimmy about eight-years. Left Forrest, played around town with such stars as "Peanuts" Whalum (Hugh D. Whalum), "Foots" Goodson, John Cotter, Bobby Graft, Oliver Nelson, Miles Davis, Clark Terry and Tab Smith.

After awhile I left town to join Lionel Hampton. I stayed with Hamp about two and a half years.

After Hamp I stayed in New York where I met players like Paul Chambers. I got to know Paul very well so I studied with him for awhile. While in New York I worked with a lot of local cats that were very good.

Every now and then I'd get a gig with guys like "Bull Moose" Jackson, Little Willie John, those kind of gigs I soon got tired of, so I came back home. Since then I've worked around town.

I still leave when someone calls from New York or wherever.

Now I'm working with my own trio, I'm thinking of forming a quintet and recording [1983].

John Mixon

I've worked with so many people in so many places, it would take weeks to write about it. So here's my little offering.

Vernon Eugene Nashville, Jr. Trumpet, piano, teacher, arranger, writer/Born May 16, 1928, St. Louis, Mo./Interviewed by Jimmy Jones.

Vernon, what were your mother and father's names?

My father's name was Vernon Nashville, Sr. He was born in Mobile, Alabama. My mother's name was Ruth Collier Nashville. She was born in Athens, Alabama.

Do you know their birthdates?

No, but my mother is 76 and my father is 74.

Where did you attend grade school?

I attended Cole School at 3800 Enright, St. Louis. I attended Sumner High School, College of Pendleton. Then I went to Ludwig Music College at 709 Pine and I went to St. Louis University on Grand Avenue in the evenings.

I went into service. After that I went to Washington University on the GI Bill and got my masters.

At what point in your career did you consider a musical instrument?

My earliest influence was in the sixth grade when I heard a cousin of mine, Leonard Boler, play trumpet. He played trumpet with the old "Bugs" Roberts Band, down on Vandeventer at the Wiggs Club. As I got older I found out that he had one of the best ears and minds in jazz.

At what point did you get serious about your career?

More or less through my four years in high school I just played because it was enjoyable. Maybe the last year in high school I was a little serious. A strong influence was a tenor sax player named John Moore. Mostly I was interested in football and art. Drew a lot and painted a lot and played football everyday.

When you came out of service, were you into teaching then, or just playing?

Well, I taught and went to school. I had a wife and one child then, and I had to get a little money together in order to eat. Later I found out if you go to Washington University, the tuition is so high you don't do much eating. But with the help of my mother-in-law, Velma Farlin, I made it. She was a very sweet woman and very helpful to me until the day she died.

So the musical career of Vernon Nashville was beginning to take shape.

I'd like to go back a few years and also state that my mother's singing and piano playing was also very influential to me. I'd like to say too, how could I forget this, my daddy bought my first trumpet for me. It cost thirty-five dollars and imposed a hardship on the family, because he couldn't really afford it. I got much of my knowledge through trial and error. I got much understanding about my instrument from Silas Stoner, Sr. He played trumpet and guitar here in St. Louis, a good musician with no formal

Vernon Nashville's (center, without a tie) band.

training. I'd like to say, the greatest music college I've ever seen is the one created by black musicians on the street.

After finishing Washington University, what did you do?

I got a job teaching music in Kinloch (St. Louis County) Kinloch High School. I stayed there for seven years.

Did you work with any name people, Vernon? Kenny Rice mentioned you the other day when I interviewed him.

There was Kenny Rice and Willie Murray. Willie's the band director now at Sumner High School.

Did you ever do any club dates?

I worked for fifteen years or so with George Hudson. Played in the Club Riviera. I was also with the Rajahs of Swing. Actually the service broke that band up, so many of us got drafted. That was in 1950, the Korean War. I do have pictures of that band. It was kinda funny, they wore turbans, little pins and things . . . felt like Hindus out there.

But basically I taught, rather than do club dates, except for George Hudson. Then I started playin' with smaller groups. For the last eight years I've been playing a type of music called rock. The only enjoyment I get out of this is, it's my group. I write for 'em . . . we have two vocalists, one female, one male. They are two very good singers.

Do you have a name for this band?

Hot Earth. Since everyone does read music, I can write for the band and everyone can read their parts.

I'm sure there are some serious things that happened, and some funny things, if you want to mention them.

One of the people I would like to mention is Leroy Cooper. He played baritone saxophone with Ray Charles after he came out of the army. When Ray Charles needed another trumpet player, Leroy Cooper came to get me. I had practiced a lot at that time and I was in pretty good shape musically. But when I got discharged I had a wife and child at home, so I didn't go with Ray Charles and Leroy. Consequently I missed an opportunity that would have led me into the musical type of life I had always wanted to live.

I got other opportunities too, a few times. Count Basie came through and wanted to fill a chair that was vacant. That was another good experience and very rewarding. The reason I did enjoy it was because I kinda half-way fit into the band.

. . . and know what was going on . . .

Yeah, yeah, it's got to jell.

Are you still teaching?

Yeah, I'm still teaching. I quit for a year because I was tired of it. I've been teaching for 25 years and it can really get on your nerves.

Especially when you're a perfectionist and have 90 beginning students.

It can get to you. You know too a child cannot play music his first day in band. It takes weeks and weeks before anything musical comes out. So he's got to make a lot of noise before he can make music. I just supervise music at Wellston now and teach two classes in high school.

You still do club dates with your Earth Band now?

Oh, yes!

Well, Vernon, I think we've covered all the things you wanted to tell me in this interview. I've really enjoyed it and I thank you so much for your time.

Just tell the young people to study hard and be serious in their music.

Oliver Edward Nelson Piano, flute, clarinet, oboe and all sax's, composer, writer and arranger/Born June 4, 1932, St. Louis, Mo., died October 28, 1975, Los Angeles, Calif.

Oliver E. Nelson was born in St. Louis on June 4, 1932. His father's name was Eugene Cornelius Nelson and his mother's name was Lucille Wilverton Nelson. He had one brother, Eugene, who was also a musician and played sax with Cootie Williams, and one sister, "Teenie," who sings and plays piano.

Oliver served in the U.S. Marine Corps from 1952 to 1954 and was a member of the Third Marine Division Band while serving in Japan and Korea.

He went to St. Louis public and secondary schools and attended Philander Smith College in Little Rock, Arkansas on a scholarship. He attended Washington University at St. Louis and Lincoln University in Jefferson City, Missouri. He also studied with Pulitzer Prize–winning composer Elliott Carter and composers Dr. Robert Wykes of Washington University and George Tremblay of Los Angeles.

In 1959 he moved to Jamaica, Long Island, New York, and later lived in St. Albans, New York.

In January 1967, Oliver moved to Hollywood, California. By 1969 he had recorded 18 albums of his own compositions while the albums of numerous famous stars carried his arrangements, and he had composed and arranged for three major network series, *It Takes a Thief, Name of the Game,* and *Ironside.* All were Universal productions.

He won three Grammy awards for best arrangements. In 1963 for "Full Nelson" (his album), in 1964 with Nancy Wilson on her album, in 1966 with the late guitarist Wes Montgomery for the milestone "Goin' Out of My Head" album, a best seller in the jazz vein.

In 1967 he was selected by *Downbeat Magazine* as Best Arranger, and Duke Ellington came in second. He collaborated with Jimmy Smith, the soul organist, with "Walk on the Wild Side" and "Who's Afraid of Virginia Woolf?"

His bright star dimmed and flickered out on October 28, 1975. He was 43 years old when he died of a heart attack in Los Angeles, and was survived by his wife, Audre, and his two sons, Oliver, Jr. and Nyles Nelson.

Edward Nicholson Trumpet, piano/Born September 9, 1935, East St. Louis, Ill./Interviewed by Jimmy Jones and Lyn Cunningham.

Edward Nicholson is a product of the East St. Louis school system. He began his musical training at a very early age, taking private piano lessons at age eight from the late Altha Caldwell, Kathryn Brown, and Jonetta Haley, and private trumpet lessons at age 12, from the late Edward Mathews and Russ Riggin.

In our interview with Mr. Nicholson, the information about his study and contributions to music is summarized thusly.

He played with the Hughes-Quinn Junior High School band directed by Mr. Tilford Brooks. Upon graduation from junior high school, he started playing with the Lincoln Senior High School band directed by Mr. Elwood Bachanan. Upon graduation from Lincoln, he was granted a scholarship to McKendree College, which he did not accept. Instead, he enrolled at Tennessee State University at Nashville, majoring in Music Education, graduating in June 1961.

Under the combined leadership of Nicholson and Richard Myrick, the East St. Louis Senior High School and the Lincoln Senior High School

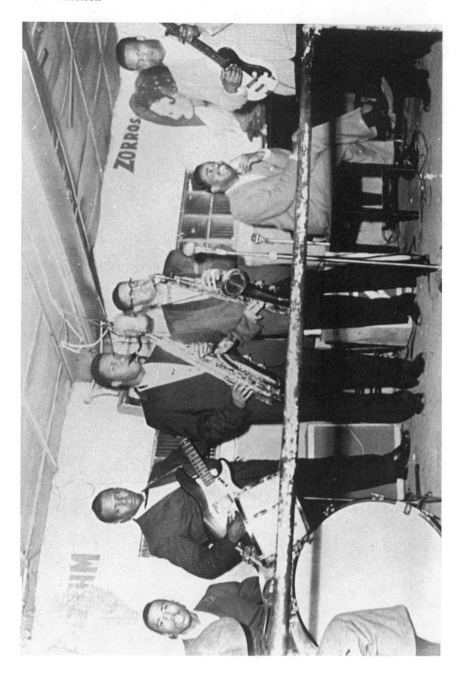

THE MANY 'BAGS' OF OLIVER NELSON

Above: Oliver Nelson composing. Opposite: Kenny Rice (drums), Sims (guitar), Nelson (sax on left) and Melvin Hughes (sax).

bands appeared on television coast to coast during half-time during a professional football game in St. Louis.

He played first trumpet with the Nashville Symphony Orchestra conducted by Dr. William Dawson, performing "Hiawatha's Wedding Feast" (1959), and appeared with the Birmingham Symphony as the pianist, conducted by Amerigo Moreno.

As a member of the St. Louis Jazz Quartet he toured college campuses in 25 different cities and the state of Alaska.

Membership in Young Audiences, Inc., gave Mr. Nicholson the opportunity to engage in mini-concerts based on black music. His music team demonstrated music from the Dixieland period to present-day music. His lectures ended with a question and answer session..

His notable appearances with the following professional musicians were most gratifying: Clark Terry, Sonny Stitt, Oliver Nelson, Nancy Wilson, Spanky Wilson, Clea Bradford, Hank Crawford, Dr. Edward Louis Smith and Dr. Andy Goodrich.

His work in District 189 at the Golden Garden School produced three very fine violinists. One of these young ladies later played with the St. Louis Symphony.

Mr. Nicholson is presently a Jazz Band instructor at the East St. Louis Senior High School.

Singleton Palmer Tuba, trumpet, string bass/Born November 13, 1912, St. Louis, Mo./Interviewed by Jimmy Jones.
We are ready to interview Mr. Singleton Palmer. Singleton, will you let me know a little bit about your background? What about your mother and father, what were their names?
My mother's maiden name was Willie Mae Folks, and she was born in Memphis, Tennessee.
And what about your dad?
Dad's name was Nathaniel Palmer, and he was born in Sturgeon, Missouri.
Your father wasn't musically inclined was he?
No, no.
Do you remember their birthdates?
I know my mother's was September 8th, but the year I don't know, and my dad's I don't remember because he died in 1916, and I was only four years old. My mother died in 1947.
When did you first start attending grade school?
Actually, now it's Cole School on West Belle . . . It wasn't nothing, it was a three-story house.
Then from grade school you went on to . . .
From West Belle I went on to the sixth grade and then I went to John

Edward Nicholson

Singleton Palmer (left) and His Dixieland Band.

Marshall's. We stayed at John Marshall's from the seventh to the ninth grade, and when we got to the ninth grade we went to Sumner.

Sumner is still the same, same name, same school . . .

Same place.

And when you finished Sumner?

Well I didn't graduate from Sumner, I was a drop-out. I got too mixed up in music.

Now since you mentioned that, at what age did you get seriously interested in music?

Well, to begin with I started taking trumpet lessons when I was eleven years old. I stayed on the trumpet until I was fourteen. At that time I had just gone over to Sumner and then I switched over to the tuba when I was fourteen.

That's that beautiful bass tuba that everybody hears about.

I think those years with the trumpet thing gave me extra dexterity on the tuba, you know?

When you got interested in the tuba, that's when you were seriously getting on the road to doing lots of things with the tuba.

I was really. I was playing trumpet in a band which was led by Mose Wiley.

Mose Wiley?

Yeah, in that band there was a saxophone player by the name of Cliff

Bachler, in fact we were all school kids, times were kinda lean and he cut out the trumpet. Looked like I was out and then he asked me if I'd be interested in playin' tuba. I told him I didn't know, that I would have to ask my dad. First I'd have to get a horn, so I asked my dad about it and he said he didn't know where we could scrape up money to buy a horn like that in those times. But finally he got me a tuba. I played with Mose Wiley for about a year, then I started playin' with Oliver Cobb and played with him for awhile. Oliver went out of town on his own, went up in Iowa, got in a swimming accident and drowned. At that time Eddie Johnson was playing piano with Oliver and the Martin twins, Chick Franklin and James Joplin. So Eddie took over the band and changed it to Eddie Johnson's Crackerjacks. And we played all over this town. The Dance Box...

Did you do any of the riverboats?

Yeah, we played on a boat called the *Idlewild*.

Where did the Idlewild *go?*

It started here in St. Louis and went to Louisville, Kentucky, and it stayed down in Louisville all summer and then we'd bring the boat back up to St. Louis. We did that for about three or four seasons.

Now I have a picture of some of the riverboats. Where exactly on that boat did the musicians perform? Was it in the front, middle or back of it?

Well now on the *Idlewild*, it was on the back of it, but on the Streckfus boats like the old *St. Paul* and the *Admiral*, etc., the bandstand was right in the center.

And you'd come back to St. Louis after you'd do that?

Yeah, we'd get back to St. Louis. In fact we'd leave St. Louis and stop at maybe Cape Girardeau, pick up some people, carry 'em about five or ten miles down the river and bring 'em back and let 'em off. We'd keep on down to maybe Paducah or Cairo until we got to Louisville. Actually there was a dance every night.

I expect the pay was kinda flimsy in those days, but how did they actually pay the musicians?

Well the pay was pretty good considering we didn't have no expenses. You ate and slept on the boat you know, so practically everything you made was profit.

Did they throw money or did they have a certain salary?

Oh, they had a certain salary, yeah. I forget what we made on the *Idlewild*, but the Streckfus boats were a bigger organization, so their payments were much better.

Did you work with any name bands down through the years that you want to make mention of?

Oh, yeah. I worked with Fats Waller. You see what Fats did, I was in Cincinnati with Eddie Johnson, and some of the top musicians would pick up a whole band intact, and they would just go under his name, you know?

*In other words he would be the leader, but he would have a band that was
already organized.*

. . .Yeah. And I played with George Hudson here for years.

Do you remember some of the clubs or places you played?

We played the Plantation Nightclub, one of the biggest here in St.
Louis at that time. Then I went on the road with George Hudson and we
played, what you call "around the horn." We played the Apollo Theater in
New York, the Earl Theater in Philadelphia, the Howard Theater in Washington, and the Sun Theater in Baltimore. We would play background
music for Ella Fitzgerald, the Ink Spots, Sarah Vaughan, the Nicholas
Brothers, and Nat King Cole, so I got plenty of exposure with George and
after that I went with Basie.

Count Basie?

Yeah, in 1947 until 1950. That's when I decided to stay home, in 1950.
We had a lay-off during the holidays and I came back and they asked me
if I wanted to play a jam session with this group there on Delmar, and I said
yes. They paid me so much for that one gig, I said shoot, I'm missin' money
on the road, 'cause in those times big bands were on their way out and it
was really lean.

Of course, when I joined Basie in 1947, they were paying fifty dollars
a night. So if you worked six nights you made three hundred dollars, if you
worked one night, you made fifty during the week. But the Theater dates
were real good because we had a chance to, instead of doing one-nighters,
stay in town for a week or two.

And I'm sure those were memorable years that you'll never forget.

That's right. I've had plenty experiences.

*Now, Gaslight Square, Singleton. Was the Crystal Palace one of the places in
Gaslight Square?*

The Crystal Palace was one of the places, but we played at the Opera
House.

*Ben Thigpen was there with you then, wasn't he? That's where I remember
Singleton Palmer when I first started coming into the Gaslight Square area,
and was trying to get down and see that fantastic Dixieland show at the
Opera House.*

Yeah, we went over there in 1958 and stayed until 1967.

That's a long tour.

Yeah, that was quite a gig!

*That means that the people were happy, the club owners were happy, and you
were happy because you didn't have to move.*

Every night seemed like New Years Eve night!

After that I guess you just did gigs?

Oh yeah, we'd maybe work a gig on Sunday, because we worked down
there six nights a week.

In the Gaslight Square days, how about recordings?

We recorded six albums while we were down there. The first one was on the Norman label.

If you did six albums I'm sure some of them might still be around or wanted.

Oh, yeah, I have people calling me once or twice a week asking me where they can get them, but they're out of print you know.

Let's see, you are still active in music as much as that phone will ring.

Oh, yeah, yeah. I wish it would ring right now! I'd be very happy, very happy.

Even though you're semi-retired you still . . .

It's not my fault.

Yes I guess we all get to that stage in life where we kinda slow down.

And too, at my age, I don't know whether I could survive doing six nights a week. But I imagine I would though, 'cause we're pretty happy doin' what we're doin'. We average two or three nights a week at different places. Like tonight we'll be down at the Missouri Athletic Club. We just finished doing the 8th, 12th, 15th of this month down at the Sheraton downtown, by the Convention Center. We do a lot of convention work.

That's because of the dues and the things they remember about Singleton Palmer. Is there any particular person that we may have left out that you'd like to mention?

I'd like to mention about my good friend Clark Terry. He was the one that was responsible for me being able to join Count Basie's Band.

Clark Terry?

Yeah, I was sittin' at home one night when I was livin' on Delmar and the phone rang. It was Terry, and he said, "How would you like to play with Count Basie?" During that time I needed work. I said oh, Terry, cut out this foolishness. I said, man, did you call me up to tease me about this stuff? He said no, I'm not kiddin', get your fiddle, get on the train and come to New York. I took the morning train and I wasn't really prepared. He told me what hotel to go to and everything, so when I got there he says the gig starts tonight. We opened at a place called Royal Roots. We went in practically without a rehearsal or anything, the very first time, you know. And I had a ball!

I'll bet that was a thrill or two.

I tell you, that Clark Terry. I also played with Harry Edison, Richard Nottingham, Earl Warren, Paul Gonzales and Shadow Wilson, oh God. And I knew Jimmy Forrest. Let's see, that's about it.

Mr. Singleton Palmer and myself have been kinda reminiscing on this Saturday afternoon, and we're going to end the interview at this point. Thank you, Singleton.

"Pops" Porter

Robert "Pops" Porter Piano/Born June 3, 1923, Chicago, Ill./ Telephone interview by Lyn Cunningham.

Pops came to St. Louis at an early age, and outside of work in other cities has lived here ever since. He is a self-taught musician; he says he learned much from other musicians and applied it to his own style of playing. Pops' last long gig was a nine-year one at Michaels in Highland, Illinois. His mother's name was Annie Ivory Porter, and his father's name was Robert Porter; neither were musical.

Pops has made no recordings. At age thirteen he played for Billie Holliday at the Sheraton Hotel in Chicago. He also played four years at the Plantation Club in Chicago between 1945 and 1949. He's played extensively in North Dakota, South Dakota, Milwaukee, and Detroit. In St. Louis, Pops played at The Oyster Bar, Hillarys, the Playhouse, and numerous places down on the riverfront at The Landing.

Kenny Rice

Irving "Mouse" Randolph Trumpet/Born June 22, 1909, St. Louis, Mo.

"Mouse" Randolph first played professional trumpet at age nineteen on the riverboats out of St. Louis with Fate Marable's Band. Following are some highlights of his career:

> *1931* Moved to Kansas City, Mo.
> *1931–1933* Worked with Andy Kirk in Kansas City.
> *1934* Went to New York with Fletcher Henderson and also played dates with Benny Carter.
> *1935–1939* With Cab Calloway, and had recording dates with Teddy Wilson (1936) and Lionel Hampton (1939). In late 1939 joined the Ella

Fitzgerald Band (formerly Chick Webb Band) until it broke up after two years.

1940s   With Don Redman and the Ed Hall Sextet.

1943   With Don Redman at the Zanzibar, New York City. Also played Cafe Society, Uptown and Downtown with Edmond Hall.

1950   With Eddie Barefield Sextet, and. toured United States, Latin America with Marcelino Guerra and recorded with Pearl Bailey for Coral Records, rhythm and blues for Victor Records.

1955   Savoy Ballroom with Bobby Medera's Band.

1957–1960   At La Martinique in New York City.

1961   Did free-lance recordings for several groups.

Kenny Rice Drums/Born November 1, 1942, St. Louis, Mo./Interviewed by Jimmy Jones.

Where were you born, Kenny?

I wasn't born in Mississippi like all the rest of you.

That's good.

I was born in the St. Louis County Hospital on November 1, 1942.

All right.

My mother was Fanny Rice and my father was Mr. Namon Rice.

What got you started in your musical career? Any teachers or musicians you want to name?

Probably the most influential cat was Vernon Nashville. You know Freck?

Yes.

He was the band director at my high school. Kinloch High. I was born in the County and raised in Kinloch. I went to Dunbar grade school. Vernon Nashville recruited eighth graders for a program he started from the high school. Anybody who was interested in being in the band could get an instrument and start practicin'. My family was poor in a sense, but I don't ever remember not having a meal. My father always had something for us to eat, and we always had a roof over us. Other than that, you got it. I was always interested in music. We were raised in church, singing, my family was very musical. My father was the main force in the family as far as music was concerned. He sang with a spiritual group called, The Wondering Four Quartet.

That was a St. Louis group.

A lot of arrangements sung by schools today, are their arrangements.

I remember them, years ago.

I was surrounded by music. We had rehearsal at our house on Saturday nights. We kids would sit in the other room or on the stairs and listen to that good singin'.

That close harmony.

Oh, you talk about getting excited!

Your preference was drums though?

I always for some reason wanted to play drums, and I wasn't gonna change either. But by that time I got to choose an instrument from Mr. Nashville, they didn't have any more drums left. He said he had a trombone or a trumpet. But my father said you will have to rent drums if you want to play. He said he'd try to work out an arrangement to rent one. But he didn't have money for none of that, I can't get you no drum. Well I cried like a baby, so I just didn't want to be in it, and I told Nashville and my father. Mr. Nashville some kinda way found out where to get one I could use, and I came up with my own money for the rent by shining shoes at the Berkeley Barber Shop on Airport Road. They loved me out there. I still go by out there and look at that little shop. So I shined shoes, made me a little money, got me a snare drum and got into the program.

Later, Mr. Nashville worked it out so that I could take private lessons from Mr. Elijah Shaw. I used to walk all the way from Kinloch to Mr. Shaw's house downtown on Cook Street.

Man, that's a long way.

It was two dollars a lesson, and that was a helluva thing back then.

A lot of shoes was payin' that two dollars.

Mr. Shaw would take me around to his gigs with Singleton Palmer. He was a drummer with Singleton's Dixieland Six. They played in Gaslight Square at the Golden Eagle Opera House. At the Crystal Palace down the street there were struggling artists then like Barbra Streisand, Dick Gregory, Bill Cosby and Lou Rawls.

All top stars now.

Mr. Shaw wouldn't let me get on the set, but he was teaching me how to set up a set when he took me around with him. And I do that to this day, set up my drums the way he taught me. Mr. Nashville really helped me as far as getting me into work.

I had a very nice childhood. There were eleven in the family. Five boys and three girls, and then we had another little brother later on. My father spent most of his time hollerin' down into the basement, "Cut out that noise." But my father gave me a few minutes after the school day to practice, after I did my share of the housework and chores.

I guess Rudy Coleman, now known as Silver Cloud and has the Silver Cloud Blues Band, heard about my work in high school. Ken Miles ask me if I played drums and did I want to play? Ken Miles gave me my first job, took me straight from house roof to Red Top.

That was a rough one.

Cryin' the blues, and you talk about some experience!

I know it.

Albert "Blues Boy" King gave me my first national exposure, went everyplace and played everything. One year Leo Goodin booked Albert into the Blue Note (East St. Louis) on New Year's Eve and New Year's night. *That's when I first saw you.*

Leo's group had Chauncy Williamson, "Little Man" (Charles Wright), and I forget who was on piano, "Albino" Red, and John Mixon. Chauncy was a big influence on my career. Leo always had a house band in his club and that was the reason for the success of the Blue Note. Everybody who was anybody in jazz came through the Blue Note. They all knew Leo Goodin.

And he was a helluva politician too.

Yeah, he was in politics all his life.

That's probably how he got a lot of connections.

Right. He had so many connections. Then we began the group, Leo's Five, and Don James really got me together. Don James was a genius.

That's right.

While I was over there I got to play with people like "Pepper" Adams, "Blue" Mitchell, Jimmy Forrest, Tab Smith, Junior Cook and Jimmy McGriff. Jack McDuff come through there. I had a chance to play with all those folks. Then I played with "Peanuts" Whalum awhile and got an offer to go with the Fifth Dimension, but Leo had this thing about not being a part of somebody else's thing, but being a creator. To this day I try to give my career to that end. I could be playing with a lot of bands and different people, but I'm trying to do my own thing.

All the people who used to come through there all got up and went to Los Angeles, but they were all sittin' right up under my drums at the Blue Note at one time.

Big name people.

Oliver Nelson still lived in St. Louis, and he came to the Blue Note and Leo hired him to play, and he made a couple of appearances backing us and Oliver loved us. Leo said he wanted to record an album, so he told Oliver to arrange an album for him. The album was, "Leo Sings the String," arranged and conducted by Oliver Nelson. I went back with Oliver Nelson's big string orchestra to New York, my first time in New York. Leo took us down to Birdland where Oscar Peterson was playing. Leo said I'm going to show you some stuff. I had always thought musicians were rich, after that night I didn't any more. Some of them were pitiful and I'll never forget that experience.

Leo and Oliver formed a company called Nolson Records. (Leo Goodin and Oliver Nelson) Nelson is Nolson. They resurrected Ruth Brown, she hadn't had a hit in years so they recorded some things. The first hit they had was on Ruth Brown but at the time her record was hittin', the suppliers wasn't pressin' anybody but the Beatles. That's when they first came to America. It hurt Oliver and Leo's company financially, so I went out to Los Angeles and got involved in writing scores for movies and things like that.

But the three brains died. Leo Goodin, Oliver Nelson, and Don James.

Yeah, and that left me. Leo died in 1965 at age 34. I still worked with Don James, but after he died, I just kept on going. I worked for Channel Four in a *Heads Up* Series with John Mixon, Jeter Thompson, and Freddie Washington. Then I went on the road with Grady Tate and then with Nat Atterly. We made an album, my first one, called, "Kenny Rice, Richard Martin Quartet featuring Nat Atterly."

What are you working at now, Kenny?

I'm doing another album, doing some things at Casa with David Hines.

This has been an evening interview with Kenny Rice at his home and it's really been a pleasure, Kenny.

Well that's it, man.

We really appreciate it.

Charles Ellsworth "Pee Wee" Russell Clarinetist, saxes, violin, piano, drums/Born March 27, 1906, Maplewood, Mo., died, February 15, 1969, Alexandria, Va.

Charles Russell was an early Dixieland pioneer. During his early childhood his family moved from St. Louis to Muskogee, Oklahoma, where he attended Central High School. There he took lessons on piano, violin and drums. Pee Wee's major instruments were clarinet and saxophones. Pee Wee studied with Charlie Merrill and gigged with the Perkins Brothers Band near Muskogee, and on the Arkansas riverboat with the Deep River Jazz Band.

Later on in the 1920s his family moved back to St. Louis, and he enrolled in Western Military Academy in Alton, Illinois. He attended the Chicago School of Music during the later 1920s and played with Bix Beiderbecke, Frankie Trumbauer, and Red Nichols. Later he played aboard the riverboats and had some dates with Herb Berger's St. Louis Club Orchestra. He studied the clarinet with Tony Sarlie of the St. Louis Symphony Orchestra, and played brief spells with Gene Rodemich, Ray Lodwig, and Joe Johnson. Pee Wee was a versatile musician and during the time when work was hard to find he traveled extensively.

Pee Wee worked with Bobby Hackett's Band in 1938. He had his own small group at the Little Club in New York with Bobby Hackett until mid-1939, and was with bands led by Eddie Condon until the summer of 1940. In 1948 Pee Wee worked the Club Riviera in New York, and also played many sessions at Central Plaza before going back to Chicago with Art Hode's Band. Art Hode at that time had Lee Collins and George Brunis.

Charles Russell moved to San Francisco in December 1948. He became critically ill in 1950 while working at Coffee Dan's Club. Louis

Armstrong, Jack Teagarden, Eddie Condon, and Art Hodes played benefit concerts to pay for the major surgery he had to undergo at Franklin Hospital in San Francisco.

Pee Wee returned to New York early in 1951, sat in with Eddie Condon in July, but didn't resume his full-time schedule until he opened in Denver in October 1951 with his own band.

He has played with almost every traditional jazz musician in the New York area, and has made guest appearances at jazz festivals and worked with groups organized by George Wein. His last appearance was with George Wein's All Stars for President Nixon's inaugural ball on January 21, 1969. On February 15 of that year he passed away in an Alexandria, Virginia, hospital, and is buried in Union, New Jersey.

Albert St. James Drummer/Born August 15, 1934, St. Louis, Mo./ Interviewed by Jimmy Jones.
Al, what were your mother and father's names?

My mother's name was Vallette St. James. My father's name was Walter St. James.
Do you know where they were born?

Yes, they were born in St. Charles, Missouri.
Do you remember their birthdays?

My mother was born September 26, 1896. My father, I don't know when he was born. He died when I was a little boy.
Where did you attend grade school?

I went to Validay. I think it was on Leffenwell and Lucas.
I see.

I also lived in the same neighborhood where Scott Joplin lived. I used to go to school at 4611 Delmar. That's where I was reared up at. I went to Vallican and I also went to Vashon.
At what point did you start playing drums, in high school or grade school?

It was in my junior year in high school that I got interested. A friend of ours, he was a drummer by the name of Clarence Tiller, he used to come around the house all the time, and he used to play and I'd watch him beat the drum and I used to look at him, you know, I got to playin'. He kept urgin' me, he found I had a knack for playin' drums, I have another in-law by the name of Pellis Davis, he was a drummer in St. Louis. Pellis Davis, he was with the big bands...
Oh, yeah, I've heard of him...

Yeah.
He's from St. Louis too?

Yeah. Right.
And what's ... He's your relative, you say?

No, he was, he was like a brother.

Oh, I see, I see. And his name was...

Clarence Taylor.

Clarence Taylor, but he kinda ... like inspired you...

He was the one.

OK. Right.

Actually I was about sixteen.

Sixteen years old when you first started. Did you play with the high school band or...

Yeah, the strange thing about that was I got to play with a swing band, that was in my last year of school, my senior year of school. I didn't play in the marching band, I wasn't equipped then, I didn't have the training. But the swing band was easy for me, I had to learn the other side, how it sounded to take a whole set of drums, so I didn't get a chance to get into the marching band. I had a chance to take some lessons up there on Boyle and Olive and I studied what drums was all about.

I see. Do you remember your first job? As a drummer and what was it like, and explain that to me.

Actually, well, I mentioned the fact of Clarence Taylor, well he also sang blues and he also what you call shuckled piano, he could play a lot too, but he could shuck and get by, you know that thing, so my first payin' job, he had a job, about four pieces, he played piano and sang and I played the drums, that was my first payin' job. And I also got a chance to take some jobs downtown on sixth and seventh street.

Yeah.

That union ... I had some friends, some were very good musicians, Jim McClennon then there was a vibe player, he played the wooded vibes, I can't call his name but he was a major influence on me, he let me come by and I played, I would teach him how to play some of the modern versions and so in return he would give me some playin' experience and I would come down and play and so he'd give me three or four dollars so that was quite an experience for me.

You were learning and getting paid at the same time.

Yeah. We'd play a lot of the dances you know, the bump and the grind.

Burlesque.

Yeah, you got it right.

Did you play at the Six-O Lounge and Dublin Village and them places down there?

I played at mostly what they called the Stage Bar down there.

I see, I see.

On Chestnut, I think it was.

Yeah, right. I was down there on Sixth and Chestnut myself.

Yeah, right! *(They laugh.)* That's exactly what I'm talking about. That was those *non-union days.*

Right. Come catch, come catch.

Right. I learned a lot in those days.

Right. And then at uh . . . About anything in your other musical career that you want to mention down through the years about Gaslight Square days and any of the big bands that you played with.

I had one experience. I never will forget it. That was playin' with Charlie Parker at the Glass Bar. We played it once, twice that is. Eight days with the great Charlie Parker. I was twenty-one and it was quite a boost, me and a friend of mine, Virgil Harris.

Yeah.

John Richoppems dead now and Cardinal Dunn. I'll never forget that. And the Gaslight, the only thing I ever did in the Gaslight was that was that we got a chance to get involved in the Club. The Club was called Club Tres Bien. I noticed they never mentioned this when they had a revue of the Gaslight area here. They had all the clubs that we played in but they didn't mention the fact that we were part of it.

The Tres Bien.

That's right at Olive and Barr.

And that was the name of the Club, The Tres Bien, and it was the Tres Bien. When you were first introduced to the Quartette Tres Bien, were you selected among all drummers?

Well, actually what happened was, Percy James, Jeter Thompson and Richard Simmons was Trio Tres Bien and they had a drummer by the name of Chuck Carter, he was very young then. OK, well Percy and I had played together with Jimmie Pharr and Tommy Dee and we remembered down the road and so Percy was sayin' that they needed a drummer and at the time we was playin' on the Gaslight Square, Dark Side, and it was between me and Sonny Hathaway that they wanted to come in the group, so first they insist that, they say what? He heard me play, he insists that you got the ears late because you're just what we need, 'cause I'd never take the chance 'cause Jeter (Thompson) and Richard knows too much music, you know, so Percy and I, my ground [sic] was fast and we did what the super cats, the cats of today—so I played my first job in East St. Louis at a place called the Faust Club.

The Faust Club. I remember the Faust Club.

Yeah, Sunday. Sunday. And from that point on, man, that was the birth of that Quartette. From that point on. We played at the Gaslight for a long time.

The Tres Bien, was it the Tres Bien Club or . . .

Yeah, it was the Club Tres Bien.

Club Tres Bien.

Right.

And it was right on the corner of . . .

Olive and Boyle.

Olive and Boyle.

It was an old theater, is what it was.

I see.

It was very unique. I'll never forget them days. But it never misses.

And you stayed with the Tres Bien until uh . . .

. . . we went all the way to the West Coast did all the recording.

Right, right.

On the West Coast we had a chance to play with everybody you can mention — It was quite a stint. It goes to show you that when you have your thing together, regardless to what the competition is, you can do your thing without playin' what everybody else is playin' when you do yours it don't really matter what they're doin'.

Right.

I really liked it there on the West Coast because on the West Coast you're an individual and they were surprised that we were all from the same city.

Yeah.

We all thought of that.

Now some of the name places, now I know you did a lot of touring . . .

You're right. We did.

Played with a lot of people. Do you remember any of those?

Yeah, a lot of experiences, especially Thelonious Monk.

Yeah, he just passed away.

Just passed, just passed and I'll never forget it because Monk was used to playin' with two groups, just the opposite, he'd play a set, he might be off an hour, well, they had to book Monk in that spot in that club just by hisself. It was too long for him. So Monk didn't like playin' them long sets and he'd go outside and stand around. At that particular time the club owners name was John T. McLaine and he was responsible for bringing us to the West Coast so he got us a place opposite Thelonious Monk and plus the fact the Columbia Records was recording us. *(He laughs.)* I'll never forget that.

Right. That was bigger, better at that time.

That was lovely, oh, God.

Yeah. Now I tell ya . . . and then down through the years did you have anything that you would want to put on tape that . . . one of the most amazing things that happened to you? In your career and then too I wanted to ask you one of the most sorriest things that happened to you possibly maybe, if you can remember.

Well I think the sorriest thing was the breakup.

Of the Tres Bien?

Well, we didn't really actually break up, but it was a difference of

opinion. We come home. But I think the most monumental thing that happened to me was, as far as the four brothers I was playin' with, was that we were able to play musically we were able to tune in on each other mentally...
Yeah.

...and do things spontaneously, you know, in that, that I'm a drummer, I may at the end of a song, without them knowin', start another rhythm altogether, an altogether other rhythm and they would follow automatically. They'd just be playin' it and you know that was sad comin' to an end. We thought it was sad. A lot of musicians I knew was drummers couldn't quite understand how Percy and I were able to follow the rhythmic thing between the two without the fight.
That was the magic, wasn't it?

(He laughs.) That's right, that's right.
Percy said the same thing.

That's right. Whoever we were with, the captain would pull me off to the side and tell 'em man I can't play with conga players. I say, well, you have to remember that in Africa and in Asia that they have 11 or 12 drummers and they beat all to a different rhythm.
Right.

Somehow you just have to guess what you're doin', you see?
And that's why their rhythm is so strong over there because they can master that.

They have rhythm, that's what it is. Rhythm is the impulse.
And I know that was one of the sorriest things that happened to you.

It was, because I was sorry from the musicians standpoint and the brothers standpoint because we always said if money couldn't break us up, what could break us up? *(He laughs.)* I think we got caught by a little individualism and it happens.
Yeah, right. I think every group has that. But you're still brothers and you're still musicians...

That's right, that's right...
...and you're still doin' your thing. Right now Al, are you still doin' the thing weekends now?

Oh, yes, I just plays off and on, nobody regular. I think I'm going to form my own trio for awhile. I think I'll go that way.
Right, right. You did a lot of the records with the Tres Bien.

I did everything, yeah.
And as far as your musical career, if you wanted to mention anything else before we close the tape about Al St. James. If you think of anything else you want to mention, you can talk about it freely now.

I'd like to say to the young musicians coming along, especially drummers, you can't get stuck in one situation like playin' rock because you got

Fred Sample, Sr.

to be able to learn the basics, because the basics will carry you through the whole thing. I've heard too many young drummers now who can't play a beat straight out. They sit down and play straight out. They're just not perfected. That's what's comin' along. They can't play that out and out swing. They can't get no jobs. Because the drum is the beat.
Right. The drum is the backbone.
    Even rock and roll, the drummer carries it.
Right.
    What I'm sayin' is, a young drummer needs to be versatile and in order to be musical you have to have an education behind you. The main thing to get is if one thing don't work for you, try something else, try to survive.
I've really enjoyed this little short interview and hopefully we have said something to inspire somebody who will read or listen to this particular part of our interview. This is Jimmy Jones and I'm ending this interview with Albert St. James.

Fred Sample, Sr. Piano/Born January 10, 1934, St. Louis, Mo./Interviewed by Jimmy Jones.
I'm interviewing a very fine singer and musician at his home. Mr. Fred Sample, Sr. Fred, will you tell me where you were born and how you got started in music?

I was born at 811 Walnut Street, East St. Louis, Illinois on January 10, 1934. I lived in one of those shotgun houses.
See straight through?
Straight through, brother.
I know the kind.
The way I got interested in music . . . when I was about nine years old we had one of those upright pianos and one of those little oval radios. I was curious about what made the music come out of the back of the radio, so when I heard the music I would go to the piano and pick out the notes because even then I had a pretty good ear, you know Jimmy, you got one. A lot of times I wish I had gone to school to learn music, but I didn't, so that's past history. The things I've learned about music I've picked up from other musicians. During my school years I was with a group called the Tornadoes, all over East St. Louis. Adel Emerson, Odel Mack, Fred Ollie, Alvin Washington, and Harold Cotton and I was playin' piano.
We did carnivals, hotel gigs, what-have-you, but in 1954 when I got out of service I started playing with Ike and Tina Turner. They came to East St. Louis, and they were at a place called Ned Loves. I didn't play with them at Ned Loves, but when they got down to the Manhattan Club I got with them.
That was on Broadway, wasn't it?
Yeah. Thirteenth and Broadway.
That was the place then. That was the place everybody wanted to come to.
I played the piano with them from 1954 to 1961 and had good musicians like Eugene Washington on drums.
Stumpy . . .
Yeah. We had Ike Turner's nephew, Jessie Knight on bass. Jackie Brenston, he was a vocal and played baritone saxophone. Had a fellow by the name of Raymond Peal on sax and Eddie Jones on tenor. Matter of fact we had Clayton Love later on. He was a vocal, but he was blowin' trombone also and we had a tight group. Tina came in by some chance, by the way her name wasn't Tina it was Ann Bullock. She came in from someplace, I don't know whether it was Tennessee or not, but she came in one night to sit in with us at the Manhattan Club. She asked Ike if she could get up and sing. She did and tore the house down. And that was it. Then Ike Turner whipped onto her, and things started happening. In 1954 we were the hottest thing around the town. In 1957 we hit the road. Our first stop was Los Angeles, California. I quit them in Las Vegas at Caesar's Palace. I haven't been back to Vegas since. Then I went to Washington, D.C. at the Howell Theater with L.C. Cook and Sam Cook. We were in Chicago in 1957 or '58 in a show with Dionne Warwick at the Regal. Then Smoky Robinson and the Miracles headed across the country on a tour.
Did you go overseas?

No. I came back home and got with Albert King.
That's Blues Boy King?
Right. Then I did some shows with Chuck Berry. After that I formed my own group. Had a little jazz trio, played at the Magic Carpet in Festus, Missouri. Then I had a quartet and played all around St. Louis and Columbia, Missouri. Also in Illinois. After that I had a duo and played private parties. I am presently employed at Al Baker's.
Who inspired you in music, Fred?
Tillman Brooks, he was a band director where I used to play in school and I think Miss Westbrooks. She had an a capella choir, I was fascinated by that.
She inspired a lot of people.
I learned by ear so I guess I was born gifted.
That's what it is, God's gift. A lot of people get degrees, but they don't see and hear what you do because they don't have the gift.
I came out to see you one Sunday and I was very impressed with the way you played. I think your father had a church on nineteenth and Central?
Yes.
It was gospel, but you were using more progressive chords. And I liked that, it made things sound a lot better. Then I wanted to get into it. I'd come over to your house and you would sit down and play and we would exchange ideas.
That's how you learn.
Steal from each other . . .
Right.
But only because it helps. Matter of fact, you still play a very important part in my life. You're a long time friend and a fellow musician. When we meet each other again, we'll have to work out something.
We'll holler along. You just made an album that had a big band.
Right, with Rueban Call. The title of it's "Misty." When I sing it's from the heart, and if I can't make you feel what I'm feeling, you don't have any soul at all.
In our conversation this evening, we got the highlights of Fred Sample, Sr. There's a lot of things we probably could have hit on, but right now we'll deal with this. Thanks Fred.

Sami Brautigan Scot Piano, vocalist/Born November 20, 1955, Florissant, Mo.
Sami was born November 20, 1955, in Florissant, Missouri, and attended grade school at Sacred Heart. She attended high school at St. Thomas Aquinas.
Her mother's name is Dorothy Brautigan and she was born on

Sami Scot

March 30, 1930. She is not musically inclined. Her father's name is Irvin Brautigan. He's a self-taught musician and plays keyboard, mandolin and wind instruments.

Sami took an interest in music at an early age and attended the San Francisco Institute of Music for one year. Sami is considered a versatile entertainer with a unique vocal style. She's worked from the south of France to Japan, from Reno's MGM Grand to Fenton, Missouri.

Sami loved music as early as age six, and by nine she was working in a professional band which played for eight years. She acquired awards in numerous competitions, local and national, and her single "Choo Choo Train" and a contract with Bull's Eye Records thrust her career forward.

Sami is small and brunette, but her talents have an emotional power that the audience can feel and empathize with.

Her repertoire is vast and she's always expanding it. It's rare that she's not able to meet 90 percent of her audience's song requests. Her opening song, "After the Loving," greets her audience, no matter where she's playing.

Eugene P. "Honey Bear" "Gene" Sedric Tenor sax, clarinet/
Born June 17, 1907, St. Louis, Mo., died April 3, 1963, New York, N.Y.

Eugene's father was Paul "Con Con" Sedric, a professional ragtime piano player.

Eugene was known for his dramatic touch in fast numbers and his tender one in slow numbers. He was highly regarded as a stylist on both instruments.

At age ten Gene played with St. Louis' own Knights of Pythias Band. In 1922 he made his professional debut with Charlie Creath, and later he worked with Fate Marable and Dewey Jackson on riverboats on the Mississippi River.

In 1923 he went to New York where he accompanied Jimmy Cooper's Black and White Revue with Julian Arthur's Band. Gene gigged with Ed Allen's band and around New York until he joined Sam Wooding in late 1923. He was associated with Fats Waller, first on record and then with Mr. Waller's touring band. From 1925 until 1931 he was with Sam Wooding in Europe. In 1932 they returned to New York and he spent a brief time with Fletcher Henderson. His association with Fats Waller lasted from 1934 to 1942. He also toured with Jimmy McPartland and Bobbie Hackett combos.

    1944   Phil Moore Four.
    1945   With Hazel Scott Show.
    1946   Formed his own band, played The Place, Smalls and Cafe Society
           in New York.
    1953   Went to France and worked with Mezz Mezzrow. He came back
           to New York and worked regularly with Conrad Janis' Band.

Gene died at age 55 at the Goldwater Memorial Hospital on Welfare Island on April 3, 1963, in New York. His nickname was given to him in 1930 when he wore a camel-hair overcoat—"Honey Bear."

Arvell Shaw Bass/Born September 15, 1923, St. Louis, Mo.

    1942   Played bass with Fate Marable on riverboats, St. Louis.
    1942–1945   In service—U.S. Navy.
    1948–1950   With Louis Armstrong's big band and small band briefly.

1950   Left St. Louis to study music at Geneva Conservatory.
1952   Back in St. Louis.
1954   Radio work with Russ Case from January to April.
1956   Back with Louis Armstrong from spring of 1954 to 1956 and appeared with him in *High Society*.
1957   Worked with Russ Case, CBS, and with the T. Wilson Trio.
1958   With Wilson and on tour in May with Benny Goodman. Stayed in Europe through September, played festivals in Cannes and Knokke. Recorded with Sidney Bechet in Cannes and Brussels. Back to U.S. and rejoined Wilson.

Arvell made many LPs on Columbia, Capitol and Verve, with T. Wilson and was in almost all of Louis Armstrong's LPs from 1946 to 1956.

Joseph "Joe" Shles Tenor sax, bass/Born January 24, 1916, St. Louis, Mo./Interviewed by Jimmy Jones.

Joe, how are you doing?

Fine, fine, Jim.

All right. Tell us a little background on yourself. Where were you born?

Right here in St. Louis, Missouri.

And your father and mother?

My mother's name was Jenny. She was born in St. Louis, Missouri. My father's name was Sol Shles, he was born in St. Louis too.

Your mother and father, were they musically inclined?

No, neither one of them were.

All right. Your grade school background . . . what grade school did you go to?

First I went to Duvall School, downtown, then I graduated grammar school from Webb Classical School.

And what high school?

I went to Soldan.

That's a prominent name here in St. Louis. After high school, when did you first become interested in tenor sax?

Oh, that was in grade school. One of the kids on the block got a saxophone. It sounded neat to me so I told my folks I'd like to have one and my dad went down and got me one.

At what age was that, Joe?

I was about ten.

Was there any particular person that you can remember that inspired you?

No, not at that time. I just kinda had a lesson here and there, but I always did like it.

And stuck with it in grade school and on into high school. Were you in any kind of bands?

Yeah, I was always in bands, but I had an alto sax and I was usually the third alto man and that was the one they could do without. This group we were playing with would get a gig and tell me they only wanted two sax men, but if I wanted to come along, I could. So I did that for awhile and this one Saturday night they got a job out to the Fenton Farmers Club, at that time, and we went out there and played the thing and the boss liked the group and hired us steady for Saturdays, so the two leaders on the gig felt they had the strength for a band, and the first guy they let go was me. I just loved it so much, but that was that. I really couldn't play much at all at that time. So I got mad and started taking saxophone lessons.

This was out of high school?

Yes, out of high school.

Do you remember the first job you had that you got paid for?

Yes, I was in the Boy Scout orchestra and there was a wedding down on Jefferson and Franklin and our group was piano, trumpet and saxophone and these people hired us and I think we were paid ten dollars, all together, but there was no piano at this place so we pooled all the money we got and bought a set of drums and the piano player played drums on the gig, so we really didn't get any money out of it but we had a set of drums.

That was the first one?

Yes.

What happened then pertaining to your music?

Well I started on the road with bands playing wherever we could, not much money but lots of fun.

And lot's of experience too probably. Are there any bands that you want to mention that you were traveling with at that time?

No. Not at that time.

And after that, what happened to Joe?

I met Jimmy Forrest here and Jimmy and I became real good friends and we started making all the rounds and we sat in every place in town in those days. Quite a name, and quite a guy too. Do you remember The Four Roses Club down on Jefferson and Market? We used to hang out there. Great piano player. Mable Griffin was her name. We made all the places on Vandeventer.

Those are names and places that all musicians remember. They bring back memories. Are there any other names or places that you want to mention Joe? When was the time you switched from tenor sax to bass?

Oh, that was my fifteenth birthday present to myself. I always admired bass and always hung out with bass players and I don't know, that was the time when rock started to get popular and they wanted all those funny sounds on tenor and I couldn't go that kind of thing.

But in the 40s I stuck with Russ David and I was down at the station with him for many years on staff there working all the society parties.

Russ is quite a man too.

One of my claims to fame is funny. It's kinda ridiculous. I was at a club in Chicago one night and Red Allen's group was there and Ben Webster was on tenor, and I got to set in for Ben that night and it was like heaven. I sure enjoyed that. He was a great player.

Are you with any group now, Joe?

Yes, I'm with Lloyd Bartlett's Trio. We're up at the University Club on weekends. On Saturday nights, and we do occasional things besides that.

What should we try to plant into the young people's minds that are trying to be any kind of musician?

Keep your ears open. No matter what you do, give it your best shot always, whether you like the group or not. You can always learn something.

Joe, I appreciate this interview, and I thank you for your time.

Carol Shoop (Lynn Carol — stage name) Pianist, vocalist/ Born November 5, 1958, Kirkwood, Mo./Interviewed by Jimmy Jones and Lyn Cunningham.

This is Jimmy Jones and we're doing another interview on Miss Carol Shoop, stage name Lynn Carol, in the home of Miss LaRue. She's a keyboard artist and singer. How are you, Lynn?

I'm okay.

Could you tell me what your mother and father's names are?

My mother's name is Beverly Aher Ackerman, and my father's name is Devere Charles Shoop.

Were they St. Louisans?

Yes. My mother was born and raised in St. Louis.

Were they musicians, either one of them?

No.

And where were you born?

In Kirkwood, Missouri. St. Johns Hospital.

And birthdate?

November 5, 1958.

And your schooling?

Grade school. Tillman, out in Kirkwood where my grandparents live and my family lives now. Kirkwood Junior High, and Kirkwood High School.

Okay. Did your musical career start in grade school or high school, do you remember?

It started in grade school in fourth grade when they tell you you can pick up an instrument. I said I want to play violin.

At what age?

I guess eight years old. So I picked up the violin. I played that for

twelve years and I taught myself guitar in the meantime and I taught myself piano. I guess in junior high I just started writing songs. They just started coming to me and I played in talent shows with the guitar and then I went to the piano. I sang in church choir from eight years old up.
I think we all did.
Yeah, yeah.
Had you really thought about being professional anytime at that point?
No, I really didn't know what I wanted to do. As Ann said, I have a God-gifted talent. I don't know what I'm doing it just comes to me.
Okay. Fantastic. But you did not at that point have any musical training?
No, just violin lessons.
Normally we would want to know about people that you would think have inspired you to do anything musically. We'd like to name those people if you have anybody you want to mention.
My father's brother Terry Shoop and his wife Nell. They both went to the St. Louis Conservatory of Music, and he kinda got me started. He had a thing about Barbra Streisand and when I was very young he got me hooked on her and I was imitating her in grade school and Petula Clark and Nancy Sinatra. I started singin' all that and he's really inspired me.
Who did you get your violin lessons from? Do you remember?
Just in grade school and I was in orchestra in junior high.
What did you play in orchestra? Violin?
Yes. Then I quit violin and went into a capella chorus in high school. I got my first professional job in high school.
With your singing or instrument?
Singing.
Do you remember your first professional job?
Uh huh. Well in high school I played coffee shops and things, you know sorta free and at seventeen I auditioned and got a job at Robotos of Japan at Westport and after I turned eighteen I started in December of 1976. I was there six and a half years.
That's fantastic. That is some kind of a . . .
First job. Yeah!
You nailed the gusto. (They laugh.) *And from that point?*
I have been playin' around town and I've been to Japan and played.
Oh? Where in Japan?
Matsuyama. That was last February and March.
Do you know how to spell that?
I got it right here. *(She laughs.)* Let's see . . .
That's where we met over there. I was there in April and May.
We met over there. We never met in St. Louis all the years we played.
Uh huh, we met in Japan.
Is that right?

It's spelled MATSUYAMA, and I am to be going back in December 1983.

Fantastic! Evidently they liked you there. And you're just getting ready to do a recording here.

Yes, I'm getting ready to make a demo tape of some originals I've written. I write quite a lot.

We're hoping to see the name of Lynn Carol around on the charts or whatever. Have you had any jobs inbetween Roboto and Japan and . . .

Yes, I played quite a few places around St. Louis, the Sheraton, the Tower Club. I just spent the summer down in Tan Tara. I was there four months. I start at the Hilton (Airport) Monday for two weeks.

Right across from the Airport. Stan and Biggies, isn't it?

Uh huh.

And in your musical career Lynn, everybody has to have a goal or something that you want to do. Is there something you want?

Yes, definitely. That's all I ever done is play music, that's how I make my living and I'm going to pursue it and I want to go all the way. Give it a shot anyway.

And what is all the way for you?

Oh, writing, recording, be a star. Have people pay to come and hear you play.

That's all the way.

That's all the way, yes.

Do you have any advice to give to people reading this?

Well when I started it was just a job to me. I didn't know what I was doing or what I was getting into. Just recently 1983, have I really gotten into the business end of it. It's very important now. Before I was just playing because I just love to sing and play. But now it's a business and I think that anybody coming up should go for what they want and believe in themselves. If they have that drive, they can do it.

And as Ann says, learn how to sell yourself.

Yes.

We thank you very much for this interview, Lynn, and we wish you all the best in your career.

Flora Bush Smith Organ, piano/Born May 23, 1912, Jackson, Tenn., died October 1, 1984, St. Louis, Ill./Verbatim answers as written to Jones and Cunningham.

Flora's parents were Reva and George Bush. Reva was born in Galena, Illinois and George in Macon, Mississippi.

Mother and father brought me to East St. Louis, Illinois at eight months old. The first instrument I remember is an old pump organ in our home. I must have made some nice sounds because my brother bought me a piano. I took lessons at the YMCA on 15th and Long, and from Lillian Pardon finished two books which were only scales, but I could play real well.

My music reading is a gift from God. Also I started adding notes and jazzing everything up.

I started in school at a very early age jazzing the school songs. Started playing at True Light Baptist Church at 11 years old. Played with a band in school with Edgar Green, Clifford King, Alex Caldwell, Jesse Brazier, Edgar Hayes and Vernon King.

We played at the theater on Piggott Avenue for Blanche Calloway's (who was Cab Calloway's sister) Show, at 15 years of age. I was the only lady jazz musician in East St. Louis all of these years. Played for almost everyone that came to town, and practically every club in East St. Louis and St. Louis. Made records with Tab Smith. Tab Smith bought an organ for me and we went in the Faust Club. Played for Don Bexlay as Bubba on *Sanford and Son*, Richard Pryor, and Lawanda Page as Aunt Ester. Called by St. Louis Local to go to Kansas City, Kansas, and Wichita, Kansas to play for Dinah Washington. Took Ahmad Jamal's place with the Caldwells in Stubenville, Ohio. Went to Montreal, Hamilton, Toronto, Canada, Greensburg, Penn., Mankato, Minn., Vandalia, Ill., Detroit, Mich., Springfield, Ill., and Greenbay, Wisc.

Played for Langston Hughes and Lincoln High School with the George Hudson Band. Langston invited me to his home in New York.

Nelson Hollins and George Lewis formed a band and asked me to be the keyboard player. The band was great. We had the great Oliver Nelson with us, we played the Mambo Club as house band, and played for Jackie Wilson, Little Jimmie Rushing, Arthur Prysock, Little Willie John and others.

In Detroit, played at all the nice clubs. Played at one of the largest churches for about 13 years, The King Solomon Baptist, and in Vegas played the Pilgrim Rest Baptist, with a 100 voice choir.

I once traveled with the Floyd Smith Band and we traveled all parts of Wisconsin and Michigan. That was back in the '30s. Dave Thomas Birdsong, Dave Kimbsell, and Clifford Basfiell was with the group way up in Stevens' Point, Wisc., where there was no blacks. We also played Rockford, Ill. with the Floyd Smith Band. Played in New York on a talent show and won first prize.

I was the first lady that had my own band. I had a good band, and kept my band working for several years. I have had a beautiful life, met a lot of nice people and was written up in the *International Magazine* as having been the only lady band leader in this area.

All East St. Louisans that have moved to Los Angeles have formed a homecoming club. They give affairs every year in October. I was called two

years straight in Vegas, to play at their affair in Los Angeles at the Cockatoo Inn. I was called in Detroit to come and play the first homecoming affair for East St. Louis at the Fischer in Belleville, Ill.

Miles Davis and I played together before he left East St. Louis. My husband and I was called by "Wild Man" Steve to come to Miami, Florida to open up his club in Miami Beach. We went and Reg Prysock was our saxophonist. Called to play in Quincy, Ill. at the Holiday Inn for three weeks and stayed there six months. Played in Sportsman Ball Park in St. Louis for the ball game. I played organ between every other inning, and George Hudson's Band played between every other Inning. Traveled with Leon Claxton Show for six months, playing production shows every day and night with great comedians, dancers and singers. Traveled from Tampa, Florida to a different city every two weeks. Went as far as Saskatchewan, Canada, as well as Edmonton and Winnepeg.

Traveled with Wild Man Steve Show and went from Tampa, Florida to Boston, Mass., changing cities every week or two. Played Atlanta, Ga. when (M.L.) King was killed. We were playing the Pink Pussy Cat. Big Maybelle was on the show. Played Basin Street East, in Boston, had a very good show. Have played for Little Ester, played at Riverero in St. Louis, with Jimmy Wilkins on the show, with Earl Garner, Chris Columbus, and Ray Brown. Played for Margaret Belafonte in a style show (Harry Belafonte's wife), also with Marva Louis, Joe Louis' wife, in a style show at Lincoln School.

Played for Roy Hamilton at the Masonic Hall in St. Louis. Played with Albert King's Band. Was called by Ike and Tina Turner to join their group while they were playing Howard Theater in Washington, D.C. Also called to play with band in Germany. Didn't go.

Played at Vegas World and the Continental Casino and the Don't Ask Lounge in Las Vegas for Kim Fuller, great jazz singer, and the Maxim Casino for Rochon Westmoreland in Vegas, a great bass player. Played for female impersonators at The Torch Club with my own band, Edgar Green, George Brazier, Harry Lewis, later Sonny Curry. Also played at Club 88 on the highway in East St. Louis with Tab Smith and Boyd Moore for strippers. Played all over East St. Louis and small cities of Ill. with Raymond Hickman's Band, James Beard and Al Hickman.

All over East St. Louis and St. Louis with Albert King. Played Houston, Dallas, Corpus Christi, Austin, and all parts of Texas with Tab Smith, and Little Willie John in Cleveland, and Dayton, Ohio.

Went to the Faust Club after it was rebuilt from a fire, with my own band, Two Jacks and a Jill, "Tee" Wiley on tenor, Buck Underwood, bass, David Hodges, drums, and yours truly on keyboards.

Opposite, top: **Flora Bush Smith.** *Bottom:* **Smith (left), Richard Pryor and unidentified go-go dancer.**

Stan Sykes on piano.

Traveled with a lady evangelist, Reverend Lillie T. Brunner for several years. We went to New Orleans, Mobile, Ala., Milton, Florida, Pensacola, Florida, Detroit, Mich., Louisville, Ky., Jackson, Miss., Paris, Ill., as well as Little Rock, Ark., and several other cities. Played gospel music for Joe Mays in East St. Louis and St. Louis area.

Young people playing now should study hard and practice daily.

Music has been my whole life. I've traveled so many places, met so many celebrities, and made quite a bit of money. My life has really been beautiful.

(Note: Shortly after this letter was received, Flora Bush Smith died in her sleep at a relative's home in East St. Louis. She was the ultimate in professionalism.)

"Sonny Hamp" *see* Clarence Hamilton

Stanley Sykes Organ, piano, writer, arranger/Born March 5, 1942, St. Louis, Mo./Telephone interview by Lyn Cunningham.

Stanley Sykes was born on March 5, 1942 in St. Louis, Missouri. His mother was Aretha (Chambers) Sykes and his father was Ernest Thomas Sykes, both born in St. Louis.

Stanley attended grade school at Louverture, high school at Vashon High, and was enrolled in the St. Louis Institute of Music during 1968–1969. He was born with a natural talent and started playing at the Nazarene Church in midtown St. Louis.

Stanley played with the Bill Tucker Group. He had his own group called the Stan Sykes Trio featuring himself, Nat Riggins, and Alvin Troup. Then he had a group called Combination 3 with Vernon Latham, Charles Gilbert, and himself. Caroline Jones also played flute at times with these groups.

Stanley's first paying job was in 1967 at The Toast of the Town on North Taylor Avenue, St. Louis. He made $15.00 a night.

His advice to up-and-coming musicians is, "Put your values in the right perspective. You have to like it and love it, and practice. Take care in the way you project yourself to the public. Have your priorities in order."

Stanley has retired from music as a profession, but still plays for his own pleasure, and keeps on encouraging others. He says, "A part of me will always be music."

Irene "Eva" Taylor Vocalist, dancer/Born January 22, 1895, St. Louis Co., Mo., died October 31, 1977, Mineola, N.Y.

Eva's parents were Orville and Julia Gibbons; she was one of twelve children.

> 1898 Worked with Josephine Gassman and Her Pickaninnies at the Orpheum Theater, St. Louis.
> 1898–1904 Toured with Gassman to Chicago and the West Coast.
> 1904–1906 Overseas to Hawaii, Australia, New Zealand, England, Germany, France, and Holland.
> 1906 Worked the Hippodrome Theater, London. With Al Jolson Show, "Vera Violetta," at the Winter Garden, New York.
> 1911–1915 Toured with Josephine Gassman, Phina and Company Show to Australia, New Zealand, and Tasmania. Toured as singer and dancer, working theaters in U.S., especially Chicago.
> 1921 Settled in New York, worked with Clarence Williams Trio, in local clubs and theaters.

1921–1922   Lafayette Theater, New York; Happy Rhone's Orchestra, New Star Casino, New York; Standard Theater, Philadelphia, Penn.; appeared in musical comedy "Shuffle Along" at the 63rd St. Theater, New York City; toured with Miller and Lyles Variety Show, "Step On It," in theaters along the East Coast; Howard Theater, Washington, D.C.; worked in show "Queen of Hearts" with Nora Bayes at the George M. Cohan Theater; recorded with Clarence Williams group on the Black Swan label, New York; appeared with Clarence Williams Trio on radio WEAF, New York; recorded on Okeh label, N.Y.

1922–1928   Recorded as Irene Gibbons, Columbia label, New York.

1928–1930   Recorded on Edison/Victor label, N.Y.; recorded on Columbia label, N.Y.C.; appeared in first NBC coast to coast radio show WEAF/WJZ; short wave broadcast to England and Europe; on General Electric shortwave radio to Admiral E. Byrd at the South Pole; recorded as Catherine Henderson on Velvetone label, New York City; Okeh label, N.Y.; and ARC label, New York City.

1932   Recorded duet with Lil Armstrong as The Riffers, on Columbia label, New York City.

1933   Recorded with Clarence Williams Jug Band and Orchestra, on the Vocalion label, New York City.

1933–1934   Appeared with the Paul Whiteman Orchestra on the Kraft Music Hall Show; recorded with Clarence Williams on Columbia label; appeared with Cab Calloway's Orchestra in the Harlem Show, NBC Network, New York City; headlined in Harlem Opera House, New York City.

1937   Recorded on Bluebird label, New York City; at Carnegie Hall with Clarence Williams.

1941   Recorded on Bluebird label, New York City; retired from active music work.

1948   Worked with Bessie Smith at a Memorial Concert, Town Hall, New York City.

1950s–1960s   Inactive except for a few engagements and a Jazz Band concert in Copenhagen, Denmark 1974.

Eva died of cancer at the Nassau County Hospital in Mineola, New York, on October 31, 1977, and was buried in St. Charles Cemetery, Huntington, New York.

Clark Terry Jazz trumpeter/Born 1920, St. Louis, Mo.

After playing with the Navy band during World War II, Terry was with George Hudson's Band in St. Louis and with Charlie Barnet on the West Coast.

He joined Duke Ellington in 1951 and has played with that band off and on ever since. His style is reminiscent of another Ellington musician, Rex

Opposite, top: **Marion Miller (left), Leo Cheers and Clark Terry.** *Bottom:* **Charlie Fox, wife of Ray Eldridge, Ray Eldridge, Clark Terry, unidentified man.**

Stewart, especially in half-valve effects. He is a modern jazz trumpeter with a technique similar to Dizzy Gillespie's.

His talents demand a high respect from members of the music world. Both Miles Davis and Quincy Jones will attest to that. Terry is always in great demand.

Terry has recorded for many major companies, and some of the world's finest artists.

Besides playing with such outstanding orchestras as Duke Ellington's and Count Basie's, he was also an assistant and first trumpet player in the orchestra for Johnny Carson's *Tonight Show*.

His own big band has performed all over the country, and has included a live recorded concert at Carnegie Hall.

Jeter Thompson Piano/Born March 16, 1930, St. Louis, Mo./Information supplied from a tape by Jeter Thompson.

This is a slight background on my career as a pianist, from the very start to where I am now.

I was born March 16, 1930 right here in St. Louis, Missouri. I started playing at the age of five. My father played piano, his name was Justus Jeter Thompson. He played in clubs in St. Louis and East St. Louis. In my younger years we had an upright piano at home, my mother sang as my father played, and my two sisters began taking lessons at an early age. I didn't want to take lessons, I refused to take lessons because I could play almost anything I heard. I also had a gift for composing my own music. I started playing boogie woogie after listening to Pete Johnson, Albert Owens, Eddie Hayward and Mattlux Lewis.

Now at the age of 12, my father entered me in a boogie woogie contest sponsored by the *Globe-Democrat* which was held at the Chase Hotel. I was the only black in the contest, and it came down to a three-way tie for first place, so it turned out I came in second. The boy who won wanted to give me first prize because he felt I had won it.

At sixteen I started piano lessons while in Sumner High. I was suspended for playing boogie woogie in the choir room, as I was very easily enticed to get up and play the piano at the drop of a hat.

I graduated as president of Sumner's class of 1947, and I attended Stowe Teachers College.

I started playing with Emmett Carter at the downtown strippers club, The Coconut Grove, six nights a week. It was myself on piano, Emmett Carter on sax, and Robert West on drums. Then I did numerous jobs with the Emmett Carter Group. We worked the Stork Club at Missouri University, then I played with the Ernest Jones Combo in and around St. Louis. I also played with Chuck Berry's Trio, and Julius Polks big band.

Then the Air Force got me, 1951. I went to radio maintenance school,

Piano master Jeter Thompson, head of Tres Bien Group.

which was at Scott Field, Illinois, and while I was there I played small towns in Illinois and also Scott Field. Then in the later part of 1951 I was transferred to Ft. Bragg, North Carolina. I met Clarence Stroven while there. He plays drums with Thelonius Monk.

Between 1953 and 1954 I was in Korea. I played in service clubs and officers clubs. I worked with Fats Waller's son on baritone. After my discharge in 1954, I was invited to play on the *Spider Burke* TV Show. Spider was a well-known disc-jockey we had at that time. I appeared on the show with Percy James who played bongo and conga drums. We sort of hit it off together, and we got us a bass player by the name of Corman Weathers, formerly with the Twentieth Century Trio, a well known trio around St. Louis, and we played at a place on Cass Avenue. Then we acquired Herschel Harris on bass, and then we had James Casey, Van Arsdale, and finally Richard Simmons on bass. One of the clubs we had was on Taylor and Eastern Avenue, and we had Oliver Nelson on sax. At different times we had Chris Woods and Charles Williams. They worked with us before going on to bigger things. Drummers included Chuck Carter and finally Al St. James.

As a trio now we played the Dave Dixon live radio show every Saturday with vocalist Leon Golden, and backed up amateur vocalists. We recorded a 45 rpm for Oscar which he distributed locally.

Then Gaslight Square in 1962 as the Tres Bien Quartette, Percy James on bongos and congas, Al St. James on drums, Richard Simmons on bass, myself on piano.

Norman Weinstrow of Norman Records liked the group and cut two LPs, which were instant hits in St. Louis and around the country; "Kiliman-jaro" and "Boss Tres Bien" were simultaneous hits on the West Coast, especially around Los Angeles.

While we were playing at the Dark Side we were made partners into Club Tres Bien. We hadn't left town yet to hit the road, but at that time we used Cleo Bradford as a vocalist. We cut a 45 record with Cleo Bradford. We also made an album with Jeanne Trevor on Mainstream, called "Pal." Then Dick Gregory came through and picked us up, and he wanted us to do three shows in three different cities with him, which included Chicago at the Tiffany Theater, at the Howard Theater in Washington, D.C., and finally the Apollo Theater in New York. On that show was Dizzy Gillespie and Bill Henderson as vocalist.

We finished up in New York. It had been a week in each city. We returned to St. Louis to find we were in great demand on the West coast. We packed up and went to Los Angeles to the It Club. They booked us there for two weeks. The club was owned by John T. McLane who introduced us to Associated Booking Corporation, to be our agent. ABC booked us for the following clubs after we finished at John T's: The Lighthouse, Hermosa Beach, California, Memory Lane and the Trident in Sausalito, California, The Penthouse, Seattle, Washington, Jazz Workshop, San Francisco, California, The Mardi Gras in San Diego, California, and Adam West Theater, in Los Angeles.

We did numerous concerts there with Horace Silvers, Thelonius Monk, Ahmad Jamal, The Three Sounds, The Jazz Crusaders, Lorez Alexandra and many other people.

Then we played Chicago, about eight times, Philadelphia, New York, Detroit, Pittsburgh, the Bronx in New York, and we were well received everywhere. We did a TV series, *Route 66*, in which our bongo-Congaist, Percy James, had a script and our other members played performing musicians.

We were in Detroit, Michigan, every New Years Eve. At that time we had about six albums on Decca Records, to date we have a total of twelve albums on Decca Records and one on Atlantic Records.

Going back a bit, my first music teacher was Aleta Ward, then I went to Miss Ellen Kentchen. She introduced me to Art Tatum who I think is Mr. Piano period.

I was told the other day that we were the only group ever to leave St. Louis and make it, there were individuals but not groups.

To date I have composed about fourteen original compositions that have been recorded while we were at Decca, they were distributed as you know, worldwide. Our records have been distributed in Australia, throughout Europe, Japan, Canada and it's something to hear yourself on the radio, coming out of New York, even today.

At present I'm writing new material I've composed, about five or six songs that have recording possibilities. We hope to sign up with a major company very shortly and continue to put music on the market, which we hope the people can enjoy and have something to remember us by.

Cornelius "Chuck" Tillman, Jr. Sax, all reeds writer/Born 1929, Port Gibson, Miss./Interviewed by Jimmy Jones.

I have in my presence a young man by the name of Chuck Tillman. Chuck, how you doin'?

Just fine.

We'll start this interview by asking, what are the names of your parents?

My father's name is Cornelius Tillman. Of course I'm a Jr., but Cornelius looked funny on the marquee.

Where were your parents born?

They were born in Mississippi, my father from Port Gibson, my mother from Clarksdale.

Were they musically inclined?

Nothing more than that they liked music.

Was there anyone in your family that was musically inclined?

No, I haven't found anyone that was.

All right. Now getting to Mr. Chuck Tillman as we know him.

I was born in Mississippi too, but we moved to St. Louis when I was very young.

And you're schooling, grade school, high school, whatever?

I actually started to school in St. Louis.

Do you remember the name of the school?

Dunbar grade school.

Dunbar grade school here in St. Louis.

Yes.

And that was your first shot at St. Louis, Missouri.

Right.

Did music come to you in grade school or high school?

I was about thirteen and there was a music teacher that was giving music lessons. We had to rent the instruments. I started on the clarinet, but switched over to saxophone, this was just briefly, because at the end of the rent period, he took his instruments back, and school was over. So I was out. It wasn't until I got into high school that I started playing again.

And the high school you attended was?

Vashon. This was after Mr. Henderson came back from service in 1946 and reformed the band. I've been associated with music ever since. After high school I went to music and arts for about a year and a half. After that I went into service, and when I came out I went to Ludwigs Music School.

In downtown St. Louis at the time?

Yes. After Ludwigs, I went to Missouri University. I was workin' on a B.A. This was after 1958. I went on the G.I. Bill.

Those guys get that from the service?

Of course, when I was in service I went to the U.S. Naval School of Music. That was across from the Naval base in Washington, D.C.

Did you do any playing while you attended school?

Oh, yeah!

Do you remember the first paid job you ever had?

Yeah, I remember. I was workin' with a group called the Jimmy Houston Band. It was all kids who were in high school together, and I think the job paid twenty-five cents. We must have had about twenty people on the bandstand. The whole band made ten dollars, and we split it.

I'm sure there are some names of people you'd like to mention from your musical career.

Well one that made quite a name for himself was Oliver Nelson, who was in that same group. Oliver and I grew up within two or three blocks of each other. We were about the same age. There was an abundance of musicians around St. Louis in the forties and fifties. Now it's almost unbelievable that those people were here.

It's a shame they had to leave to acquire some kind of fame.

We used to be able to go down to local 197 and see someone who would be able to tell us some things on the instrument. The musicians union was quite a brotherhood. Everyone was very congenial. They passed along information, and they'd sit with you and tell you what you were doing wrong, how things were supposed to be done, and what was expected of you as a musician. This came from older musicians who had found out by trial and error. You could look up to them. They were fine musicians.

And the name of some of the musicians you worked for?

I worked with Jimmy Forrest, Ernie Wilkins, Edgar Hayes, Tommy Turntine and Stanley, Tommy's brother, but I think the first person who ever taught me the circle of breathing, was Clark Terry. He showed us how to breathe continuously without appearing to take a breath. Naturally you got to take a breath, there's just a way to do it.

Then there was Rufus Webster, a piano player out of Minneapolis, a fantastic player. It was a very good learning time, during the forties, but life will be life and it takes different turns.

You know we were talking about the different phases of the senses?

It's just that the ear is the only part of the body you can't turn off, not only do you hear through your ears, you hear through your fingers, you hear through your bones. The vibrations you hear in your body, control your emotions to a certain degree. You are able to control people if you're able to manipulate these emotions, because they can't turn it off. He can close his eyes and not see you, he can close his nose and not smell you, but it's rather hard for him not to feel you, that is the vibrations of you as the music enters the body through many different areas. Music plays an intricate part in a persons well-being.

In other words, a person is blessed with hearing.

I wouldn't like to lose any of my senses, but if I could only keep one, I believe hearing would be the one.

That would be a difficult decision. Chuck, I know you've had dreams in your life of doing great things in music. What does it take to be a musician?

Well the aim is determined by the individual. You must be determined, have perseverance, have faith in what you're doing, and of course it helps if you have your fair share of talent. But discipline is what a musician has to have! Music is a reflection of ones emotions. Instruments are much harder to discipline than voice, to get across their emotion.

Is there anything we haven't covered that you would like to mention?

I've worked with practically every band that's been through St. Louis. That goes from Dewey Jackson to Ike Turner.

What advice, as we're closing this interview, would you give any musician that is studying?

If he desires to play music, all facets of it, keep in mind that that's what he wants to do. You only get so much from a teacher, so be open to knowledge wherever you can and whenever you can. Ask questions.

We are going to close this interview at this time, and thank you very much, Mr. Chuck Tillman.

Randall Wayne "Randy" Tobler Trombone, medical doctor/Born June 20, 1958, St. Louis, Mo./Telephone interview by Lyn Cunningham.

Randy Tobler was born on June 20, 1958, the son of Patricia Ann (Primo) Tobler and Robert Harold Tobler, both born in St. Louis. His father has played trombone at Muny Opera for over 28 years, served as head of music for Lindbergh Schools, personnel manager for the Muny, and contracts for the Fox Theater in St. Louis. (See Robert Harold Tobler.) Randy's mother sings, although not professionally.

Randy started playing the trombone at age ten. He studied formally (his father trained him) but he also studied with trumpet player Bob Ceccarini. Randy's schooling consisted of Dressel Grade School, Sperreng Middle School, and Lindberg High School, Kennerly, Missouri. He attended University of Missouri–St. Louis as an undergraduate, majoring in biology, and attended medical school at Washington University. He's a member of Alpha Omega Alpha, a curator-scholar and an OB-GYN at Barnes Hospital.

At 15 years of age Randy had a group of his own from a stage band and played a wedding reception for one of the teachers at a local hotel in the neighborhood for his first paid gig, netting $20.

At sixteen he joined the Musicians' Union (2197) and played at Six Flags, a local theme park.

> *Professional Accomplishments:* "St. Louis Brass" (Christmas album); Commercial recordings for McDonalds; Home Box Office production *(Burlesque U.S.A.);* started with Bob Kuban from 1974 until 1981, and still plays for him when he's not on call at the hospital; played for Yul Brenner's *The King and I;* Tex Beneke; chorus line; broadway shows; The Muny, shows at the Fox Theater, "Days, Summers, Nights"; Six Flags; on *The Admiral,* 1974–1979; with Russ David, Jack Engler, Johnny Polzin, Buddy Marino; Circus's Ice Shows; the Ice Follies and various other St. Louis groups.

Randy's advice to younger musicians: "First of all, develop good basic skills. Develop sound. Above all, be able to read music. Develop a good sense of pitch. Should learn standards and be able to offer consumer what he wants. Need to practice always, alone and with your group.

Robert Harold Tobler Trombone/Born October 4, 1934, St. Louis, Mo./Telephone interview by Lyn Cunningham.

Robert Tobler is a teacher of applied music in the Lindbergh Music Department. He also teaches part-time at University of Missouri–St. Louis and Webster College. His mother is Edna Amelia (Elschinger) Tobler, born in St. Louis, and his father is Harold Herman Tobler, also born in St. Louis. His father was a professional musician, and played the saxophone, clarinet and piano; his mother had no musical background but played piano occasionally.

Robert attended Scullin grade school in St. Louis and also Immanuel Lutheran School. He attended Beaumont High School. He received a B.A. in music at Washington University, a masters' degree at Southern Illinois University–Edwardsville in school administration. He was professionally taught by Ralph Abbetiello and Dorothy Ziegler.

At age fourteen Robert had his first paid job—a wedding—playing with Leon Schankman. He played trombone and received one dollar in payment. At age thirteen he played with the St. Louis Philharmonic Orchestra, and played with them between the years of 1947 and 1953.

He has played with Ralph Marterie in 1959 or 1960; with Tex Beneke when his band was based in St. Louis, when he needed musicians over a ten-year period from 1971 to 1979; with Nelson Riddle; and with the St. Louis Symphony as an extra.

Robert was the principal trombonist with Muny Opera for 27 years, played for the Ringling Brothers circus when it was in St. Louis, and The Ice Capades. He has also written two books for Mel Bay Music Publications, made television and radio commercials, and free-lanced industrial tape-recordings.

His advice to aspiring musicians is: "Learn your instrument very well, study with the finest teachers available, play all forms of music every opportunity you have, work for total versatility and go where the jobs are. The trombone has been good to me."

As of 1985, Robert was playing for the Fox Theater Orchestra, and was personnel manager for the Muny.

Henry James "Mule" Townsend Piano, vocalist, guitar, harmonica/Born October 27, 1909, Shelby, Miss./Interviewed by Lyn Cunningham and Jimmy Jones.
We are doing a book on St. Louis musicians and since you're getting a lot of recognition, we'd better include you in what we're doing.
Well it would be kind of a sad thing not to.
We're not going to leave you out, I'll tell you.
I would be kinda disappointed, you know.
So Lyn will give you some questions now.
First, Mr. Townsend, what day, month and year were you born?
1909. October, 27th.
And that was in what city?
Shelby, Mississippi.
All right. Now what were the names of your mother and father?
My father's name was Allen Townsend. My mother's name was Omelia Blount Townsend.
Do you have a middle name, besides your nickname?
Yes. James.
Do you know where your mother was born?
Yes, my mother was born in Shelby, Mississippi. My father I don't.
Were they musicians?
My father was.
What did he play?
He played a button box.
A button box?
An accordion.
Oh, a button box is an accordion? That's great! Did he play for himself, in a group, or . . .
No, he more or less played for himself. That way he could imitate all the noises musicians make.
Back in them days it was just good to play anything and have fun.
That's right.

Yeah, any kind of fun was O.K. All right, what grade school did you go to, Henry?

It was in Shelby. I don't really remember the name.

Did you go to high school?

Wait please, let's correct that.

It wasn't in Shelby?

No, I went to school in Cairo, Illinois. We migrated from Mississippi into Memphis into Cruthersville. During that time it was one year and you were gone again. And then into Cairo and we settled there for awhile.

Moved up the river. Now, did you go to high school?

No. My grade was the third grade.

He didn't need high school anyway, I can tell.

I would have liked to have had it then though.

Yes, I know. We would all like to have more than we have, Henry. What was the first instrument that you played?

Guitar, no, harmonica.

All right. And then guitar.

And then guitar.

And then the piano. Now, do you remember the first paying job that you had?

No, I really don't. My brother and I were working as little kids down in Southern Illinois . . .

What was his name?

Charles Morris Townsend. And we would entertain, we were just little children. I don't remember the months, years, or anything.

And that was in Cairo, Illinois?

And the musicians back in those days played for room and board, whatever, didn't they, Henry?

Yeah.

So that's the first job you had. What year did you come to St. Louis?

I came here in 1921 or 1922. I believe it was 1922.

Did you have a regular job and play music on the side?

Do you mean at that time?

Uh huh. Since you were only eight or nine years old then what was the first job you had in St. Louis after you grew up?

Well I tell you that's going to be hard to answer too. The first job was on Jefferson Avenue between Biddle and Carr Street. It was a house where a guy sold unlegal drinks and had parties and things, you know what I mean Jimmy? It started out as a house rent collection thing you know.

You play and they donate so much and get the rent up?

Yeah, get the rent for them.

Yeah, all right. And you didn't get any salary there unless it happened to be your rent.

Unless it happened to be my rent and then of course I did. It stemmed from that and the pay started later on as they found out this was profitable. Then the people would hire us for no rent, and if you drank you could get half a dollar cash and all you wanted to eat or drink, and if you didn't drink you could get a dollar or a dollar and a half for your work.

That's good. O.K.

That sounds like the same thing the other people we've interviewed said. They worked for a little of nothing, but they were heard and playing for so many people, there was a chance you might be heard, meet the right people.

The publicity, the exposure.

Right.

How old were you when you got married?

Oh, twenty. Somewhere around that age. I'm embarrassed trying to keep up with that kind of thing.

Same wife you have now?

No, of course not.

Do you have any children?

Yes.

How many do you have?

I'm going to accept five.

Five.

Most people don't want to accept none.

What year would you say you actually went out and got a job playing the piano in a club?

Well the first time I done piano for pay, was in a studio in Aurora, Illinois for a recording. I got paid for the work.

You were making a record at the time?

Yes.

Do you remember how much you made?

Five or six hundred dollars maybe, which was a big amount of money then.

Are any of the kids musically inclined, Henry?

Yes, I've got a boy who is real talented, but he studies looking and finding himself.

What does he play Henry?

He plays bass guitar, he plays piano.

That's nice.

There's a big demand for that good bass player.

There sure is. Outside of this recording you have here, have you made any other recordings lately? Or is this a late recording?

This is the last one I made in the States.

Where were you when you were out of the States?

Oh, Switzerland, Sweden, Germany and Austria.

I'll bet the people were very receptive too.

Oh, beautiful!

They say they're very nice.

It's amazing how much more receptive the people are overseas than they are in the States.

Well it's like LeRoy says, we take it for granted. Some people take their own home for granted and don't appreciate one another. You know?

That's true. How many recordings did you make over there?

I made three albums.

Do you remember the name of them?

One of them was with the Fox label, the other two was with Swingmaster. One was "Cut Back Blues"—Swingmaster.

If you were giving advice to a younger musician now, what would you tell them?

I would tell him by all means get what he could out of it. If you have a format for it you can be more diligent than if you have to learn it all from the ground.

You learned your instruments because you were determined to learn them.

That's right.

It wasn't really a teacher like we know today.

No, of course not. Because it was something I wanted to do.

Henry was self-taught and a natural. Many great musicians were self-taught.

And I'm inclined to say, most of the better ones.

You're right, Henry.

I don't try to put anyone down, or wouldn't, but the guy that goes for reading it, it's beautiful, it's great, but when he reads and settles for it, if it's not on paper I don't do it, he's in bad shape. He's not himself.

That's what I think, Henry.

He's not himself at all, he's not creative at all.

You've got to hear it up here, and feel it in here.

That's right! If the wind comes along and blows it out of his face, he's got to quit playing.

That's true.

You're going to receive an award for Mr. Henry Townsend from the National Arts Council in Washington, D.C. on Friday 13, 1985.

I should be in Washington, D.C. from August 11 to August 14, 1985.

Is there anything else about Henry Townsend you want to note?

No, not off hand. I enjoy entertaining as much as people enjoy my entertainment.

You love people and they love you.

That's right. That makes it a success. If you apply yourself all the way to what you're doing, you can't be too big a failure. I'll entertain until I can't entertain. That's a field I know, it's what I know best. A fellow asked me if I wasn't doing this, what would I do? I told him I'd probably ease it onto the side and instruct people to do what I am doing. But I couldn't leave this.

It's a part of you.

Too much a part of me to walk away from.

I know what you mean, I'm in the same boat.

It's been part of you, and that's the way it has to stay.

I guess that's all Henry.

Mr. Townsend, we thank you for your time and your interview today and we enjoyed your concert very much.

That's okay, that's okay.

Anthony Joseph Viviano Vocalist/Born October 17, 1948, St. Louis, Mo./Interviewed by Jimmy Jones.

Tony, what's your full name?

Anthony Joseph Viviano.

What were your mother and father's names?

My mother's name was Dorothy Cusumano. My father's name was the same as mine, I'm a Jr.

Where were they born, Tony?

In St. Louis, Missouri. My mother was born in 1915, my father was born in 1910.

Either one of them musically inclined?

Not really, not really. My father could sing, but he never took up a career.

Your birthdate and place?

I was born in St. Louis at Normandy Osteopathic Hospital on October 17, 1948.

Are you married?

Yes I am married. I have two children (one girl and one boy).

Now, at what age did you become interested in music?

About three days after I was born. I became interested in it I guess at about the age, as far as I can remember at least, four.

Four years old?

Three or four years old. My older brother Joe would sing all the time in the living room, just swing his arms and sing all the time to some old records, 78s. "I'd Like to Get You on a Slow Boat to China," "Somebody Else Is Takin' My Place," all them old tunes and that's what happened.

Well, Joe, was he really, was he kinda the inspiration for you trying to sing?

Definitely. My brother Joe is, in fact you were there that night when he was there.

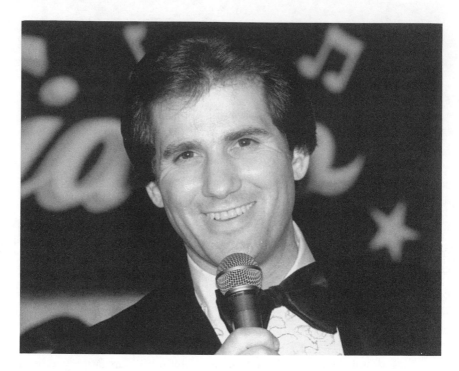

Tony Viviano

Yeah, yeah, yeah.

He was the one that taught me how to sing on the truck. The produce truck.

Well, tell me about that Tony, I mean tell me about . . .

When he started singing at home, I would sing when he wasn't there, I couldn't sing in front of him, you know, so I begin to start singing on my own there at home. Elvis Presley was out doin' his rock and roll, a few of the others, but he was basically into Frank Sinatra. He liked Sinatra music.

Right.

In 1958 he bought two albums on Frank Sinatra and in those days, you got sixteen songs on one album. You had a good time. So we wanted to get a radio for the truck and my father would not allow us to have a radio on the truck. He says forget about the radio, go to work. That's it, you go to work. You can go rock and roll later.

Yeah, yeah. It seems funny now. (They laugh.)

So we'd get up at 12 or 1 o'clock in the morning and go down to produce row here in St. Louis and get things, get the truck loaded and by the time we'd hit the highway we'd start singin' them songs. We go through Alton, East Alton, Woodriver, Godfrey, way out in Hardin, Illinois and there ain't no radio, so we had to sing. What we did, we memorized the songs at home, since dad wouldn't let us have a radio, we memorized the songs at home, took them in our minds and we sang them on the truck track for track. And in our minds we'd flip the record over and we'd sing the other side.
I see, I see.

Then in 1959 Bobby Darin come out with, "Mack the Knife." We learned that album. In 1960 he did "Clementine" and we learned that album. By the time we got home, we were doin' Louie Prima and Fats Domino. That's how it was. We kept movin' all the time but I still was into the rock and roll, don't get me wrong, I was still doin', I would go and I would sing at private little things like a splatter-platter party that KXOK would have at Chain-of-Rocks Park. Things like that, singing to the records, but I never thought I'd ever take it off and do other things, what we're doin' today. That's the roots of it there, that's how it really began, my brother Joe, Bobby Darin, Frank Sinatra, you know.
Did you ever have a professional teacher, Tony? Or was this kinda just like a gift?

Well, I found out that I could get some good applause for singing some songs and takin' it off like that, I thought that I would go and get voice lessons and I went to this gentleman in Clayton.
And his name is. . .?

Bill Harder.
Bill Harder.

And he told me the very first lesson that I didn't need voice lessons, that I needed work in a nightclub. He says, go to work. I says but I want to know what is going on in my throat. I want to know how to hit a higher note or come down gracefully, or whatever. So he gave me another lesson and he told me to go to work, find a job, and that was it.
Said you didn't need nothin'. (He laughs.) *Do you remember your first paid job?*

Paid job. Very first paid job. Well, let's go back. The very first time I sang, this is a good one, *(He laughs.)* my Uncle Vito was a very big strong man, he looked like you Jimmy. *(They laugh.)* I think he was a little bit bigger than you. He was a very large fellow and he was what you'd say, he was like a rough character. That was my mother's brother, and he took me to a bar with him, he was gonna meet a friend of his. This was the first time I ever sang in front of the public.
How old were you?

I was, back then, seven or eight.

Really? (He laughs.)

Yeah, and at that time Perry Como had a hit on the hit parade, the top charts back then. It was "Catarina." (Tony sings a little bit of it.) So, he knew I liked that song. He knew I had it at home so he gave me, he come up to me and give me a fifty cent piece. He said I want you to put it in the juke box and play "Catarina." So I went over there and punched the buttons off and he said there's that stage over there, which was even with the bar, I want you to go over there and sing it in front of all these people. I said, you are crazy. I said there's no way I'm going to get up and do that one, and he reaches over backwards there and started taking his belt off. Now, if you don't get up there, and he meant everything he said.

Yeah. (He laughs.)

So I got up there frightened and I sang it, and I got a big applause for it and it was kind of a good feeling and I wound up singin' three or four more songs that day. But that's one thing and I never wanted to be forced into it you know, but he made a big threat about it and I got up and did it.

And at that point was when you kind of got the feeling to maybe give singing a try.

Not back then. It never, it never...

It hadn't hit you yet.

No, it didn't hit me. I would sing on the truck with my brother Joe, these songs, these Sinatra songs and he would tell me, you think you sound like Frank Sinatra because you're singin' exactly what you heard at home, but really, your voice is your voice. See? So he says he felt the same way. He thinks he sounds like Sinatra. But it's not, you're picking up the same mannerisms or what have you. So but we just had all kinds of courage on the truck singing and you sound like you're in a studio because you're in the cab, you know, like a shower, so to speak. So we just did it that way. I guess what really hit us, what really got me started was ... another thing, my older, I have another brother Sal, a younger brother. Joe's the oldest and then comes Sal. Sal was in high school at the time, goin' to De Andres High School. He liked Elvis (Presley). He looked like Elvis. He used to imitate Elvis in the corridors and lunch halls and everything. Hold up a broom like Elvis Presley's guitar. So I was into Elvis too ... I liked Elvis too and I liked the smooth suave Sinatra-type songs and I went through high school and I was up for a play one time to sing between the intermissions. There was many times I was gonna do it, but I never did it and then college come along. I was goin' to college. You always feel like, well, you can sing but somebody's got to discover ya...

Yeah, yeah, yeah.

Like in your backyard, there's an agent gonna drop out of the sky and say I want you, like Elvis Presley. *(They both laugh.)*

Yeah, sure.

So I didn't bother with it, I kept working, I was in the produce business. I went to college, two years at Florissant Valley and then I started out at SIU in Edwardsville (Illinois.) Soon as I started out there, I quit right away and I wound up in my own business. The produce business and I built it up and it got to be a very big business. At that time, I'm going back now, before that I was, see I was in the produce business at the same time I was in college, OK? And I took a break for the Easter break and everybody goes to Ft. Lauderdale. So when we got down there, I went with a buddy of mine and that's what kinda kicked off when I met Milton Berle. We walked into Dean Martin's place, had a nice meal there, and the friend I was with, Mike Varel is his name.

All right.

Dean Martin's restaurant called Dinos. His first cousin was the maître d'. Dean Martin's first cousin and Mike, my friend, behind my back, tells the first cousin the maître d' tells him that I like Dean Martin, that I've got every one of his albums, that I go see all of his movies, and that I watch his TV programs...

Settin' you up...

Settin' me up to get me up there and sing with this piano player who was from Peru and the stage was even with the bar. It was really a beautiful set up there. So after our meal, the maître d' invited me to the bar, both of us, and he got me a drink, a green drink, crème de menthe is what it was, beautiful, and we had a nice time there and he says something to the piano bar, to the piano man there, it wasn't a piano bar, the piano was up like on the piano bar and he starts playin' "Everybody Loves Somebody" and I couldn't sit still. I'm just singin' it at the bar, you know and the maître d' knew everything I did from Mike, so in return he said I want you to get up there and sing. I says no way. I mean people were really decked out nice. So he insisted that I did, so I went up there and sang in front of 350 people. "Everybody Loves Somebody," "King of the Road" and "I'm Not the Marrying Kind." And after that we had a good time and I got ready to leave and I met this talent scout from New York.

Oh.

And uh, and he in turn told me, the way he said it was I had a talent there that you could really get something rollin'! I said sure, we're leaving, come on Mike, let's go. So we hopped in my convertible and we went to the apartment that we were staying at. Fifteen dollars a week. *(He laughs.)* It was a nice place really. It sounds terrible but back then it was like a boarding house and you paid 15 dollars a week. The only bad thing about it was community showers and community kitchen. But it was alright, it was two blocks from the beach.

Right, right.

Let everybody else pay the forty dollars a week.

Yeah, sure, right, right. (They laugh.)

So what happened, the next morning I took Mike to the airport, after that I went back to the hotel, put on my swimming gear, drove down to the Fountainbleu, between the Fountainbleu and the Edenrock Hotels and I laid out in the sun. And the next thing I knew there is sand kicked, some of, this guy's kickin' sand in my eyes. I looked up and it's the same gentleman from New York that I met at Dean Martin's. He said I been following you all morning. I said you have? He said, yeah, I want you to come over and meet some friends of mine at the hotel next door to the Edenrock which was the Montclair Hotel and he introduces me to Don Rickles' mother and staying there was Ann-Margret. I didn't meet her, but she was staying there at the time. She was doing a show down there, so he thought that everything was hunky-dorey. Like he wanted to take me to New York or what-have-you, but he could do something for me. To cut this thing kinda short, I sang in front of all these gals down there, older ladies, and he made me stand on a diving board and I was singing some Tony Bennett songs at the pool there at the Montclair and later that afternoon he invited me, he said he wanted to take me out to eat. He said to meet him at the Fountainbleu at 8 o'clock. I got to the Fountainbleu, I'm driving this old '64 Chevy Convertible with spots on it, I pull up with these ladies and they got these gowns on and everything and I figure I don't belong here, you know. I said, I'll get this guy and we'll go out and get something to eat. So I parked the car, the guy said he's gonna park it and I walk inside and one lobby leads into another lobby into another lobby . . . how the hell you gonna find this guy?

Yeah. (They laugh.)

So we finally run into each other and he says come on I want you to meet another friend. I said I got the car waitin', he says forget about the car. We're going to eat here. I said OK. So we walk into this place called the Gee Gee Room and he walks . . . I said who we gonna meet? He says come on, I'll tell you later. I said, tell me, I'm dying to know. He says come on I want you to meet Uncle Milty.

Milton Berle.

Milton Berle. He walks up to Milton Berle and he says, he walks up to him and introduces me to him. Says Milton, I want you to meet a good friend of mine, Jack O'Brian, and he walks away. By that time I'm shaking hands with him and he said, Mr. O'Brian, I'm very glad to meet you, I understand you're a boxer. I said no, no. My names Tony Viviano and I'm from St. Louis, Missouri and he says Tony, I know all about it. Sit down, I'm pullin' your leg. So I sat down with him, his nephews, he had his niece there and a nephew and his gentleman, his talent scout by the name of Mr. Miller, OK. We sat there and had a beautiful meal. Steak and lobster.

Yeah.

He had this all set up for me and he said I hear you're talented and I

want to see you. I can't believe this whole trip. My buddy went back to college and here I am down in Miami for a couple of more days and this doesn't seem right, you know. You know I feel like I belong in the truck.
Yeah, it's new to you.

Yeah, it was real new to me and it was comin' into me almost too fast and we had a beautiful meal. Mr. Miller gets up and Mr. Berle was just a perfect gentleman the whole night and we had a good time, and Mr. Miller gets up and walks up to the bandstand and gives me this fantastic introduction sayin' Tony Viviano, live from St. Louis, Missouri, and he's going to come up and sing a few songs and I said, my God, I don't even know what keys are. I don't know what modulation is in anything and I got up there and I chatted with boys that were there, and we did, "My Way" by Frank Sinatra, "I Want to Be Around to Pick Up the Pieces" by Tony Bennett. Just those two, I think it was, and Milton Berle said right then and there, he said that you're going to go to Vegas. I said no, you got to be nuts. At that time I said I didn't want to go because . . . that was in 1971. '71 it was. Milton Berle was playing at the Playhouse down in Miami and I just felt like I didn't belong, you know. I told him I had just heard the news that a lot of entertainers are into drugs and are into heavy drugs. This Rodger Miller I heard was taking a hundred and sixty-two pills a day. I said I don't want to have nothin' to do with that. I don't need that kind of life. He said you just come on out, we'll make sure everything runs smooth for you. So, I couldn't get away. The produce business was so big I couldn't get away. This was . . . when I met him it was in January of '71. February went by, they wrote me a letter. Come on, your ticket's waiting for you at Lambert Airport, we want you to come out. I didn't get out there until my brother Jerry, who was in college in Columbia, came home, he took over my route for me, and I took off. July 8, 1971. And I was out there for 5 days. I got out there and Mr. Miller met me at the airport. By the way, Mr. Miller's son owns Lollipop Records in New York.
Oh.

OK. His son is the guy that wrote that song "Ah Ha, Don't Let the Rain Come Down." Remember that?
Oh, yeah.

His son wrote that, so he met me there and the hotel was free at Caesar's Palace, brought me straight there and everything was set up. I put everything in my room and came back to meet him in the lobby there and I get a message that he had an emergency call, he had to leave. I don't know, he had to go back to New York or something. Something strange came up and very important. Milton Berle wasn't there, he was back at the Playhouse again. I missed him. So here I am stuck in Las Vegas, ready to audition for nobody.
Yeah.

And nobody's there. So that evening I saw the Tony Bennett show. He was appearing at Caesar's and the next day I get up and I try to make some contacts to these people and I couldn't, so I was really disillusioned, I was really upset about it cause here I left my business to come out here and try this out.

Everybody's giving you the . . .

Giving me the . . . so that afternoon the very next day I met Tony Bennett at the pool and I tell him the whole story about Miami's incident down there. He tells me who to see and who not to see. I get on the phone and speak to this gentleman by the name of Sidney Gathard. He says blah, blah, blah, you got an agent? I said no. He said well, I'll talk to you later, boom. I call him back and I said Mr. Gathard you don't understand. Mr. Bennett told me to call you. He said fine, you got an agent, I'll talk to you, otherwise I can't talk to you. You got to have somebody to represent you here, because if I hire you and then you split, I'm stuck and uh goodbye. I called him for the third time. I said you do not understand what I'm saying. I came all the way from St. Louis to come out here and audition here at Caesar's Palace through Mr. Miller and Milton Berle. He in turn again said get Mr. Berle's agent, get Tony Bennett's agent, but get an agent. OK. I know nothing about keys, right? All I know is, put the needle on the record and play it and sing it.

(J.J. laughs.)

So, I'm upset, so I got to get to Tony Bennett. How in the heck are you gonna get to Tony Bennett? That's tough. All I know is that he is performing there. So I go to the Coffee Shop and I meet one of the Golddiggers that was performing in the show and I started talking to her and she was the lead Golddigger, the lead singer, the lead vocalist. Francine was her name. Francine says you are my cousin, I'm gonna get you backstage. So you gotta go two floors up to go backstage and come down, see? And she got me backstage and the stage manager thought that I was the cousin. She takes me into the green room where Tony Bennett is getting ready to do the show. He was watching television. In fact he was watching a special for Louie Armstrong who just passed away back then and people were comin' in and out of the door and he was cussin' and sayin' get the hell out of here I want to watch this program and they had Peggy Lee on there singing some of the songs a little tribute, everybody was doing a tribute to him.

Yeah.

So, the stage manager comes in and says Francine, you're on. He looks at me and says, you, you're out. Get out. You don't belong here. Tony Bennett says, that's alright. He's OK. Mr. Bennett, he says, nobody is allowed backstage. He (Tony) said its alright, I know him, it's my friend Tony. I thought, man I'm in now. Here I am standin' there watching this special with Tony Bennett. I feel like an idiot watchin' this special with Tony

Bennett, his agent, all his stage men and a few minutes go by and he takes me back to the bar and he says, Tony, I understand the whole thing. I understand you called Sidney. . . . I said I called him three. . . . He says I know you called him three times. He said meet me here between shows. He's got an 8 o'clock show and he's got a 12 o'clock show. He says meet me between shows and I'll talk to you about it and I'll tell you what I can do for ya. So I said OK. So I left and I said you'd better explain it to this manager because this guy's hot. He don't want me around here. He said you tell 'em. So I walked out, I told the manager, before I leave I want you to know Mr. Bennett wants me back. And he was so mad. Oh God, he wanted to throw hands, he really was so hot. I said just to let you know he does want me to come back. So I leave and come back fifteen, twenty minutes ahead so I don't miss 'em. I sit there and I'm watchin' the show live up against the curtains. I couldn't believe how these sound men were crankin' him up on these high notes, but they were . . . that was amazing, that's another story in itself. So I meet Tony Bennett, we talk, we even sang a song together. "Something in the Way She Moves" (Tony sings it) "Attracts Me Like No Other" . . . We did that and he told me to see somebody up in New York and the trip to Vegas was free and I didn't want to go through another one of these ballgames and I never did take that trip but he did set me up. He told me to go across the street and see Harry Mills of the Mills Brothers and Bob Newhart down the street so maybe you can get lined up with Dean Martin and somebody can do something for ya. Cause I was doin' some imitations of Dean Martin in front of the Golddiggers which they thought was pretty good.
Right, right.

So I did and Harry Mills and Bob Newhart got me to audition along with Tony Bennett at the Riviera. I sang there with a sixteen piece orchestra.
This is nice.

This was really nice. No music. I didn't know how to read it. All they did was play it for me. So after I left Vegas, you know. I came back here to St. Louis and I was just wantin' to get to work someplace because I know I can do it now. They got the trip, you got the trip, you got something goin' for ya.
Right, right, right.

So '71, '72 comes along and I'm working in these little pubs, it's called the Topper. The old Topper was on Natural Bridge, the new one is in Riverview on Chambers. We sang there a long time. On Friday and Saturday nights. The piano player's name was Don Kamp. No money, I just sang for nothin'.
No money, just tryin' to get that name out there.

I was just singin' and we had good crowds and then one night, Friday

or Saturday night if I wanted a date, I went out and they could get a little upset. They'd call my mom up and say where's Tony? He didn't show up and we want him *(They laugh.)* it wasn't that there was no money it's just that I had a date.
Yeah.

So he said he wanted me to be there every Friday and Saturday. He wasn't gonna pay me anything and I said well at least give me a PA system. They had two cracked speakers and a microphone that looked like it had been run over by a Mack truck.
I can imagine. . . .

So what happened, I sang there and somehow I just . . . oh uh, your friend Charlie Carpenter he was workin' with some guy Merrit Reed. Merrit Reed was the guy who came over, for just try-out use, a speaker. We tried these speakers out, and these older folks, since I was singin' older songs thought that I was a rock and roll band all of a sudden. So they started callin' me names and everything, get this rock and roll loud speaker. We don't want this loud stuff. And when they heard it, it was nice but the boss did not want to pay for nothin', so I quit singing.
Knowledgeable about what is going on musically and they know nothing about what's happening really, but they are in charge of everything, and that's sad really.

So I left the club and I went about half a mile up the road to a club called the Bissell Lounge. Had a lady piano player. Some set-up cracked speakers, microphone all . . . so I turned around and I bought me a P.A. system. Fourteen hundred dollars for it. I paid something like seven hundred fifty dollars for it. It was a nice unit. I asked the guy if he minded if I brought it up and he said no, I don't mind. She was gettin' paid twenty-five dollars a night. I think the most persons that came in there was about three or four on Friday, on Saturday night we'd have about eight or nine, you know, and we got workin' in there. We started rehearsing with this lady. She knew a few people for singing like in Hill Day or U City Fair at the Square and I started singing with her and it was goin' pretty good. I don't know too much about music, all I know is, I can sing it and you play it. Later on I realized what was going on, she was playing the melody and I'm singing the melody. It came out OK but it's not what you really want, you know what I mean?
Yeah, right.

But I didn't really know any better at the time. What I did, I kept working there and I didn't drink all I drank was 7-Up and the drummer he had to pay for his own beer, he didn't get paid and the joint started getting packed every Friday and Saturday night. I heard the waitress say there's another 800 dollar night, there's another 600 dollar night, there's another 700 dollar night and I said I'm not gettin' nothing. . . . I been bringing my

P.A. system up here, every Friday and Saturday night and you're not giving me change for a quarter? You know what I'm saying.
Yeah.

I just told her politely, just give me something for just bringing the stuff up here. I understand I'm gettin' myself a little name goin' which is good for business. P.R. So he gave me 10 bucks. Big heart. Ten dollar bill. I'm not gonna do nothing 'cause he put an ad in the paper. Wow! So I think I worked another two weeks, three weeks. It was all through the spring, is what it was. Then the summer came along, that's what it was, and then a gentleman came in from Alton, Illinois. He owned a club called The Midtown Lounge. Kid you come over to my club and I'll pay you $75 a night, just for you. He said how long you booked here? I said, uh *(They laugh.)* uh, well uh, I'll have to get back with you right away *(He laughs.)* and it was the very next week I quit that club. No, I take it back, I worked another week and then I let everybody know where I was going. *(He laughs.)*
Right.

And everybody went over to the Midtown across the bridge, see I didn't get really mean about it, it's just that . . . .
That's business.

That's pure economics, that's what it is. I want to make a livin' now.
Right.

Who's gonna pay for the P.A.? So I went over there and they booked me there for 17 weeks, straight ahead, and I had a great time. After that we came back across the river and we went to the Ramada Inn at Bellefontaine and 270. Worked there for 42 weeks straight. Left there and went to a club in Belleville, Illinois called Fishers Restaurant. You know Fishers is a very nice club. Worked there for six or eight weeks. Left there, went to Schien-horsts Hofamberg Inn in Clayton. Highway 40 and Clayton Road. We were there for about eight, nine weeks. Left there and we went to the Chase Hotel at the Steeple Chase with Paul Stanth and he had the comedians with him that opened the show. After that I went to the Ramada Inn over here. But we kept climbing the ladder and went back to the Ramada Inn with Jimmy Becker. You know Jimmy Becker?
Oh Jim? Yeah, yeah. Very good friend.

We did the Ramada Inn again for thirty some odd weeks. It was like another home plate. It was right close to home. So then I got out of it for awhile and I was doing private parties, weddings, singing in churches . . . parties, you know, private parties, charities, the UNICO, the Marriot, pro-duce row dinner dance, got married, went to Hawaii you know on the nice vacation we had, by the way the Hawaii trip was damn near free. We got a gentleman, a friend of mine that knew a guy, that knew a guy in the airlines. The flight, in other words, it only cost us from Los Angeles to Hawaii, Hawaii to Los Angeles. The trip from St. Louis to Los Angeles was free, you understand. So that was the way it went. One of the gentleman, one of the owners of a club that would never hire me. He would never, ever hire me. We've asked him to come in to see me at the Ramada Inn. He'd come in, he'd see the whole show, he'd stay the whole night. He'd come in another night, he'd sit there with some of his waitresses, see the whole show, the whole night. He did this, I don't know how long I don't know how many weeks I'd say out of the 42 weeks we were there he came in at least a hundred times, I don't know how many times, and he would never hire me. He'd see the place packed and everything and he would never hire me. So I even walked up to his club one night with my girlfriend, she was my girlfriend at the time, by the way my wife's name is Billie. Put that on there. *(Billie laughs and says, by the way)* Billie and I went up there and talked to the guy and said, look don't pay me, just pay the musicians, put me on for just three weeks, two weeks, no pay. But if it does good for you then start paying me. I said that's all.

You can't beat that.

You can't beat that. He said I don't like to make changes and if I get up here and you get real popular then you'll want to go someplace else and I got nobody. I said you got be kiddin' me. I ain't goin' nowhere. I live right here. This is the finest club around. The name of his club was Rizzo's Top of the Tower. And he wouldn't hire me. All the other musicians said, yeah it's a great gig, try to get it and he wouldn't hire. So I'm married now in 1978. This was in '79. I meet him at a stop sign. His big Cadillac pulled up and he had this big dog in the back seat and he rolled that window down, the power windows went down and he says, what are you doing now? I said I'm singing with Russ David which I was at the time, the county Parks and Recreations, all around Queeny Park, North County, Hemann Park in U City, all of them, and he says OK and he took off. Next thing I know is, he called my cousin who delivers the produce to his place. A.J. Catamaro. He said have your cousin Tony call me up. I called him up and he told me he hired an organ player who was actually an organ salesman, he only knows 12 songs to sell the organ. I need you to come on up and help me out. He's actually in his older age and he comes up with his high school picture and all this kind of stuff. *(He laughs.)* It was really a funny sight, it really was. So here we are up there with this Wurlitzer organ, oh it was a mess. It was like putting perfume on a pig. That's what it was, so I just, I got up there in a tux, 'cause he was in a tux you know, we were all dressed up and if I wanted something done in B Flat he said OK we'll do that in F. If I wanted something in E Flat he said OK we'll do that in C. He said you don't understand. I can only play in C, F and G. I'm the one that plays this thing and I make it sound good, you gotta match what I play.

(J.J. laughs.)

So I told Joe the first night, I said that's no good. He said well you stay one more night, do me a favor and stay one more night. I said if I can take it because I'm ... oh man.

It's like whippin' a dead horse. So the next night went by and I told Joe Rizzo, I said get rid of him and call me when you get rid of him and I'll come up here with my own accompaniment. So he was contracted with this guy from October all the way through December. Couldn't get rid of him. So I started in January after the first.

Finally.

Started up there with Ernie Hays, you know who Ernie Hays is?

Yeah, yeah.

Plays for all the hockey teams, and ball clubs in St. Louis and Don Fette. They would substitute because Ernie had the baseball games. So he got going with me, got me started up there, with that big Baldwin Organ and then we got rollin' and we didn't know whether the Cardinals were going on strike or not, so they didn't go on strike so Ernie had to go to the ballgames and Don Fette was pretty busy so I looked for another piano player. Which I did. I got another piano player and his name was Eric Lindstrom. I worked with him and we stayed there, you know. But it worked out very well for us and Jerry Burger would show up and different writers would show up. It's nice, I'm just glad to see it's gettin' off the ground now. So after that sixteen and a half months Sarky Webbie calls and wanted me down at the Mayfair. Instead they changed their mind and they opened up with Marty Bronson. Then after that they called me and said come on down, so I did, I brought my band down and then I pick up an excellent gentleman by the name of Kenny Rice. So now I got three in the group, well before Kenny Rice at Rizzo's Top of the Tower, I picked up Freddie, saxophone player, there was three of us up there, then we picked up Kenny Rice and we were down at the Mayfair. We were there for 21 weeks. We left there, we took off a month in August and then we went to the Plankhouse. We worked at the Plankhouse for one month. Then we went to Kansas City for two weeks. Casconies, north of the river area which is an excellent club. After that we came back to the Plankhouse and we were booked all the way through New Year's Eve. We left there, we took off in January and we started in February 1982 at Stan and Biggies at the airport. We were scheduled to be there for one month and they were going to bring back Ollie Ramond instead he put me on for February and March. After March he put me on for April and May. When that was over, well during the month of May we were working at the Tower Club Tuesday nights only and if that went he was going to put me on for the summer, which he did, so currently we're at the Tower Club at Westport Plaza on Thursday, Friday and Saturday nights. That's where we are now. So.

Did you ever do any recording, Tony?

I did do a recording. In fact I went into Technosonic and I brought a

record in there with me, it was already a pre-recorded record, took the music off it and put my voice onto that music. Thirty piece orchestra.
How did it go?

It's going very well, very well. I use it in my resume when I send it out.
You did.

Because I couldn't afford a thirty piece orchestra.
How well I know, I know. (They laugh.) One question I think we've probably forgot. How long have you been with the Local 2197 in St. Louis?

Since 1974.
I know you intend to extend your new career as far as it . . . as far as you can go.

I'm not finished, no, no you keep going.
(J.J. laughs.) Everybody has a dream or a vision or whatever, they should have anyway. I do, everybody should have and I know you do and. . . .

Well, let me flash back here a little bit. When I was in Vegas that was 1971, I went to Vegas again in 1977, and through some connections I met Elvis Presley's conductor Joe Gershaw who told me to forget about trying to sing all the time, to learn what the musicians are talking about, pick up an instrument and learn it. Get a guitar or something so I came back home to St. Louis and I bought a guitar and I learned it. On Channel 9 they teach you how to play a guitar and I learned it and I can converse with a musician on keys and modulation. . . .
All right.

Changes but currently there's this movie I'm kinda interested in. They're making the life story on Bobby Darin.
Right.

And I'm kinda of excited about that.
I was hopin' we would kinda mention that too and we want to inject that whenever we're talking about Tony Viviano.

What else, maybe you might have something. . . .
But in our closing, we are getting near the end of our interview, I'd like to, what we try to, is there anything you would advise any of the people who are striving or studying, any advice that you would give them of your past experiences, that maybe would help some person who is trying to do anything at all musically?

The main thing is to not give up, I found that out. You can't give up, cause you give up.
In other words, once you set your mind or your goals, you have to hang in there.

Don't give up. Do it. Don't be a tryer, be a doer.
Right. Is there anything you want to put on this particular tape before we end the interview?

If there's anything you like to ask me. . . .
I think we've covered Tony from birth till now and places, times. . . .

Oh, there's many stories I could tell you about singing on the truck, sleeping on potato sacks and all that kind of stuff, but you know. . . .
But this is the main one that we got now. This is Jimmy Jones and I've been in the home of Mr. Tony Viviano and it's been an enjoyable evening, we're hoping what he said will be read by many, many people and we hope it will help someone.

Another thing I would like to say is, I owe quite a bit to the musicians who have been backing me up this past two and one-half, three years. They earn a lot of praise because they are fantastic musicians, they really are. *Anyone in particular?*

Kenny Rice, Freddie Delgaudio, Jimmy Kreisman, Gary Gatlar, Jimmy Jones. Thank you very much.

Following are three important dates in Tony's career:

> *December 1983* Opened the "Carol Channing Christmas Show" at Westport Plaza, St. Louis, and played one week with his own band.
> *March 1985* Opened for Domenico Modugna (original artist of Italian hit, "Volare") at the American Theater, downtown St. Louis, with his own twelve-piece orchestra.
> *April 4, 1987* Opened at the Chase Hotel for Julius LaRosa and Pat Cooper with Tony's twelve-piece orchestra for the UNICO Benefit.

Mitchell Wadley Bass player/Born St. Louis, Mo./Handwritten interview by Mitchell Wadley.

I was born at (St. Louis) city hospital and raised in St. Louis.

My mother and father struggled drastically to survive throughout the years. We were a big family of six girls and six boys.

My father was a man that loved many things, he loved to fish, building homes, and most inspiring to me was music. My mother told me that Jake had an Indian friend named Do-Ci, that played harmonica and that they would go down to the railroad tracks and make many people happy.

When I was about thirteen years of age, my mother sent me and my sister to Montgomery, Alabama, where she was raised, to make money in the field. About three years later we came back and periodically we would go back and forth. Being in St. Louis there wasn't very much to do, because of the construction taking place and people were like scattered chickens all around. I didn't have many friends, like some of the others because we were always raised to going to church. So my parents put us in a Catholic school. After coming home I would always pick up my father's guitar (which I called a music box) and he would hear me stroking, and seldom I would get scolded.

About my nineteenth birthday, my father died of pneumonia. After the

Mitch Wadley

funeral arrangements, and we all got over the hurt, my mother said, "Son, I'm going to give you your dad's guitar." (Boy was I happy!) She said, "[Your] father said [you] may be famous one day."

At that time my mother didn't have very much money, so I couldn't afford a new set of strings (three were missing), so a few months later a family moved in upstairs from us named the Martins. I asked if they would need any help, so they let me, and one of the sons named Vincent ended up being my friend. So I would go up to his house and he would be playing songs that really sounded good. I told him that I had a guitar, but three strings were missing, so he gave me a set and we started working together. I would play things that he showed me, ended up being bass lines. So I wanted a bass so bad that I saved all of my money that my mother gave me for lunch, and that year at Christmas I got it. People would come from all around to hear us and would throw money that would mount up to getting the amplifier costing $50.00. I practiced every evening, and Vincent inspired me so much, that of this day I can truly thank God for being gifted because now I'm inspiring Vincent.

And I went on learning from everyone I could, like Oliver Sains, Clayton Love, Fred Sample, Jimmy Jones, Ike Turner and James Brown.

Now I'm playing gospel music in church, and doing studio sessions, and hopefully I'll get that big break in producing!

Jimmie Walls Drums/Born February 10, 1921, East St. Louis, Ill., died 1968, East St. Louis, Ill./Information from his aunt, Bessie Walls.

Jimmie was born in 1921 in the East St. Louis area. He went to grade school in East St. Louis, and then later he decided he wanted to go to Chicago to go to high school, where he did quite a bit of studying. After coming back to East St. Louis he played with a lot of different people, and then he decided to form his own group, and that group worked St. Louis Metro East, Brooklyn, Cahokia, Belleville and the Scott Air Force base area.

Jimmie had a brother. The only person I know in his family that was musically inclined was his brother Huston Walls who was a saxophonist. Huston was a little older than Jimmie. He was born in 1918. Huston studied under Edgar Green.

Jimmie Walls created the nickname of "Big Thunder," the reason being, he would take both drum sticks and make a loud, deep, melodic tone on his drums. Even though he was kinda small in stature, that would classify him as a big guy. He was a quiet man, but when he was on the drums he was called Big Thunder.

Jimmie worked many places in this area, a place called Scotties and another club called the Bamboo and I'm sure that his band was noted all around the St. Louis area.

He was devoted to his mother after his father passed away. He moved back home to take care of her, and he looked after her until he passed away. At that time he was living on the corner of Nineteenth and Trinley.

Jimmie died in 1968, but he died leaving a beautiful memory of being a very fine musician, and a very talented person. He backed a singer called Luther Ingram who made it big.

Eugene Clifford "Stumpy" Washington Drummer/Born January 10, 1931, Pine Bluff, Ark.

Stumpy's family moved to St. Louis when he was eight months old. He attended Denver Side, John Robinson, Dunbar and Lincoln High School. He received a private pilot's license from the Lake Side School of Aviation. He was a member of the U.S. Air Force for one year and he was honorably discharged.

Stumpy became interested in drums when a brother returned from the U.S. Marine Corps. He studied under Wheety Morris, a renowned drummer, and played in the metropolitan area with various bands until the early '50s. Stumpy joined the Ike Turner Kings of Rhythm band during the rock and roll years, and stayed until the group recorded a hit tune, "Tore Up."

George Brazier (left), "Stumpy" Washington, Jenise Staton, Jimmy Jones.

The band left town and since became known as the Ike and Tina Turner Revue.

Stumpy stayed in the city and formed the Caravan's Orchestra and worked the Metro area for a few years. After dispersing the group, he joined the George Hudson Orchestra for a few years, and then left the orchestra because of his job as an over-the-road truck driver. He is still in that field.

He has worked with, recorded and traveled with such musicians as Billy Gayles, Clayton Love, Albert King, Jackie Wilson, Chuck Berry, Lloyd Price, Little Willie John, Gatemouth Brown and many others.

He is married, has children and is still living in the East St. Louis area and still plays occasionally.

Hugh D. "Peanuts" Whalum Sax, trumpet, piano, bass violin, drums, vocalist, composer and arranger/Born September 8, 1928, Wilberforce, Ohio.

"Peanuts" Whalum was a member of the Wilberforce Collegians Orchestra which won a band poll in 1947 and played Carnegie Hall in New York City. He played first trumpet, doubled on tenor sax and did vocals with the 18-piece band. He earned a B.S. degree at Central State University at Wilberforce, Ohio, in 1948.

Peanuts moved to St. Louis in September of 1949 and was enrolled one

Eugene "Stumpy" Washington

semester at the Lincoln University School of Law at Jefferson City, Missouri, in 1950, and another semester at St. Louis University School of Law in 1958.

He is affiliated with Local 2197, American Federation of Musicians, and has played with Count Basie, Lionel Hampton, George Hudson, John Cotter, and others, including the "Peanuts" Whalum Band and Trio.

He's been on stage in Carnegie Hall, New York, Savoy Ballroom, and Apollo Theater, New York City, Kiel Auditorium, St. Louis, Civic Auditorium, Nashville, and others. His club dates have been in many cities: New York, Chicago, Milwaukee, Cincinnati, Cleveland, Dayton, Columbus,

Springfield, Ohio, Sacramento, and most recently these clubs in St. Louis: Fedora, Union Station, The 7th Inn, Cheshire Inn, Al Baker's, Greenbriar Hills Country Club, and Old Warson Country Club.

Television and radio credits include KSD-TV, KMOX-TV, KTVI, KETC-TV, and radio station KMOX.

His recording credits are: arranger for "Pow, Jeannie Trevor Sings" on Mainstream Recording Company Album #5605. Peanuts also performed on saxophone and piano with the quartet Tres Bien on the same album. He recorded "St. Louis Is" (original composition), and "I Remember You," piano and vocal, Norman Records.

Over the years, in between his music, he has worked as a cartographer, school teacher, automobile tire salesman, automobile salesman, insurance salesman, and health inspector for the City of St. Louis.

He has been married to Veronica Whalum for the past 36 years. They have seven children.

Mae Florence Wheeler Jazz vocalist/Born May 15, 1934, Memphis, Tenn./Telephone interview by Lyn Cunningham.

Mae Wheeler was born in Memphis, Tennessee on May 15, 1934. Her mother's name is Amelia Lucille (Adams) Warren, born in Crystal Springs, Mississippi. Her father's name was Darde Smith. He was born in Forrest City, Arkansas. Mae's mother and grandmother were singers. Her father was not a musician.

Mae started her singing career at age three in Memphis and her family moved to St. Louis when she was four years of age.

Mae attended Lincoln Grade School in Richmond Heights, Missouri, Douglas High School in Webster Groves, Missouri, and Forest Park Junior College in St. Louis for two years, taking general courses.

Mae has a natural-born talent, but she studied with Maxine Brucestarks, Kenneth Brown Billups, Wirt D. Walton, and Mrs. Bonner. She has worked with most of the St. Louis musicians and a great many others, such as Sonny Stitt at The Gallery in East St. Louis, Pearl Bailey at Westport Plaza, Arthur Prysock in *Carousel*, with Russ David on his radio show, and has traveled with a gospel group performing at RKO Radio City, The Palace Theater, and The Apollo and New York City, and The Ted Mack Show, with Chick Finney on the "Stars of Tomorrow" in St. Louis, Missouri.

Mae's first paid job was at the Kiski Social Club and Cosmopolitan Ladies Social Club in 1955. She received twenty-five dollars. She has made no recordings as of yet.

Mae's advice to younger musicians is, "Have determination, always give your best, always continue to grow and learn the things to always make you better. Learn to read music and study theory. Practice and learn to

"Peanuts" Whalum

believe in yourself. Help others to grow. And last but not least, trust in God."

Thelma "Tee" Wiley Saxophone/Born November 1923, East St. Louis, Ill., died November 1978, Belleville, Ill./Handwritten interview by her nephew Joe Wiley.

[Thelma] began playing saxophone at the age of 18. After taking a couple of lessons she began to play by ear.

The first group she played with in 1941 included her two brothers, Milton Wiley and Raymond (Jack) Wiley. Other members of the group were Floyd Naylor, Frank Gully, Ervin (Broz) Woods, and Joe Coleman. She played with this group for approximately two years.

She then joined Ben Thigpen's Band. She played with Thigpen for six years.

She played with Tiny Davis' band for two weeks at the Circle Bar in St. Louis. Tiny Davis offered Tee a job to tour with her band, but she turned down the offer.

She played with Ben Thigpen's Band longer than any other group. Other bands she played with included Hattie Harriet's all woman band, Tab Smith, and Flora Bush, the pianist and organist.

Noted musicians and singers who she set in with included Clark Terry, Bob Graf, Jimmy Forrest, Stan Getz, Lester (The Prez) Young, Miles Davis, Floyd Naylor, Lee Howard, Freddie Twin, Chuck Berry, Ike Turner and Dinah Washington.

She was a very versatile musician. She played jazz, classic, rhythm and blues.

She played throughout St. Louis and East St. Louis, Illinois.

Ernest "Ernie" Wilkins Piano, saxes, composer/Born July 20, 1922, St. Louis, Mo.

Ernie's mother started him at an early age on piano. He attended college at Wilberforce University. Ernie joined the Navy for three years, playing at the Great Lakes Training Center with Clark Terry, Willie Smith, and Gerald Wilson. He was with George Hudson's Band in St. Louis, with Earl Hines' last big band in 1948 and then returned home to St. Louis.

1951 Joined Count Basie.
1955 Settled in New York.
1956 Gave up playing entirely except for an overseas tour with Dizzy Gillespie. He wrote arrangements for Tommy Dorsey, the year before Dorsey's death.
1958–1960 Worked for Harry James Band, and did scoring for record dates and continued to write for Basie.

Wilkins contribution to the Basie Band during the 1950s was an important factor of its success. He also helped modernize the Harry James Band.

A list of his LPs are "Trumpets All Out," "Top Brass," "Flutes and Reeds," "Clark-Wilkins Septet" on Savoy label. He played with Basie on the Verve-Roulette label, Harry James on Capitol–MGM label, "Candido," ABC label, "J. Cleveland," "Dinah Washington Sings," "Fats Waller" and "Sarah Vaughan in the Land of Hi Fi," all on the Mercury label.

Ralph Williams Guitar/Born September 26, 1921, St. Louis, Mo., died 1984, St. Louis, Mo./Interviewed by Jimmy Jones.
Tell me Ralph, when were you born?

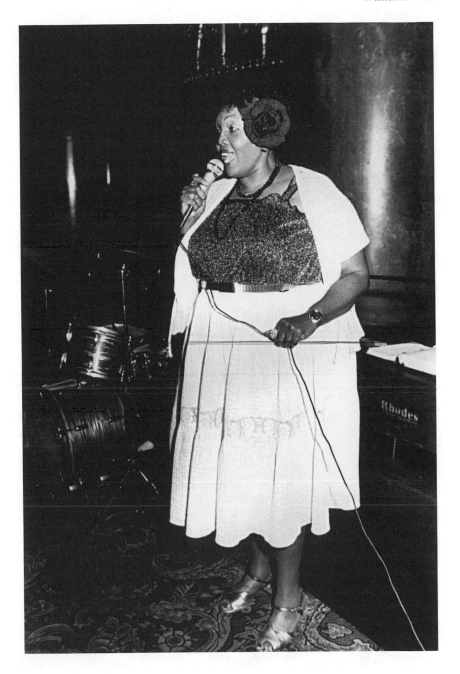

Mae Wheeler

"Tee" Wiley

Ralph Williams (center)

I was born September 26, 1921 at 3422 Pine Boulevard in St. Louis, Missouri. After I went to school I was introduced to a group called the Spirits of Rhythm. They consisted of five young men who left St. Louis and went to New York and made it big. Their names were Douglas Robbins, Douglas Daniels, Webber Daniels, Buddie Burton and Leo Watson. *Who was your musical inspiration in childhood, or did you have one?*

There was a man around here that was a terrific banjoist, he was Sherman William's father, and he also played guitar. Then there was Professor Moseby. The funny thing is Jim, my father was able to get my oldest brother violin lessons under Professor Moseby, my sister took piano, but when it

came my time the country was like it is now. Only we didn't have a recession, we had a depression.
Perfect timing, Ralph.
So I learned everything there was to learn out on the street corners.
Was your father a musician?
Back in Arkansas. He played drums and sang, but he wasn't a professional. He and my cousin U.S. Smith played camp meetings and whatever.
Yeah, I know, on the yard.
Then I met Calvin Ponder who had his base down at Booker T. Washington School here in St. Louis. He and his wife, Martha Davison, were on the *Gary Moore Show.* Anyway we left and went to Chicago and formed a group called The Black Cats. That was Sherman Williams, Henry Steward, Henry "Frog" Morris, myself and Calvin Ponder. Then it was back to St. Louis and up to Michigan City, Indiana. Then the war broke out and the group broke up.

I went into the service and was attached to an all white band. Then I got out of service and came back home for awhile and then went back to the coast. Then I went to Chicago and on to New York and got with the Orioles. Our last big hit was "Cryin' in the Chapel." The first song that made the Orioles was, "It's Too Soon to Know."

When I joined the Duke Ellington group there were some St. Louisans in that band. There was "Shorty" Baker and Wendell Marshall. Wendell was a bass player.
I haven't interviewed him yet.
I don't think he plays anymore, but he was a terrific musician.
Were you with the Ink Spots?
Yes, I was with them when I became ill in 1976. Sonny Till was with that group, he and I worked together. The last time I was in Australia I was with the Ink Spots.
The Ink Spots were like the Mills Brothers at that time. They were worldwide known groups.
I don't think many people know this but there were five Ink Spots groups. Five different groups and all of them making money all over the world, so that proves to me that they had to be one of the biggest organizations ever. Isn't that something to be able to take five groups and keep them going all over the world?
Like you say, they must have been doing something right.
Like with us, you know how hard it is to handle so much work. Here at home we can't, we just don't have time. We're only one person.
That is why I want to bring attention to St. Louis. We have here prominent musicians that are as good or better than some of the musicians that are paid a big salary and come in here from other parts of the country.
That's true, it's true. Like Jesus said, "I go to my own, and my own

receive not." Like when Clark Terry came to town and played at the Chase with that big band. Our own musicians could have been that big band. *Now that is what really irritates me about it.*

Like I was down on the Becky Thatcher. It was supposed to be Singleton Palmer's band and I looked around and Singleton wasn't even there, but they had a big Dixieland thing. This is a mockery.

I went to San Diego one time, and I was staying at Archie Moore's home, he was from St. Louis, the light heavy-weight fighter, and we were talking about things. He was a champion, but the only way he could make it was with his fists.
Just like we all do.

I had to leave here to make it with my art. They talk all this talk, but it's not fair. And Josephine Baker, she had to go to Europe. There's so many. All the managers end up millionaires, but we end up paupers. It's sad, but it's true. If I hadn't been a veteran, if I got ill I guess I'd starve to death. And Jimmy, this is what a musician's life is all about.
I thank you so much for your time and the information about your life and musical achievements. It has been a very pleasant afternoon talking to you.

I've talked to people who have worked overseas and those people accept us for what we are, people. We are people, we are people. . .

Terry Williams Organ/Born February 8, 1937, East St. Louis, Ill.

Terry Williams started his musical career at age 14. His father was a professional pianist, and his mother, grandmother and grandfather all played piano. This background played an important role in the life of this musician.

Terry Williams grew up in East St. Louis and led a very active life. He attended Lincoln High School and excelled in sports, particularly track. His spare time was all spent in the band room, where he was surrounded by the greats in music . . . Miles Davis, Eugene Haynes, Wendy Morris (who was a drummer for many years for Jackie Davis), Della Reese and Jimmy Jones, and many others of great talent. The bandmaster, Edgar Buchannon, taught and influenced all of these musicians, inspiring them to greater heights. Their vocal teacher, Daisy O. Westbrook, added her great talent to their development and has never been forgotten by any of her students. Terry was a soloist in the a capella choir and received many awards at state competition meets.

Terry formed his own combo in high school. Eight months later he was called on to play piano for Chuck Berry. That gave Terry his first taste of nightclub exposure, but that still didn't satisfy his desire to play jazz.

After a brief stay with Chuck Berry he joined a rhythm and blues band, Johnny O'Niel and the Hound Dogs. He toured with that group for about

Roland Clark (left) and Terry Williams

four years. He continued playing with R&B groups for many years, polishing his talent until he finally made contact with the jazz media. This happened when he was called to play piano as a fill-in with a tenor sax man named Jimmy Forrest who was working at the Club Riviera cocktail lounge. This was the moment of truth, and needless to say the ultimate goal for Terry. Jimmy Forrest like his style and ability and asked him to think of joining him in Denver, Colorado. Jimmy Forrest became ill and was away from music for almost six months. Once again Terry was out of jazz. But not for long.

Terry received a call from Tab Smith, who was a veteran recording

Terry Williams

artist. He told Terry that his regular organist, Flora Smith, was leaving him to go to Detroit and that he needed a replacement. Terry was chosen to replace her.

After a few weeks at Club "88," they made a tour through Indiana, Kentucky and Tennessee. Terry remained with Tab Smith until Tab's untimely death.

Terry once again formed a trio and started working clubs. He worked the New Frontier and Chilies Baby Grand Club.

After the death of his grandfather Terry opened a jazz nightclub in St. Louis called Mr. Mellow's Room. It became a meeting place for jazz lovers.

One night Louis Jordan, who was appearing at Geno's, dropped by to catch the show. He was more than pleased with what he heard. Two days later Jordan's organist, Big Jake Patton, became ill and Louis asked Terry Williams to take his place and finish the engagement.

After that Terry was booked into the St. Louis Playboy Club and stayed there for three years. The Playboy Club was the meeting place for all the stars. Every week brought in a new name: Jimmy Smith, Shirley Scott, Nancy Wilson, and Clea Bradford. They spent their time between shows with Terry.

Terry has since played the Billy Eckstine Show at Kiel Auditorium along with Timmie Rogers and the St. Louis Symphony Orchestra. Terry Williams name has become a household word in Kansas City, Missouri, the home of some of the greatest musicians of all times.

Robert Edward "Juice" Wilson Violin, sax, clarinet/Born January 1, 1904, St. Louis, Mo.

Juice's family moved to Chicago when he was three years old. He played the drums in elementary school, and in 1912 began studying violin and played for dances. He finished his career as one of the most outstanding jazz violinists.

> *1918–1919* Played with Fred Keppard and Eddie South, and on the Great Lakes excursion boats.
> *1919–1928* Played with James P. Johnson, Lucky Roberts and various bands in the East and was a jazz violin accompanist on records for blues singers.
> *1929* Went to Europe and Noble Sissle and remained in Europe.
> *1930* Joined Leon Abbey. Gave up violin for alto sax and clarinet. Toured North Africa.
> *1937* Went to Malta where he remained seventeen years with various bands.
> *1954* Worked in Lebanon, Italy and Gibraltar in American bars.
> *1960* He was playing in the Safari Club in Tangier.

Charles "Little Man" Wright Saxophone/Born June 17, 1927, Arkansas/Interviewed by Jimmy Jones.

This is Jimmy Jones and I'm in the home of Charles "Little Man" Wright. Where were you born, Charles?

I was born in Arkansas on June 17, 1927.

What were the names of your mother and father?

My father is Charles Wright, my mother is Emma Wright.

Were they born in Arkansas?

Yes. My father is still living, my mother is deceased. The only grandparent I can remember is my grandmother Fanny Knox. I don't know very much about my family.

Were any of them musically inclined?

Yes, my uncle Columbus Knox played clarinet. Another uncle, Charles Perry played a trombone. That's where I got my first horn, but I never could do anything with a trombone. My father plays violin and guitar. He's not an educated musician, but he's got talent and he can do a lot with a guitar and his violin.

You moved to this area at what age, Charles?

Five. I entered grade school at Dunbar on West Madison in East St. Louis, Illinois.

When did you first become interested in music?

I became interested in music at age ten. We had a fellow named Jimmy Forrest who lived across the street from me at that time, and at the first touch of his horn I knew I wanted to become a saxophone player. The country was in the depression at that time, but my mother bought me a horn at a pawn shop in Granite City, Illinois. It was soprano, but it was the curved soprano. Dave Barrett taught me the scale.

Now this Barrett, is that the doctor?

Yes. The late Dr. Barrett.

Everyone in East St. Louis can relate to and remember Dr. Barrett.

He taught me a method. Gave me ideas, told me what books I should buy, but this universal method took me all week on the saxophone, it was like getting a degree. I studied that for years. At this point I didn't have a job, I just studied, studied, studied. I came out of service in 1945 and went to Ludwig School of Music. Miller Brister from Ludwig got me a job with Eddie Randall's Seven Blue Devils. That was my first professional job.

Do you remember your first paid job?

Yes, that was at the Harlem Country Club in Brooklyn, Illinois. I got four dollars a night. I was getting my experience, so the pay didn't really matter.

There was a fellow around here named "Candy" Johnson, he went to Dunbar too. He told me to learn every scale that there was. Later on through the years I found out that this was the main thing in playing. About a month before he died, I was working down at Hannigans, and he came down a couple of nights in a row and said that he was glad to see that I was playing.

What were some of the big name groups you played with?

I worked with "Snookem" Russell, Tab Smith, Count Basie, Abbot King, B.B. King, and Ray Charles, also a few bands that are not known of today.

At this point you hadn't formed Leo's Five yet, because that was one of the greatest things in this area.

No that was during the sixties. We had Larry Proto, Kenny Rice, Don James and we had the great Eddie Fisher.

The masterful Eddie Fisher.

I wrote seven tunes on that Leo's Five Album, "Cookin' with Jessimae," "Leo Five Soul" and all of those seven tunes I had planned to do something with, change the pattern, change the form.

So at this point in the interview we know you worked for a lot of clubs and name bands, and we also know that you're still one of the best saxophone players in this area. I think everybody could take lessons from you. Everyone knows your name.

Well I can't say I'm one of the best saxophonists in the area . . . It's just a matter of style, everyone has a different style.

And no one can take that away from him. It's a God-given talent.

Sure. We must think that we are always going to be better, that's the only thing that keeps us going. I still believe that someone is going to listen to me. Without that we would have nothing to look forward to.

By the way, how did you get your nickname? Why do they call you "Little Man"?

Because I was small in stature and my horn looked bigger than I did.

I want to thank you Charles, and your family, for allowing me to come and take up a bit of your time and for this beautiful interview.

Jimmy, it's been a pleasure and let's meet and talk again sometime. Maybe we can put some other things together and exchange ideas. To have the exchange of ideas and feelings to one another, this is important to me.

Karen (Mooney) Zelle Vocalist, piano/Born April 19, 1957, St. Louis, Mo./Telephone interview by Lyn Cunningham.

Karen (Mooney) Zelle was born in St. Louis, Missouri on April 19, 1957. Her mother is Loretta Marie (Howett) Mooney, and her father is James Thomason Mooney, both born in St. Louis. Both were singers, but not professionals.

Karen attended Corpus Christi Grade School, Corpus Christi High School and Jennings High School. She went to Webster College and Community College for one year studying theater and music (piano theory) and graduated from the University of Missouri at St. Louis.

She started singing in 1976, at age 19, with a rock group called Babylon. In 1978 she was with a Top 40 dance group called Spankin, and was with another group called Fame between 1980 and 1983.

She started with Bob Kuban's Brass in March 1983 and was still with them as of 1985.

Her first paid job was a friend's wedding in 1975; she was paid $20.00.

Recordings: In 1982 she was back-up vocal on a country record with Jerry Loman. She has done TV training films for Maritz (1982).

Her advice to young musicians is, "Try to get along with the people you work with and learn from them, you can always learn something from everyone. Some things may be bad, but that's also a lesson."

Fred H. Zettler Trumpet/Born February 13, 1933, St. Louis, Mo./Interviewed by Jimmy Jones and Lyn Cunningham.
This is Jimmy Jones and I'm in the home of Mr. Fred Zettler. We're going to start our interview with Fred. I want to say good evening, Fred.

Good evening.
And we want to find out about your mom and dad. What were their names?

My father's name was Herman Zettler. No middle initial and that's my middle initial, Fredrick H. Zettler. My mother's name was Georgia Ida, maiden name, Nagel.
I noticed just a minute ago that we were mentioning grandpa.

Yeah, I didn't know him very well, he was quite old when I . . . he was about 65 when I was about four or five.
Uh huh.

His name was Oscar. (Zettler)
And he was affiliated with the big symphony?

I was told that he played violin in the St. Louis Symphony.
Fantastic. When were you first . . . grade school first?

Grade school . . . well, I was, I guess we ought to go back to Wellston. I was, I lived on Myrtle in Wellston and went to, I guess it was Myrtle Grade School, I don't know what the heck it was, it was in Wellston anyway, up to sixth grade.
Okay.

And that's where I began music. At the Hugo's School of Music in Wellston. My first teacher was Ray Bates. I was 11 years old when I started, so since I was born in 1933 that makes it about 1944.
So we should get your birthdate, month and year now, I think.

Yeah, Thirteen, February 1933. (February 13, 1933) That's my birthday. I remember that my dad got me the horn from Hugo's School of Music, just a few months before I was 11, on that Christmas, because I remember a guy named . . . what's the trumpet player at Hugo? Anyway one of the Hugo brothers was the brass person . . . it was something like Eric or . . .
But Hugo was his last name?

Yeah. Hugo's was the biggest school of music then, and he said we'll have him playing, "White Christmas" by Christmas. I played it a week after. Bad timing.
That was your introduction to music. Eleven years old?

No, I was interested in it earlier, but only because I was, my wife might disagree, but I was introverted. I needed things personally, by myself, and

I had seen things and heard things, and like I said, I said I saw Harry James with a trumpet and I heard the sound of it, and that's what I wanted. When my dad took me to the music studio, I remembered it very well, and it was the old time music studio, you know. They had hardly any instruments around. They had pictures of people playing them and whatever, and I said that's the one I want and it was Harry James with a trumpet.
Yeah.

That's what it was and I do know that I knew what it sounded like, but I had no idea how hard it was to play.
What was the first paying job that you had, do you remember?

Oh, yes! Oh, yes, very well. I was fifteen years old. As a matter of fact, Don Muckerman from St. Louis School of Music Service, president of that, hired me for that, and it was the prom night for Berkley School, and what might be interesting to you is, that Joe Riggs which you may or may not know, was the alto player, and that was his first job. Of course, he was about thirteen. And Joe is working in Vegas now. He was Harry James' band manager for fifteen or sixteen years, and he's now a musical director in Vegas. I was on one side of Muckerman and Joe was on the other, and he would take the music and say, "We're going to play this tune," and well, we didn't know the tunes, he'd put 'em up there and we'd play. I don't know if it was very successful or not, I don't recall that we got very many jobs. We didn't get any recording sessions.
Was that the first job?

Yeah, we made seven dollars.
Isn't that fantastic?

It was a lot for us.
That sounds like no money, but it was some money at that time.

You're right.
You could buy quite a lot with it.

You didn't have to go ask pop for a buck. It meant something then, not now.
Down through the years Fred, you've had some experiences that you would want known. Were there any big bands, that sort of thing . . . or any recordings?

Never had any recordings that was a commercial effort, you know. I have some down there that I'd be embarrassed to play for you, but on occasion play for myself, remembering . . . No, I played with a lot of good musicians, like I mentioned. I remember the first band I ever had was in high school. We called it the Top Hatters. In fact I even have some of those cards around, and ever once in awhile I look at 'em. Yeah, we had a big top. We had our stands that were made like top hats and we had a bunch of spangles on it and everything. It was terrible, and we didn't make any money, but then we didn't deserve it.

You don't have a picture of the band, do you?
Yeah, but it would be of very poor quality. Yeah, I do have one from my aunt's wedding, as a matter of fact.
We might be able to reproduce that.
Do you have one of the little cards?
Oh, yeah. In fact I have a card that Harry James signed.
What's the name of some of the clubs that you played around the St. Louis area?
We played Gaslight Square for Joe Bose. I had a band there for about two and a half years. Then we worked the Bow Club on Locust between 11th and 12th. The Den of Iniquity, and then the Hilton for about 17 weeks. The Purple Orchid, over in Granite City, Illinois, The Club Imperial. Everybody played that, Ike and Tina Turner. 'Course they made money. Yeah!
No, when you're talking about playing places, of course we played everywhere. Anything built in the last 40 years.
Sometimes people have humane things they do in a community that are not generally known. You can feel free to tell us about whatever . . . if there are any names of musicians that you would want mentioned, teachers, tutors, or . . .
All great teachers. I do want to mention Ray Bates, he's dead now, but he was my first teacher. I had him for about five years. I also studied with Eddie Bower and a lot of other people. Those were the people who had the greatest impact on the way I play.
I see, and that's important.
I guess it's important, I'm not workin' that much, but I could I think. The other thing I would like to mention is that St. Louis born musicians, there are so many magnificent ones. I earned my living playing hard for about seven years. That began on Gaslight Square. When I say earn my living, because I was working during the day too, but I was making most of my money at night, but thinking back to the people I met because of it . . . it means more to me now than the money. The money meant most to me then. When we were working Gaslight Square, Tommy Smothers was workin' for George Edick who owned the Emperial Club. Bad weather had canceled out the main act and that was when the Smothers Brothers were on the rise and they were the replacements. Anyhow, I was doing a dumb thing I had put together on money, funny. And I had ended with the old tune, "Funny, Funny, Funny What Money Can Do." There was hardly anybody in there when we started the last show and I looked across the way and saw a beautiful woman, who was Tommy's then wife, and a tall dark-headed, good looking guy who was Tommy's manager and Tommy Smothers. I looked at him and thought, oh hell. Here we were, going to do this show, and look who's out there. It wasn't that I wasn't proud of what

we were doing, but we were doing things on a shoestring, you know, and maybe he was too at that time, but it didn't seem like it, 'cause you'd see him on TV and this and that. We played the show and I did this little number. This is the truth. After the last show, we shut it down and went downstairs to the dressing rooms and changed. I was an MC, playing trumpet, all those dumb things you do when you're desperate for money. I got cleaned up, (I always take my horn with me) came out in my mackinaw and a big muffler around my neck, and I'm trying to sneak out because I could see they were still there at the bar, and I heard George Edick say, Fred, Fred, I got somebody here who wants to meet you, and I thought just what I said a minute ago. ____! I put my horn down, took my hat off, turned around and Tommy was three feet away from me with his hand out, like that. "Listen," he said, "I want to tell you something. I'm due at a party tonight, I got everybody on me, but I wouldn't leave until I told you how much I enjoyed that piece of stick you did up there." That's a true story.

Isn't that beautiful?

He was very nice. I thought, he really did want to say that to me. Tommy was complimenting me on a piece of stuff I put together. I offered it to him but he said it wasn't the kind of stuff that he and his brother did, but he really enjoyed it.

When you say shoestring budget, you mean it was a tight budget, right?

Well, yeah. In the beginning when the Roaring Twenties opened in Gaslight, it was pretty big and did pretty well, but like everything on Gaslight, everything just went down. I have my theory on that but I'm not going to tell it. The thing is I read all the editorials in the paper, that wasn't it.

We kinda know.

The thing was, what we had when we opened, we had really great second string players, not the people that were on TV or whatever. I remember there was Gus Van our comedian from Van and Skink, from the old Ziegfeld Follies. I mean, they were the people. The comedy routines and everything. Well Gus Van came down, old buzzard, I don't know how old he was but he was probably older than he looked, acted younger than most of us, was the supreme professional. They have the times up there, have to go so long, can't go no longer than in their contract, and he was beautiful and it always worked out. Everything worked out and if somebody screwed up, they just kinda covered, didn't get upset, like Jackie Mason, didn't jump up and down and act like a fool. I mean everything was just so smooth.

Just kinda blended it in.

It was fun to work with the older professionals.

Have you taught any music at all?

Oh, yeah, sure. Never for any official school system. Mostly private.

What clubs have you played at around town in the last few years?

Last few years? Not many. As a matter of fact mainly single engagements, mostly on the East Side. I had a group for about 19 years, it was my group.

What was the name of that group?

Cornucopia. But my drummer who was with me for the 19 years died in March of 1980, and the guy who was playing keyboard, Don Daughtering, moved to Bowling Green, Kentucky, and it wasn't the same group, so . . . but I met Jerry Brown on Gaslight Square and he's gone through all the club dates with me, we even played a place down in South St. Louis called the Cabana Club. It's now a Jehovah Witnesses Church, and believe me, even though I don't believe in Jehovah Witnesses, it's a better place.

It's a vast improvement?

Yeah. The Club Cabana, I remember it well. It was a burlesque comedian that started that thing down there, I don't remember his name. I got out of the service about 1955 when Mark was born (my oldest son) and I went to Harris Teachers College. I went to Washington University first, I couldn't afford it, then I went to Harris. I used to work at the Grand Theater. Of course I was hungry, had a wife and kid, and this guy wanted to know if I'd take the evenings for him. That was fun too, but that theater is gone now. The whole building is gone. It was Spanish Pavilion and whatever it is now. Yeah, I think they got it all sewed up down there because I was down there too.

I know what you're saying'. I think we should ask Fred about the statements that he would want to make to people or younger musicians, maybe what it would take to make a good musician, or what music is all about.

Well I have a couple of things to say if you're going to talk about that right now. Basics. I'm so tired of having young people come in and ask me what a waltz is, a drummer that asks what a waltz is, or a bosa nova, and I'm not saying anything against it. The fact of the matter is, we have so many young people out there that learn to do this little portion of what it is to be a musician, but they don't really learn to do what it is you have to do.

Right.

And that means beats. What's a good drummer? A good drummer to me, I don't care what he's playing if he has a good obligation to the beat. That's important to me. If a guy wants to come out and put on a big show, fine. But you better have somebody over there keeping the beat, because if you don't have a beat, you don't have anything.

That's the bottom line.

But that's the thing in all the instruments.

Like you said, it's the basics they're going to forget and that's what they're going to need.

I feel the most important thing is to be a fine musician. When you're talking about St. Louis, I think there's a couple of things I ought to mention. There was a group, it was a non-union group, but they were all kids. Bob Hoffmeir, they called it the Bob Hoff Band. He played the accordion (are you going to quote me?)

Yeah.

. . .Okay . . . rather badly. But the thing is, in that band he had Joe Riggs, who when you look into that, you'll find out how good he was, and Rich Daughtery. He had Jimmy Hayslip, he was fifteen years old, the youngest boy in the band. The thing is, we had three trumpets, three trombones, three saxes. Jimmy was fifteen years old when I met him in the Bob Hoff Band. We were a bunch of teenagers. It was the band going. It was the only band going that was definitely better. Jimmy Hayslip loves Dixieland, he works here right now (1983).

We'll find him.

But he was with Pete Fountain in New Orleans for about five years. Now going on with that other thing, Bob Hoffmeir also played 5th saxophone, but the most important thing about it was when we had Joe Riggs on the alto, and Roger Berger who still plays here and plays so well always. We had Rich Dancoler, we had Jerry Brown. In the trombone section we had Jimmy Hayslip, Rich Dancoler, who is a St. Louis musician and Jerry Brown played beautiful trombone and also is still playing around town, he plays electric bass and some other things, but we had a dynamite trombone section.

What would you advise young people coming up?

Work hard and practice the basics. The people who really did something with their music knew what the basics were.

We want to thank Mr. Fred Zettler for letting us have this moment of his time this afternoon.

Afterword: Music

African music was, is and always will be, the real basis of jazz. Different cultures in different parts of the world sometimes have difficulty under-standing this, because they interpret from different points of view, depending on their circumstances, their mode of life, their personal feelings, and why they use the music the way they do.

Music is a feeling. It is not just a beat or a rhythm, but the echo of a human voice crying to be heard through the centuries, yearning to communicate, to erase the prejudice and form the bond of love with feelings. These feelings are put into the instruments and the voices and when one listens, if one listens, no one can deny that the primitive feelings come through, that the vibrations stir the heart and somehow satisfy the human soul's longing to be happy, peaceful and free.

In our civilization today, feelings have been stifled, put behind a wall. People are not quite sure if they should let themselves go and enjoy the music that seems to leave their insides naked to the world. It is the basis of all experiences. Music is an integral part of everything, from birth to death. You don't have to be anything special to feel the power of it, it knows no boundaries. It is always there in some form, for one purpose or another.

Musical feelings celebrate, add pleasure to love, and live with you constantly from a baby's first cry until that cry ends at Heaven's gate at the end of life. It knows no race, creed or color. It is understood and revered by all as a way to get through each life with as much joy as possible. It doesn't matter if it's primitive or classic. It's the truth of humanity and in some form or another, it will always be right there for us to use and love. A constant friend. A moving force to listen to or participate in. A vehicle to tell stories, release feelings, express faith and all the myriad of other things that are hard to say or that there seem to be no words for.

During the earliest immigration to America many different influences in music were brought to our shores. Like the people themselves, it was a melting-pot of individual musical traditions. There were the work songs, ballads, popular music, church music, brass bands, all of which served their various functions for the pleasure and musical education of America.

215

Glossary

Ad lib Improvise or blow.

Axe An individual's instrument.

Back Accompaniment.

Back beat Secondary rhythm accent.

Band man Jazzman who excels in ensemble playing.

Barrel house Style of piano playing—"blue," seductive, syncopated, or rhythmic.

Battle Competition between two orchestras or instrumentalists.

Blackstick Clarinet.

Blewy Misplayed note.

Blowing group A group that uses tunes that they all know.

Blue note Flattened third or seventh note of scale. Impossible to show in written music.

Blues Song form, style and harmony originated by black Americans.

Bone Trombone.

Boogie-woogie Jazz or swing generated by eight-to-the-bar rhythms. Can be solo or orchestral.

Bop Also known as bebop or rebop. A way of describing staccato two-note phrase.

Boss Applied to jazzmen or their performance; authority, excellence.

Box An old, upright piano found in clubs and bars.

Breakdown A jazz dance originated by blacks, 1920–1935. Also applies to the fast music they danced to.

Bridge A refrain usually placed in the middle of a song for the featuring of accompanying ensemble.

Buck Trying to outplay the other fellow.

Bucket-o-blood Cut 'em up, shoot 'em up nightclub.

Burn To play music intensely and expertly.

Busy Said of a supportive and energetic drummer.

Cakewalk The dance or the music for it.

Call and response "Call" by a singer is answered by an instrument.

Canary Woman vocalist.

Carve To play better than someone else in musical competition.

Catgut Name of material used for strips on many stringed instruments.

Chance music Permits musician to play sections of a composition in any order he chooses.

Charts Arrangements, mental or written.

Cheat In jazz, stretching to cover limited musical skills.

Chicago style Replacement of tenor sax for trombone (as in 1920s New Orleans style).

Chops Technical ability on a given instrument.

Clambake A jam session.

Clincher Decisive happening, the end, fastening together musically.

Clinker Error in playing, missed note replaced by goof.

Coda Tailpiece or ending or a passage.

Collar the jive To understand what's being said. To be hip.

Cook To play with rhythmic inspiration.

Cook him (out) Best him musically.

Cool Early 1950s term for jazz, any soft introverted sounds.

Crank it up (behind a singer) Play behind a singer.

Cue Notes or words signaling singers or actors after rests.

Cut out To leave or depart.

Dada mama Drum roll.

Day gig Alternate job taken by jazzman for monetary reasons.

Dig To understand, to study diligently, recognize, listen to, hear.

Dirt Hot, earthy, driving jazz.

Dirty Robust, somewhat rough tone production.

Dive Worse than a nightclub.

Dog or dog tune Song of questionable musical quality.

Drive Musical power or energy.

Dues The things you put up with to get what you want.

Eight-to-the-bar Boogie-woogie.

Fake (it) To play a piece without music as though the music were in front of you.

Fanfare A flourish of trumpets.

Flügelhorn Brass instrument with valves similar to the trumpet.

Fluff To play a wrong note.

Frontline The featured group with a small band, up to eight pieces.

Funky Dirty music with blues feel, notes and tones distorted.

Gig A job.

Gone Out of this world, musically.

Goodie A good old tune.

Groove Preference, style, pleasurable routine.

Groovy All right. Fine.

Gut bucket Unrestrained brand of music played by small bands in dives.

Gutty Earthy music.
Hard bop East coast modern jazz style played by black jazzmen around 1954.
Harlem A popular swing music style with pronounced rhythm and earthy tone quality.
Head The melodic verse of a song.
Hide beater A drummer.
Hime (Hame) Any job outside the music business.
Hit Starting a song or a starting time for a job.
Hot Traditional jazz, not modern jazz.
Idiom A fragment or portion of music that is indicative of a style or period. A way of expression.
Improvise Music made up at the moment, not from memory or written music.
In the grove Carried away musically, inspired.
Ivories Piano keys.
Jam Improvision of hot music in groups.
Jam session A gathering of musicians improvising hot music after their regular jobs.
Jazz A musical form created in America characterized by skillful improvisation, distinct rhythmic punctuation and an original approach to instrument and music.
Joint A nightclub or living quarters.
Jook (Juke) String band that played in roadside inn-brothels, also dancing down to music.
Juice Joint A night club.
Jump Lively, animated music or dance.
Kick it around To improvise music freely.
Kick it off Leader of band stamping his foot at desired tempo for the musicians to begin playing.
Kitty Container for tips, very young girl.
Knocked out Superb, excellent, exciting.
Lame Square, but not beyond redemption.
Lay Back To fall behind rhythm.
Lick A musical or rhythmic line that is used for a "clincher."
Like Replace comma in jazz parlance.
Low-down Slow intense jazz in the manner of blues.
Mice Violins.
Moan To play or sing soulfully.
Moldy fig Modernist's name for Dixieland jazz admirer.
Moving out Playing jazz dynamically.
Noise Unwanted sound. Bad playing.
Oldie An old tune.

One-night stand One-night gigs in night clubs, theaters, etc., travel all day, work all night. Very tiring schedule.

Opener First tune of a set.

Original Tune composed by member of group, not a standard.

Paper Sheet music.

Paperman A musician who reproduces the score faithfully.

Party piano Boogie-woogie piano style.

Peck horn An alto horn or mellophone.

Peep To read sheet music.

Picker Player of bass or guitar of any string instrument.

Pickup Introductory note or notes leading into chorus or tune.

Piece Musical composition.

Pipe Any wind or reed instrument.

Pop A tune enjoying success at the moment.

Porkchop Slow barrelhouse style of jazz.

Quote To insert a phrase from another tune into one being played.

Race In the '20s and '30s, rhythm and blues was called "race" music.

Ragtime Ragtime was invented to describe the new syncopated piano style that developed among Missouri pianists.

Rag Initially a piano piece, sixteen bars, popular until 1928.

Raga Scale found in Eastern music.

Range Highest to lowest notes a particular voice can sing.

Rebop Highly technical and cerebral modern jazz ca. 1945. Also known as "bop."

Reggae An urban music style and dance originating in Jamaica in the 1960s. Closely resembles "rock steady." North American popular, Afro-American, Jamaican. Original Jamaican lower class music, expresses beliefs, classes, values, fundamental concerns and extreme social discontent. Western melodic-harmonic bass, West African sound ideals, original principles, American popular and rock music mannerisms with preference for high volume, particularly in bass.

Rhythm and blues R&B, simple harmony, rhythm, methodical popular music or jazz originally intended for black audience.

Riff An exercise through chord changes.

Rip Effect used by reed and brass instruments. Starts at lower note and hits written note hard and staccato.

Romp To play jazz or dance.

Rugcutter Good dancer.

Run Rapid succession of notes.

Sand A Harlem jazz dance step.

Scat Originally a succession of meaningless syllables sung to fill in when the vocalist couldn't remember the lyrics. Now it has become a part of jazz.

Scream Effect produced by playing upper register with great volume.
Screamer Jazzman producing scream-like effect with trumpet.
Scuffle Term for dancing, to get along.
Secular music Music other than that for the church.
See around the corner To read music expertly.
Session Unit of time in which musicians play several pieces.
Set One unit of a session on the stage.
Shake To dance, laugh, or cry uncontrollably.
Shit Equipment, instruments, music, etc.
Shuffle Southern dance, slow, boogie-woogie rhythm.
Single Performer working alone, usually singer who plays piano.
Skins Drums.
Slap-tongue To strike the tongue against mouthpiece.
Slush pump Trombone.
Smoke 'em out Playing music excitingly, to do anything extremely well.
Snake hips Animal movements of the body in jazz dancing.
Solid sender A musician or anyone who provides excellent entertainment.
Soul Inborn quality of authenticity.
Soul brother A fellow musician.
Speakeasy A 1920s nightclub.
Spiritual Afro-American religious folk song; solo and refrain design.
Spot Nightclub.
Stick Clarinet.
Sticks Drumsticks.
Stomp To dance or play jazz; also, very nearly synonymous with "swing" (stamp).
Straight Classical, serious.
Struggle To dance, to dance badly, or play music badly.
Style A distinctive presentation in the construction or execution of music.
Sweet Gently played music.
Swing Jazz oriented popular music.
Swinger A piece of music that provides pleasure or excitement.
Swinging High term of approval, anything a jazzman likes.
Tag A musical phrase added to end a song or performance.
Tailgate New Orleans style of trombone playing. Musician had to sit at the back of wagon or truck because of the length of the trombone slide.
Take five Five minutes rest for musicians.
Take it out Conclude the piece.
Takeoff Improvised solo.
Talk When instruments imitate the human voice.
Tear down To dismantle equipment after a performance.
Thing A musical performance, composition or conception thereof.
Threads Dress.

Toilet Worse than a dive.

Too much Getting beyond belief.

Tore up Distressed.

Tough Great.

Trad Dixieland or New Orleans style.

Trip-up When a musician plays a wrong note and it definitely shows.

Truck To dance, the dance.

Trucking A dance introduced in 1933 at the Cotton Club.

Vamp A continuous refrain at end of a song that allows for last-minute statements from the soloist. Chord used as a filler until soloist is ready to continue.

Wail To do anything well musically.

Walk Lively, four beats to the bar rhythm.

Whip that thing Play that instrument.

Wipe out To best in musical competition.

Woodshed Taking the time to practice on what you used to know.

Sources of Information

All information not listed was taken from verbal sources.

The Argus Newspaper, St. Louis
Chicago Sun-Times
Detroit Free Press
Detroit News
Detroit Public Library
Encyclopedia of Jazz, Vol. 2
Florissant, Missouri, county library
Kansas City Star, Kansas City
Local Musicians Union 2197 of St. Louis
Long Beach, California, library
Los Angeles Examiner
Main County Library, St. Louis County
Memphis, Tennessee library
Metropolitan Toronto Reference Library
New Orleans City Public Library
New Orleans Times Picayune
New York Times
Personal data and information from St. Louis musicians and their family
    records and personal interviews
Record Research Magazine, Olive Brown, Nov. 1956, page 12
St. Louis Globe-Democrat
St. Louis Post-Dispatch
St. Louis Public Library, St. Louis
Toronto Star
Toronto Sun
Who's Who in America

Index

by *Teri Haines*

Entry numbers in **boldface** indicate photographs.

Boler, Leman 76
Boler, Leonard 126
"Bolo Blues" 55
bongo-conga drums 66, 90, 167, 168
Bonn, Germany 11
Bonner, Mrs. 196
boogie woogie 166
Booker T. Washington school (St. Louis)
  202
Booker T. Washington Theater (St. Louis)
  4
Bose, Joe 211
Boss Tres Bien 168
Boston Blues 29
Boston MA 124, 161
"Bottomland" 79
Bow Club (St. Louis) 211
Bowden, Len 56
Bower, Eddie 211
Bowling Green KY 213
Bowman, Lanky 31
Boy Scout orchestra 155
Boyd, Eddie 110
Boyd, James, Jr. 12, 15
Boze, Martin 41
Bradford, Clea 132, 168, 206
Bradshaw, Tiny 14
Brazier, George 16, **17, 18,** 161, **194**
Brazier, Jesse 20, 23, 159
Brennan's Restaurant (St. Louis) 107
Brenner, Yul 172
Brenston, Jackie 150
Brister, Miller 207
Bronson, Marty 189
Bronx NY 168
Brooklyn NY 25, 193
Brooks, Tilford 129
Brooks, Tillman 151
Brown, Channa 66
Brown, Charlie 15
Brown, Gatemouth 194
Brown, James 30, 192
Brown, Jerry 213, 214
Brown, Kathryn 129
Brown, Olive 23, 24, 44
Brown, Ruth 142
Brown, Wiley 81
"Brown Eyed Handsome Man" 10
Brucestarks, Maxine 196
Brunis, George 143
Brunner, Reverend Lillie T. 162
Brunswick (label) 93, 99
Buchannon, Edgar 203
Buckner, George "Bubba," III 25
Buckner, Houston 26
Buckner, Joe 26, **28, 29, 75**
Buckner, Milton "Milt" 31

Buckner, Owen 31, 64
Buckner, Teddy 93
Buckner, Theodore Guy "Ted" 31
Buffalo NY 24, 32
Bullock, Ann 150
Bull's Eye Records 152
Bunch, Dick 32
Bunts, Howard 31
Burger, Jerry 189
Burke, Mose 31
Burlesque 145
Burlesque U.S.A. 172
Burnside, Archie 78
Burton, Buddie 201
Busch Stadium (St. Louis) 79
Bush, Flora 198
Business College of Sikeston 81
Butler, Floyd 38
Butler, Jack 73
button box 173

C

Cab Calloway's Band 73
Cab Calloway's Orchestra 164
Cabana Club (St. Louis) 213
Caesar's Palace (Las Vegas) 150, 183, 184
Cafe Nostalgique 25
Cafe Society (New York City) 140, 153
Cahokia IL 193
Cairo IL 135, 174
Caldwell, Alex 159
Caldwell, Altha 129
Call, Rueban 151
Calloway, Blanche 159
Calloway, Cab 73, 139, 159
Campbell, Burns 78
Campbell, "Little Milton" 88
Campbell, Wilbur 72
Canadian National Exhibition, Toronto 25
"Candido" 198
Cantor, Eddie 6
Cape Girardeau MO 135
Capital riverboat 90
Capitol (MGM label) 154, 198
Caravan's Orchestra (St. Louis) 194
Cardinals (St. Louis baseball team) 189
"Careless Love" Show 80
Carl Fisher bass 20
Carnegie Hall (New York City) 25, 164,
  166, 194, 195
"Carol Channing Christmas Show" (West-
  port Plaza, St. Louis) 191
Carousel 196
Carpenter, Charlie 186
Carpenter, Theodore "Wingie" 31

242   Index